Father Augustine Maydieu, O.P., and Louis J. Putz, C.S.C. on the campus of the University of Notre Dame

In 1953, the late Father Augustine Maydieu, O.P., visited the United States to learn about the position of the Catholic Church in America. Father Maydieu returned to his native France convinced that he had made a significant discovery of the particular genius of the Church in the U.S. Unfortunately, Father Maydieu died an untimely death soon upon his return.

The eventuality left Father Louis J. Putz, C.S.C., of the University of Notre Dame, in charge of completing Father Maydieu's investigations. It was a task not only of determining an approach to the study, after countless conversations with men across the country, but also of finding the very best specialists for each phase of the study.

Father Louis J. Putz, C.S.C., is equally at home in Europe and the United States. A specialist in history and theology, himself, he is professor of theology at Notre D' me. He is also founder and presently P. esident of Fides Publishers Association and one of the outstanding churchmen in the country in forwarding the cause of a responsible lay apostolate. Born in Germany, he entered the Holy Cross Community at Notre Dame, completed his theological studies in France, became an American citizen and joined the faculty at Notre Dame.

THE CATHOLIC CHURCH, U.S.A.

THE CATHOLIC CHURCH, U.S.A.

EDITED BY

LOUIS J. PUTZ, C.S.C.

CONTRIBUTORS

John J. Wright, D.D.

Gustave Weigel, S.J.

Henry J. Browne

Edward A. Ryan, S.J.

F. D. Cohalan

Harry J. Byrne

Frederick G. Hochwalt

C. Joseph Nuesse

John L. Thomas, S.J.

Edward G. Murray

Joseph N. Moody

Edward O'Rourke

Dale Francis

Joseph B. Gremillion

Robert E. Lucey, D.D.

George N. Kramer

Edward Marciniak

John La Farge, S.J.

John A. O'Brien

Jane Marie Murray, O.P.

Paul Marx, O.S.B.

John Tracy Ellis

Vincent J. Giese

Jordan Aumann, O.P.

Walter J. Ong, S.J.

FIDES PUBLISHERS ASSOCIATION

CHICAGO 19, ILLINOIS

Nihil Obstat: Rev. John Quinlan, S.T.D.

Imprimatur: Leo A. Pursley, D.D., Apostolic Administrator
of the Diocese of Fort Wayne, Indiana

Library of Congress Catalog Card Number: 56–11629

Manufactured by American Book-Stratford Press, Inc., New York City

I

Contents

Preface

BY LOUIS J. PUTZ, C.S.C.

Hᴏᴡ ᴅɪᴅ *The Catholic Church, U. S. A.* come into being? In 1953 the late Father Augustine Maydieu, O.P., visited the United States for the express purpose of learning about the position of the Catholic Church in America. He had previously planned similar monographs on the Church in Ireland, Italy and Germany. It did not take Father Maydieu very long to appreciate the particular genius of the Church in the United States and the fact that few people, even in our country, were aware of the strength and vitality of the Catholic Church on American soil.

Father Maydieu returned to his native France convinced that not only had he made a significant discovery but that the world should hear about it. Unfortunately, Father Maydieu died an untimely death soon upon his return. This eventuality left the present editor the whole responsibility of pursuing the task.

Whether this book will ever reach the European market is problematic. There are potent reasons, however, for publishing a work of this nature in the United States. Even to

---

Louis J. Putz, C.S.C., teaches theology at the University of Notre Dame and is the President of Fides Publishers Association.

vii

the American Catholic, the Church is not well known. He may be familiar with the Church as it is strongly entrenched in New England, but unaware that it differs completely from the Church in the missionary wastelands of the deep South. If he knows the Church as a member of a great cosmopolitan and urban parish in New York City, he may be far from appreciating the closely knit national parish of Chicago or an almost one hundred percent Catholic rural community in Iowa. The Church differs widely, depending upon the locality and region.

Institutionally, the Catholic Church has benefited greatly from the American cultural and economic climate. It is a free institution in a pluralistic society, a phenomenon quite recent in the long history of the Church. The Catholic Church prospers in this environment, and interest in the Catholic Church is on the increase, if the popularity of a Bishop Sheen, or the presentation of Catholic themes, involving priests and nuns, on the movie screen, or the appearance on best seller lists of books by Paul Blanshard are any indication. This interest may be inspired by a fear of the growing strength of the Catholic Church or it may have a commercial motive at its base, or it might reflect a genuine tendency towards a religious system which inspires confidence. Whatever the source of the interest, it signalizes the growing importance of the Catholic Church. For this reason it is highly important that accurate information on the Church, in a fairly digestible form and presented by authors eminent for their knowledge in the field, be made available.

The Catholic Church, U. S. A. is divided into three parts. Part one presents the history and structure of the Catholic Church in the United States. It tries to establish the course of events that brought the institution of the Church, as it is now structured, into being. The second part reveals the geographical diversity of the Church on a regional basis. Part three shows the influence and impact of the Church on the national community in areas vital both to the United States and to the mission of the Church.

Admittedly, there are gaps in this presentation of the

Church in the United States. The great network of the Catholic Press is not specifically treated, nor is the great work of institutional charity given adequate coverage. Since these are areas the ordinary person comes most easily into contact with, there is less of a mystery in formulating an adequate idea of their place and function in the life of the American Catholic. Admirable personal and group efforts have been left out in order not to obscure the picture of the central reality. A book of this nature could easily develop into an encyclopedia, but this, of course, is not our intention.

A sincere tribute needs to be paid to all the contributors who have given so generously of their time and competence to make this book available. It has been a source of inspiration, and if the reader will benefit as much as the editor has from reading the manuscripts, he will receive a real appreciation and knowledge and above all else love of the Catholic Church.

Introduction

———— ◆ ————

BY JOHN J. WRIGHT, D.D.

IT MAY strike the uninformed as a curious fact, but it is
nonetheless true that Catholicism sometimes seems an
unknown quantity in the American community. Despite
widespread and sometimes even violent criticisms of Catholicism; despite the considerable publicity which Catholicism
and things Catholic receive in the popular press, the movies
and other media of American information, Catholicism is in
many ways the least well or, at least, accurately known of the
myriad religions whose names are familiar to Americans.

Dean Willard Sperry, of the Harvard Divinity School,
demonstrated this strange truth some years ago when he
wrote his book "Religion in America." The dean wrote in
response to an invitation from the Cambridge University
Press to contribute a volume on American religious life to
a series of books prepared to help the English public understand certain American institutions. Dean Sperry undertook
to explain in a general way all and in a particular way many
of the 256 religious groups in America, their nature and their
place in our community. He obviously could comment

———————————————————————————

*John J. Wright, D.D., is the Bishop of Worcester in Massachu-
setts. Bishop Wright is active in the Lay Retreat Movement,
the Liturgical Movement and in the general field of lecturing
and writing on the social teachings and apostolic directives of
the Holy See.*

xi

knowledgeably and objectively on all the religious traditions
in the American community, from Adventism to Zoroaster-
ism practically,—all, that is, save one. That one was not a
recent importation from the Orient nor a passing fringe-
form of any obscure cult in the hills of the South or the
exotic towns of the West. The one exception was Catholicism.

Dean Sperry himself confessed, with disarming humility,
his inability to interpret Catholicism in America to his English readers. He clearly appreciated how embarrassing this
inability was, especially since, as he admitted, he had lived
all his life surrounded by large numbers of Catholics and in
a community where Catholic institutions are not only many,
but long-established and quite public. And yet he avowed
that his own knowledge of their understanding of themselves
by his Catholic neighbors would be only that of "the average
Protestant householder."

The knowledge of Catholicism possessed by such a person
is thus described by Dean Sperry: "The average Protestant
householder knows Catholicism only outwardly: by its substantial churches; by the crowds pouring from its doors at the
end of a Mass; by the police directing traffic at such a time—
an attention seldom given to a neighboring Protestant congregation and, if the truth be told, not always required by its
smaller numbers; by the arrangements which must be made
to allow maids to attend Mass; by the early dinners in Lent
or during a Novena preaching mission (by the way what is a
Novena?); by vague rumors that the *Index Expurgatorius* is
not observed on news stands or in bookstores; by disgruntled
comments in conservative clubs at the growing strength of
the Irish vote; by the loyal patronage which parish priests
accord professional baseball games; by the intransigence of
the Church in the matters of birth control and divorce, and
its scepticism as to the 'noble experiment' of prohibition. In
all these respects we look at Catholicism with mixed emotions of envy and perplexity. Its customs are not ours, the
two ways of life do not always 'mesh' like well-oiled gears.
There is, however, one thing we cannot do: we cannot ig-

nore that which we do not wholly understand. The massive
fact of American Catholicism is too considerable to be dismissed by studied indifference."

And so, in order to be fair and to complete his picture of
religion in America, the dean adopted a device that was
clever but revealing. He chose to let the mysterious Catholics speak for themselves. However, in the hope that their
spokesman might be someone with a mentality somehow ap-
proximating that of himself and of Protestant readers generally, he selected a convert to Catholicism, Mr. Theodore
Maynard, to interpret the Catholics to him so that he in turn
might present American Catholicism to his English readers.
He boiled down Maynard's "Story of American Catholicism," being careful to attribute almost every proposition to
Maynard, referring to him as "our chronicler." Writes
Sperry: "I shall refer to the author as our 'chronicler,' and
shall introduce my own comments by the gambit 'one' or 'we.'
In this way I shall hope not to make the author himself
chargeable for my Protestant second thoughts."

Thus by a combination of courtesy and caution Sperry
could conscientiously describe some 30 million of his American neighbors with something like accuracy and at least
attempted understanding. Mormonism, Christian Science,
Vedanta and Rosicrucianism would seemingly have presented no comparable difficulties!

It is this astonishing confession by an urbane and friendly
critic which prompts the contention that, for all the publicity it receives, Catholicism is almost an unknown in large
areas of the American community. Perhaps even more distressing is the fact that the place of Catholicism in the American community is largely unknown to Catholics themselves.
I cannot myself forget how George Schuster's "Catholic
Spirit in America" came to me as a revelation when first I
read it, unaware as I was of the full story of the dramatic
place of Catholicism in the early history of America's political and cultural formation.

As a practical conclusion from this initial fact, the relatively unknown part of Catholicism in the national life, one

is tempted to suggest a self-study project by Catholic Americans themselves in order that they may discover their own heritage in America. Their complex contribution to the national community is much more intimately identified with the American reality and ideal than they or their neighbors usually suppose, and their impact on the minds and customs of their fellow citizens is considerably greater than seems to be understood at home or abroad.

In recent years it has again become almost a stereotype to speak of "fear of Catholicism" and to take it for granted that Catholicism is disliked—or held suspect by large numbers of American citizens. The response to Paul Blanchard's lectures and books warrants the suspicion that Catholicism is an object of a certain misgiving in large areas of the American community. So do some of the articles and editorials which appear regularly in typical non-Catholic religious periodicals, even literate ones like *The Christian Century*. So, finally and notably, do anti-Catholic attacks like the hurtful article which presumably a responsible writer like Joseph Harsch wrote in the Christian Science Monitor at the time of the McCarthy hearings, an article purporting to give "reasons" why Catholics are allegedly given special treatment in Washington investigations.

It is important to analyze the roots of these mixed sentiments of fear and fury which cloud up discussions of Catholicism in the American community. Such analysis reveals that most of our difficulties stem from almost the same circumstances as do our advantages. I mean that the very factors which, from one point of view, make us so readily *American* apparently operate, from another point of view, to make many Americans nervous about us.

For example, the Catholic Church in America is probably still thought of as an "immigrant" church. To be sure, the other religious traditions in America are also importations from abroad except for a half-dozen denominations which have sprung from the native soil and which, oddly enough, are not usually thought of as being particularly American. Everyone, I think, knows the sense in which Protestants, even when relatively close to their European origins, can be nativists, while Catholics are frequently thought of as "immigrant." The distinction between nativist and immigrant is arbitrary, but it is a clear and fairly widely accepted practical distinction, even if sometimes ridiculous.

I might cite a personal example. My mother was born in Boston. So was her mother before her. Yet a Swedish lady who lived near our house when I was a boy and who came to this country when she was already married, used to speak of my mother, with great neighborly affection but heavy Swedish accent, as "the little Irish woman with six children."

This alien air which has surrounded Catholicism in so many American neighborhoods has resulted in many short-range disadvantages, but it should be a long-range source of strength to the Church in a nation which is, in its roots and idealism, itself entirely "immigrant." The hierarchy of the Catholic Church in America illustrates, at least in its ancestral origins, how similar to the American civil pattern is the make-up of the Catholic spiritual community in this country. Catholicism in America has been served by bishops who, by origin or descent, have been the sons of just about every national group represented in the national life: Austrian, Belgian, Canadian, Cuban, French, English, Dutch, German, Hungarian, Luxemburger, Irish, Italian, Mexican, Polish, Scotch, Spanish, Swiss and Eastern European. One of our bishops blended Negro and white blood in his veins. To the extent that America herself has been made strong by a plurality of racial strains, the Church in America has certainly shared the elements of that strength as well as of the genius of America by reason of her parallel diversity. One feels that this may prove of great significance both to the Church and to America in the future, especially if any effort be made to splinter the unity of the American community.

Perhaps related to this first point is a second of even greater significance. There is a sense in which the Catholic Church in America has been from the beginning and is still "proletarian." Rural America has been and remains largely Protestant, with exceptions which prove rather than violate the rule. To the extent that this is true, any "peasantry" which we have in America is Protestant rather than Catholic. Catholicism has been largely identified with the working classes and the cities, though not with all the cities, of course. Perhaps the word "proletarian" is not the happiest or most exact word to use in this context; all I mean is that Catholicism in our country is a religion with deep roots and powerful support among the so-called "working classes."

This also is illustrated in the hierarchy of the Church. One should not exaggerate the significance of this fact, but it remains interesting nonetheless that, as Archbishop Cushing pointed out in a talk to a C.I.O. Convention, the "democratic," not to say proletarian roots of our bishops are dramatically exemplified in the family backgrounds whence they come. Of all the bishops, archbishops and cardinals in the history of the Church in America and down to the moment of writing, not one is the son of a college graduate. Not one comes from what most people would consider a "privileged class."

Our bishops and our clergy are the sons of farmers, millworkers, coal-miners, dock-hands, day-laborers, tradesmen, shop-keepers and other types of working men, including "white collar" workers, but in each case "workers." It would seem then, that, if this is the century of the "common man" in any Christian and democratic sense, the Catholic Church, both through its spiritual chieftains and through the broad masses of its devout working people, should have a congenial place in the American community and should make a powerful contribution to the spiritual direction of a community so largely industrial in its character.

There may be a reflection of the truth behind these same truths in the interesting coincidence that the most recent Democratic administration and the present Republican administration of the national government have both found it somehow appropriate to name Catholics to the post of Secretary of Labor in presidential cabinets from which Catholics are otherwise too often strangely absent.

A corollary of this "proletarian" character of the Catholic

body in the American community is that our people are, as we have noted, chiefly urban in their background and interest. This fact, too, may well account for some of the prejudices against Catholicism.

Catholicism is largely urban, but America is not. Rural America's suspicion of the "city slicker" is a favorite subject of caricature and comedy, but it corresponds with something quite real in rural American character. Anyone who watched the telecast of the investigations in which Senator Tobey of New Hampshire pursued with righteous wrath the people involved in "big city" political scandals must have noted the clear inability of Senator Tobey to comprehend how God could permit situations to develop in a city of five million which do not occur in a New Hampshire town of five hundred—or do they?

In any case, recent Congressional hearings revealed a tension between rural and urban America. To what extent this antagonism carries over, however falsely or inappropriately, to the relations between "urban" Catholicism and "rural" Protestantism, it is difficult to estimate. It is a point worth notice, however, in any study of the place of Catholicism in the American community.

On the other hand, Catholics themselves obviously feel completely at home in the American community. They have not merely come to terms with the basic postulates of that community, but have even been accused of undue attachment or at least uncritical devotion to some of the practical corollaries and by-products of these postulates. On this point Dean Sperry writes with sympathetic insight. He says that the people of no church are more vocal in unqualified affirmation of their 100 percent patriotism than the Catholics, and he makes it quite clear that these protestations are completely sincere and justified by events. However, he observes that in matters of national policy the Catholic Church in America sometimes seems to many Protestants too uncritically patriotic. He considers that our "instant loyalty" to the Federal government is in part a vote of thanks for the opportunities which this country has given the Catholic Church and he quotes utterances of our clergy which say as much. "What one misses, perhaps, in these utterances," the dean observes, "is a strain of sober, critical second thought upon all of our American institutions."

Catholicism has played one part in the American community which distinguishes it from all other religious traditions, and yet which has also given it an authentically American characteristic. It has perpetuated strong strains of many of the national cultures of the Old World, while reconciling them with one another in the pattern of the New World. It has done this work of reconciliation without eliminating anything valid and of value. If it be true, as is sometimes said, that Catholicism in America has as yet produced relatively little by way of an indigenous Catholic culture, it is also true that precious cultural heritages have been preserved in the United States by Catholic peoples, to take their own spiritual good and of the considerable enrichment of the American community. Not long ago a non-Catholic doctor, who grew up in a Maine town, remarked that the French speaking Catholic priest of his native town was the only intellectual companion with whom his father had felt at home in the Yankee town. He remembered the priest as the representative not only of Catholicism in his community but also of a rich cultural heritage to which his own travels had introduced him.

Nor has this broadly cultural influence of Catholicism been limited to the influence of a few gifted individuals. Catholic people as a group have exercised a more refining and spiritualizing influence on the general traditions of the community than they themselves ordinarily realize. The American observance of Christmas and of the other sacred seasons is a case in point. For example, Theodore Maynard reminds us in his book, "The Catholic Church and the American Idea," that the observance of Christmas was proscribed in Boston as late as 1856 precisely because it was looked upon as a Catholic aberration. Christmas Day was studiously made a work day; even in 1870 any pupil who stayed home from school on Christmas Day was severely punished

or even expelled. The family of Emily Dickinson was sus-
spected of being secretly Catholic because they observed
Christmas in Amherst. We owe it to the influence of the
Irish with their Christmas candles, the French with their
family and parish observances, the Germans with their Advent wreaths and Christmas trees that these prejudices were
eventually eliminated and that the Catholic observance of
Christmas became so typically "American." The late Cardinal O'Connell used to tell of being rebuked by one of his
grammar school teachers who lost patience with him for
speaking of "Good Friday." "Every day is good," this Puritan schoolma'am insisted.

We fortunately need not assume responsibility for some of
the more recent developments in the American observance
of Christmas and Easter, but the manner in which these
festive seasons presently loom so large in the American imag-
ination we owe in great part to the Catholic influence.

It is only fair to note that occasionally persons outside the
household of the Faith regret that our influence along spiritual lines is not even greater. Here again Dean Sperry
proves a friendly critic when he writes that many miss in
American Catholicism any wide concern for the contemplative life. We Americans are too practical, he asserts, too
much given to action without reflection. He contends that
Catholicism might have been expected to correct American
culture at this point. He quotes Archbishop Ireland as evidence that we have not been disposed to provide such a mystical corrective: "An honest ballot and social decorum will
do more for God's glory and the salvation of souls than
midnight flagellations or Compostellian pilgrimages."

It is only fair to recall the context in which John Ireland
was speaking and the immediate problems to which he was
addressing himself. It is reassuring, moreover, to detect in
the catalogues of Catholic publishing houses a very remarkable increase in strictly spiritual literature, most of it deriva-
tive from the Catholic traditions of other countries but not
a little of it revealing the native genius of our own land. It
is noteworthy, too, that the Catholic Lay Retreat Movement

is continually extending its numbers and its influence, and that "days of recollection" are now conspicuous in the calendar of present-day Catholic institutions, clubs and parishes.

Catholic scholarship in the American community is a subject of frequent analysis and debate. So many recent studies have appeared on this point that there is probably no need to discuss it here. The most recent of these are marked with a forthrightness and objectivity which argue well for the prospects for reform or improvement where these may be needed. They justify the hope that we are beginning to come into our own, little by little, in the world of scholarship, despite the real disadvantages of a financial kind under which most of our educational institutions do their gigantic work.

It must be confessed that, except for a few familiar names, the authors who have most impressively related the best chapters of our cultural history in America have often been friendly neighbors rather than our own writers. One thinks of Francis Parkman, Willa Cather, even Longfellow on occasion.

At the moment it is difficult to deny that our place in the American community is under attack. The numbers of those who join in the attack and the permanent significance of what they have to say are open to question. The *fact* of the attack and the lines it follows are clear; the latter are new in their direction.

A century ago the attack on the Catholic Church in America was essentially pornographic. The creeds of Blanco White and books like *Maria Monk* remain fair samples of American anti-Catholicism in the last part of the last century.

Today the attack is largely political, or at least pseudo-political. There is a professed misgiving in some circles as to what use we could make of political power if we became a majority in this and there are even charges that our professions of fidelity to the Constitution and to American political idealism involve an "interim ethic" which we might put aside should we acquire greater numbers and sufficient power.

It is exasperating to be perpetually issuing assurances that Catholics are sincere sharers of the constitutional and other American traditions which we consider ourselves to have helped establish, indeed, to have inspired in no small degree. It is idle to plead the evidences of our support of America and her institutions by the same means which others employ in the support of these. It is beneath our own dignity to argue, as we so often do, from the statistics of our representatives in the Armed Services and in other posts of trust. These considerations are received with cynicism by any who need such arguments.

On the other hand, there are undoubtedly many things Catholics can do to persuade others (and perhaps ourselves!) of our major and beneficent place in the American community. For one thing, it is well that we keep clear the rather obvious fact that we are here in America to stay. This basic premise is by no means as well understood as it should be; the points we have considered concerning the "immigrant" air attributed to the Church would indicate as much.

Then, too, we would do well to extend the influence of our good works, our corporal and spiritual works of mercy, in the widest possible measure. It is very difficult for essentially good people to resist the logic of goodness in others. The work of Catholic religious sisters frequently dispels more prejudice than could be handled by more hours of speeches than we should care to give or hear. A recent book by the Jewish father of a cerebral palsy child quotes the illuminating remark made by a non-Catholic doctor when he was obliged to tell the parents of their child's unfortunate condition. "Try to place the little boy with Catholic sisters," the doctor said, adding that thus the parents would be doing all that their hearts could desire to protect the little boy. It is an eloquent testimony to one side of Catholicism which has favorably and powerfully impressed most members of the American community from the beginning.

Finally, we can perhaps be a little more conscious of the

need that we develop certain potentialities of Catholicism in this country which, rightly or wrongly, many people think have been neglected. Our mightily organized activities and impressive organizations will lose nothing from more frequent emphasis on the organic nature of the Church. Perhaps the present flowering of the Trappist and other contemplative communities in our midst, together with a new American interest in spiritual literature, closed retreats and vigils before the Sacrament, will both increase and emphasize those mystical resources of our people which they themselves occasionally under-emphasize and their critics do frequently forget. In this connection the Liturgical Movement is making a special and providential contribution in America.

Those who love the Church will pray God to prosper the intellectual apostolate among us. The difficulties of the intellectual vocations in the service of the Church are many and familiar; they are the same in America as they are elsewhere. Good works are usually much more easy than the long, hard road of study, consecrated learning and dedicated defense, by written and spoken word, of the truth taught us by the Divine Intellectual, the Incarnate Word of God. The traditional temperament of the typical American, a willing doer of the Word more often than a rapt listener, has helped make scholarship a neglected field among us.

It is through the intellectual apostolate that, please God, we shall best increase and intensify the international ties and interests which increasingly operate among us as counteractives, sometimes badly needed, to our American isolationism and as corollaries of our Catholic supranational idealism. On the level of good works Catholicism in America has a remarkable record of authentic Christian "world-mindedness"; the Catholic American part in the support of missionary work and the characteristic generosity of Catholic America to world relief appeals are impressive evidences that we have not acquired any nationalistic spirit so narrow that it leaves us unmindful of our brothers' need.

Perhaps we are not always equally mindful of the need in

which we stand, a need for inspiration and even instruction by our Old World kinsmen in the faith. The liturgy and the love of the Saints have always served to keep us somehow close to the lands whence we came. But now there are enheartening indications that on the level of scholarship and the various areas of the intellectual life Catholic America is making new international friendships and associations. This very book is perhaps a modest witness to that new and welcome direction. Nothing could be more constructive for America or consistent with the spirit of Catholicism.

PART I

———— ❖ ————

THE CATHOLIC CHURCH

Her History, Her Structure,
and Her Inner-workings
in the United States

CHAPTER ONE

An Introduction to American Catholicism

———— ❖ ————

BY GUSTAVE WEIGEL, S.J.

A NY STUDENT of current American affairs will necessarily be drawn to a consideration of the vibrant reality of the American Catholic Church. In the United States, of the total population of over 160,000,000, the Catholics are slightly less than a fifth and slightly more than a third of the 85,000,000 Americans who formally adhere to some recognized religious group. Within the class of religious adherents, the importance of the Catholics is greater than their numbers indicate, because the Catholics are knit together more effectively than the others. Their disciplined corporate zeal makes them more conspicuous in religious life and activity.

American Catholicism, first of all, is Roman Catholicism, with no desire to be anything else. Sometimes this banal truth is not recognized beyond the frontiers of the United

---

Gustave Weigel, S.J., is Professor of Ecclesiology, Woodstock College, School of Divinity, Woodstock, Maryland. He is a frequent contributor to Theological Studies, Thought, Gregorianum, America, New Republic, American Scholar, *and* Revista Universitaria *(Chile).*

States. The writer knows of a South American Bishop who said that he would rather have American Protestants proselytizing in his diocese than American Catholic priests, because he felt the latter would inculcate an illegitimate form of Catholicism. This state of mind is unfair, but it does point to something very real: Catholicism in the United States is quite different from Catholicism below the Rio Grande. The causes for the differences do not imply non-identity of faith. They are explained by differences of history and cultural background. Let us in our introduction merely select three over-all traits which distinguish American Catholicism from Catholicism elsewhere.

First, Catholicism is not something traditionally inherent in the American way of life. For a Greek Orthodox, to be Greek means to be Orthodox, so that a non-Orthodox Greek is no true Greek. No American at any moment of the life of this country believed that to be American also meant to be Catholic. There have been and there still are many Americans who believe the opposite, namely, to be American means to be non-Catholic. This position however is no longer soundly tenable either in the abstract or in the concrete. Yet it is true that American Catholics have always been a minority in this land; an insignificant minority in the first days of the republic and an important minority in our own time. Hence at no time was the established cultural pattern of America inducive of Catholicism, although the vision of the Constitution effectively made religion an unhampered force for the individual and individual groups. Moreover, the phenomenal rise of American Catholicism during the last hundred years was caused by the immigration of men and women from different and foreign cultures. Catholicism became definitively American only after 1914, and there are still isolated Catholic groups which have not become thoroughly absorbed into American civilization. Bilingualism is more common in Catholic communities than in their non-Catholic counterparts, though bilingualism is a disappearing problem in Catholic circles.

In consequence of this basic fact, we do not find what is

common in Europe where there is the spontaneous tendency to take for granted that the individual member of the civic community is an adherent of the religion of the national culture. Such a spontaneous assumption leads to dangerous misunderstandings. In many so-called Catholic countries, in spite of the supposition that the overwhelming majority is Catholic, the fact is evident that the vast mass is Catholic only in a cultural sense. If they have religion, it will most probably be Catholic, but the majority is not infrequently removed from religion. To substitute population statistics for Church statistics is a woeful error.

The American Catholic has explicitly chosen to be a Catholic. It was not thrust upon him by a culture. It is true that family influences have conditioned his choice, so that we expect certain communities to bring forth only Catholics, yet if the individual wishes to become a Protestant or an indifferentist (as almost half of all Americans are), this is easily possible. No social condemnation will fall upon him. You must always ask the American if he is a Catholic or a non-Catholic; you cannot take it for granted that he is one or the other, no matter what be his background. This explains why so many Catholics have drifted out of the Church. The environment and the history of the land did not exert any pressure because of which they felt compelled to retain a thin, nominal, allegiance to Catholicism. It is not uncommon on the American scene to find families with Catholic and non-Catholic branches, although in the beginning they were all either Catholics or non-Catholics.

This explicitly chosen adhesion of American Catholics to their church makes Catholicism a vital thing. It is theirs not only because they once were exposed to it but because they want it here and now. In consequence they make sacrifices for it, because they are by their continuously exercised choice attached to it. The impressive material aspect of American Catholicism has its root in this explicitly willed allegiance to the Church. The thousands of churches, the universities, hospitals and institutions of American Catholics are monuments of the self-sacrifice of all the Catholics. They built all these

things in less than a century, not in the course of ten. They
built them not with the ample legacies of a few rich men,
but with the many pennies of the poor. The generosity of
American Catholics for Catholic causes is matched in very
few places of the world.

Another consequence of the non-identification of Catholicism with American culture is the American Catholic's attitude to religions which are not his own. There are very few
Americans who live in a community where all the members
belong to the same church. As a result, the American Catholic lives, works and plays with non-Catholics. Intermarriage
is an unavoidable characteristic of such a milieu, though in
America it is not so frequent as one might spontaneously
suppose. Yet religiously there is so little contact between
American Catholics and non-Catholics. Many a European has
a better knowledge of American Protestantism than most
American Catholics. Many a European Catholic is scandalized by the small efforts made by American Catholics to
attract non-Catholics religiously. The American Catholic has
kept quite aloof from non-Catholic religious life, yet nonetheless it is impossible for him to entertain fantastic notions
concerning Protestants; he knows too many. He certainly has
no ill-will for them, and he contributes to their organizations
of charity. He cannot conceive of them as the great enemy,
although this is the attitude of many Latin Catholics in Europe and Ibero-America. In many instances there is collaboration between Catholic and non-Catholic groups, but this
never takes place on the plane of religion itself. The frequent
American meetings of a purely civic or quasi-religious nature
will bring a Protestant minister, a Jewish rabbi and a Catholic priest together on the platform, each of whom will say a
public prayer. However, this phenomenon is essentially cultural, not religious. But the result is that almost all American
Catholics have at some time or another bowed their heads in
prayer led by non-Catholic clergymen. Likewise Catholic
priests and Protestant ministers dress alike in public. It is
impossible to distinguish them, though we must not forget
that the majority of Protestants do not usually wear the

Roman collar. The American Catholic takes religious plural-ism as an obvious fact. He is not disedified nor scandalized by it. His own love of religion makes him prefer to have his neighbor in some church rather than in no church at all. The general effect is that the American Catholic is much more tolerant of non-Catholic religions than members of European communities where only one religion is effectively present. This tolerance may be interpreted by some superficial ob-servers as a diminished allegiance to Catholicism, though such an interpretation would be very wide of the mark. Catholic tolerance is caused by an exercise of charity rather than by a defect of faith.

The second generalization to help us in our consideration of American Catholicism can be expressed by describing the American Catholic as more activist than contemplative. It is not mere whimsy to say that most American Catholics be-lieve that our Lord was not altogether fair to Martha and too partial to Mary. The American preacher urges his hearer to activity and moral endeavor in a program of concrete works. He does not dwell on dogma which is taught routinely in the synthetic form of the catechism, once and for all. Church for most Americans means something to do rather than some-thing to think about. It is a trait of all Americans to be cold and suspicious of intellectual schemes, especially when they are brilliant pieces of dialectic. Their prime interest is in the practical program attached to a thought scheme. Hence it is logical that the life of an American Catholic parish is a con-stant whirl of activity, and this explains the greater vitality of the American parish in contrast to the European. The school the Catholic boy attends is in the majority of cases the parish school. The organization to which he belongs is a parish chapter of some national union. His father and mother be-long to societies which arrange social meetings in the parish hall. The larger boys form athletic teams on whose uniforms is sewed the name of the parish, and often enough the instruc-tor of the team is one of the parish priests. The constant need of money for parish and diocesan projects brings the Cath-olics together in all kinds of fund-raising enterprises ranging

from simple games of chance to elaborate theatricals. The
youth organizations plan and conduct dances sponsored by
the religious society to which they belong. Catholic life in
America is intensely active, and many of the activities which
of their nature are not religious, have assumed for Catholics
a religious meaning. In consequence even their genuinely religious exercises are tinged with this activism. The American
Catholic uses language for his religious life which indicates
this activism. He is always "going" and "making"; he "goes"
to church, he "goes" to communion, he "goes" to confession,
he "makes" a retreat.

To many a European this materialistic approach to the
sacred is understood as infantile and anti-intellectualistic.
Such a formulation of the facts is misleading. The American,
Catholic or non-Catholic, is no opponent of thought. His
universities, so many and so lively, produce and communicate thought. However, because of the English roots of his
culture, the American judges thought by its practical con-
clusions rather than by its abstract premises. In doing so, he
is only applying the maxim of our Lord who taught that by
their fruits you shall know them. That is why the clearest
example of American thinking is the disciplined organization
he erects for concrete tasks. The organization builds on
thought and through thought, with the result that American
activity is highly rational. In fact, he becomes irritated with
the lack of rationality of the *modus operandi* of non-Americans. However, in all such organization, abstract principles
must cede to efficiency. Thinking is judged by the end prod-
uct, not by its inner logical consistency. The American has
seen that logically perfect systems can be treacherous or even
harmful, and he refuses to see the *summum bonum* in mere
logical consistency. This is not anti-intellectualism. It is an
anti-apriorism which insists that thinking must enrich life
rather than make life submit to the strangling power of "self-
evident" abstractions. Hence Americans frequently engage in
works which are declared to be impossible by some philosophy or some generally assumed principle. He is bold enough
to do so because he knows from his own experience that a

priori impossibilities are very often a posteriori possibilities.
That is why the American considers no traditional scheme
or customary pattern of action as sacrosanct. Within a very
conservative framework, he is willing and ready to change all
the time. This is the American paradox. Without being a
revolutionary, the American is always changing in the hope
that by experiment through trial and error he will better
achieve his traditional goals.

This general attitude is shared by American Catholics. All
visitors to this country are struck by the absence of intellectualism in general American Catholic life. It is true that everywhere small but promising groups are now springing up
with a hunger for the intellectual, but as yet they have not
deeply tinged American Catholicism. It is a known fact that
Catholics do not adopt scholarly careers in great numbers,
and as a sector of the total community the Catholics fall far
below the proportion they should have in scientific pursuits.
It is also true that the Catholic universities in general produce very few scientists and scholars. Even in the sacred sciences the American contribution has been slight, in spite of
the large numbers of seminaries and seminarians. The American Catholic has for a long time rested content in looking to
Europe for the development of philosophy and theology.
Only in the last twenty years do we find isolated efforts to
work productively in these fields, and the results up to the
moment have not been spectacular. Often, too, the best work
is done by foreigners who have established themselves in the
United States.

It is hard to explain why this is. We cannot explain it by
saying that the Catholics are economically hindered. Certainly the general Catholic population belongs to the low-in-
come groups. Yet the generosity of Catholics is such that they
will finance any worthy cause. In the smaller Jewish community many poor boys and girls dedicate themselves to
scholarship. They find the financial means in the many foundations which exist for this purpose, and these are available
to all.

Nor can we lay the whole blame on the Catholic schools.

More than half of our Catholic student population studies in non-Catholic universities and colleges, but this group does not produce more scholars than the Catholic-university group.

Perhaps the explanation is to be found in the origins of the Catholic community itself. The Catholics of today are in very large numbers the sons or grandsons of Europeans who came to this country in order to improve their economic and social positions. The importance of having and earning money is thus unconsciously inculcated by the Catholic family. In America, no less than elsewhere, the scholar is not highly remunerated in terms of dollars. In America rather than elsewhere, there is no social prestige attached to the status of a professor or scholar. The doctor, the lawyer, the clergyman, the politician, the business man, are civic idols, and in these guilds the Catholics are prominent. Professors on the other hand are considered to be dreamers and incompetents. Today they are called "egg-heads," quite in accord with a well-known American saying: he who can, does; he who can't, teaches.

Consequently the two values which attracted the first immigrants, Catholic and non-Catholic, were money and social prestige, and both are unlikely to produce scholars. For the Catholics there is an added difficulty. Those elements of Catholic youth with signs of a scholarly vocation, were directed to the priestly or religious life. However, though there is no dearth of vocations in America, priests and religious are led by the imperious necessities of concrete Catholic life to become pastors, administrators and organizers. Those who do teach, for reasons of economy have many other occupations or heavy teaching loads and they do not lead truly scholarly lives. They communicate what is commonly accepted without engaging in the labors of productive scholarship.

The general picture is not too pleasant, but there are signs of an awakening to a lack in American Catholic life, and there are younger groups anxious to dedicate themselves to lives of study and contemplation. Only the future can say if they will fulfill their promise, but it is already true today that things intellectual are more highly considered than twenty years ago. Books in abundance, readily available to all, plus the felt want of a Catholic intellectualism, may perhaps do what the teaching fraternity did not do; create a representative group of Catholic intellectuals.

One consolation the American Catholic draws from his own intellectual poverty is the reflection that it is the price for something valuable (in American eyes, more valuable), the vigorous life of the Church on the level of the non-intellectual. When the American Catholic visits Europe he is delighted and impressed by the flourishing intellectualism of the European churches, but he clearly sees that it affects only a very small group, while the vast masses are lethargic in their realization of Catholic faith. In fact, Catholic intellectuals often take a pharisaic attitude to the "people," considering them quite incapable of true Catholicism. Such an attitude is clearly sterile snobbery produced by a cowardly inability to communicate the gospel to every creature.

The third and last guiding generalization would state that American culture is highly respectful of religion and piety. It is safe to say that nowhere in the world with the possible exception of Ireland is the religious in so high esteem.

This general thesis comes as a surprise to many Europeans who uncritically believe that America is the incarnation of materialism, the land of the Philistine, the proper home of the tawdry and the vulgar. Nothing is far from the truth than this conception of the United States, and it must be flatly said that the man who believes in such an idea is very ignorant. Religion was and is an important factor in American life. We need not defend the dubious opinion of some Catholics who wish to prove that the Constitution was directly derived from religious principles. Many of the founding fathers of the republic were not very religious men, and the notion of God which pleased their leaders was a deistic construction. However, the religious roots of life in America were too strong to permit the authors of the Constitution, even had they so wished, to ignore religion, much less oppose

it. From that time on, religion was always a respected phase
of American life. It has at times taken bizarre shapes; it has
often had little to contribute to the activities of the moment;
but it was never attacked. Instead, it has always been given
deferential treatment. Of course, individual religions have
been persecuted by groups and mobs, but never with the
consent of law nor in odium of religion itself. The attacks
were made because concrete religions were considered un-
patriotic or corruptive religions. Anti-Catholicism has constantly made itself visible in America, nor are we surprised
when we see it flare up momentarily even in our own time
but this is not an attack on the concept of religion as such.
Anti-semitism is by no means dead in the United States, but
it is not dynamised by an opposition to the Jewish faith.

It would be wise here to say something concerning the
American separation of church and state. This famous phrase
means one thing to a European and another to an American.
The old European liberals used the phrase in a conscious effort to eliminate religion as a force in public life. The phrase
meant the reduction of the church to a place in public law as
a social union subject to the government. The liberals were
not satisfied with the mere separation of the two things but
tried to make the church subservient to the state, which was
turned into a secularistic leviathan, with no morals by which
it was to be ruled and with no God to whom it was subject.
The old liberal slogan was really the apotheosis of the state.
In America this was not so. The Declaration of Independence
begins with a profession of faith in God as the creator of all
men, and the first article of the Bill of Rights attached to the
Constitution prevents the state from any interference with
religion and the free exercise thereof. The whole function of
the Constitution is to restrict the powers of government and
to arrange things so that the state would never be apothe-
osised. To this day the American tradition has ever been to
suspect government in order to keep it a pliant instrument of
the people rather than to have it be their lord. In the Constitution the people put religion beyond the state, not the
state beyond religion.

From the first moment of the application of the Constitution to American life we find this understanding clearly made manifest. The Congress had its chaplains, and so did the troops of the nation. The churches were exempt from taxes and clergymen exempt from any military duties other than spiritual. Religious marriage was recognized as civically valid, and in many states it was the only recognized form of marriage. Public officials entered into their offices by taking an oath on the Bible. All the Presidents once a year proclaimed one day to be set aside in order to give thanks to God for favors received. The state was under religion but religion itself was beyond governmental power. The Constitution could only speak of religion in general, because no single church of the many in the land represented the religion of the citizens as a whole. The constitutional separation of church and state was made to assure the liberty of the church, not its exile from public life. Politicians and statesmen from the beginning until now have always been sensitive to religious opinion. Nor has there ever been a movement hostile to faith. Religion is presumed to have a right to criticize the government, and such criticism is never rejected as impertinent. It is not false to say that the churches are the conscience of the nation, and the government is the instrument of a nation with a conscience. Where the churches agree, the government will obey—but agreement is so difficult where 250 different churches exist.

This spirit pervades not only political life but also social life as a whole. A man's faith is sacred and must be respected by his fellows. The American stage, screen and press carefully respect religious conviction and religious symbols. The rare jests about clergymen are always kindly, and more a sign of friendship than hostility or contempt. It is a general presumption that a man believes in God, and has some religious connection, even if only desultory and informal. The clergy are really a privileged class. They travel on the nation's railroads (all of which are private) with a 50 percent reduction of fares. Very many shops and business houses will give them rebates on their purchases. They will be treated by doctors with little or no fee. When queues are formed in restaurants or public gatherings, the clergy are usually escorted to places without awaiting their turn. No nun will ever have to stand in a crowded bus or tram; from all sides men and women will offer them a seat. (This great deference to the clergy is certainly one element in the explanation of the large numbers of American vocations to the priesthood and the religious life.)

In such an environment piety can evolve freely. In the American Catholic Church it has evolved, but it has taken on the modality of the culture of the land. Now the American has a horror of manifesting deep emotions of a personal kind. Piety is considered as primarily personal, and hence it is presumed to be in bad taste to flaunt it in public or even to discuss it. This does not imply any shame because of personal piety or faith, but rather a respect for the holy. A constant reference to one's own or another's religion is considered vulgar and ill-bred. According to American mores religion should not appear in the market-place, not because the market-place is not subject to religion, but because it is not dignified enough to house the religious. The colorful public processions of Mediterranean Catholics are not forbidden by American law: they simply grate on American sensitivity.

Because of the limiting action of American culture, American Catholic piety is peculiar. No visitor to this land is left unimpressed with a visit to a metropolitan church in the busier parts of the cities. Day and night, at all hours, he will find Catholic worshippers at prayer in silence and devotion. The very silence of the church is a living silence, not the silence of an empty tomb. If a visitor attends a Catholic service he will again be impressed by the mannerly conduct of the people. There are no wanderers gadding about; no youths standing at the church-door eyeing the girls who enter; no chattering or conversation. If the visitor comes from certain countries, he is surprised at seeing almost as many men as women present in the pews as well as at the communion rail. But the same visitor will be shocked to find a collector at a table at the church-door demanding an entrance fee. (It really is not a universal custom nor it is an "entrance fee.") He will also be surprised that confessions should be heard only on Saturday afternoons and evenings, but the American Catholics have been disciplined so that they will go to confession only on that day, and they will go in large numbers. In general the visitor will be pleased with the decency of the churches, some of which are extremely beautiful.

In spite of the fact that American Catholicism is chiefly metropolitan and numerically weak in rural areas, Sunday mass attendance is very high in comparison with most European countries. Exaggerated statistics are sometimes given, but it is not an imprudent conjecture to suppose that about 50 percent of the Catholic population assist regularly at Sunday mass. The Friday abstinence will be observed by the vast majority of Catholics, so that all American restaurants have special meatless menues for that day. The last Catholic custom which the man drifting out of the Church will relinquish, will be Friday abstinence. Only when he has considered himself definitively out of the Church will he begin to eat meat on Fridays.

But the European visitor who sees all these things: the many communions, the frequent confessions, the impressive attendance at Sunday mass, will say that these are only externals. What is the state of mind in the Catholics who do all these things? The visitor probably is thinking of intellectualism, and since this is generally absent in American piety, he will find American devotion childish. He will be confirmed in his opinion when he sees the popularity of the non-liturgical novena devotions held everywhere and often with a commercial aspect of miracle-mongering. If he reads the typical diocesan weekly paper, he will note a saddening mediocrity of content and a mass appeal in its format. Many a visitor goes away with the conviction that the American church attendance is merely mechanical with no inner force.

Such a conviction can bring evidence in its favor, but it is not justified by the total reality it is judging. In the first place, it is certainly better that our Catholics go to mass rather than stay away. The material element is the first desideratum, even if not the whole demand. Secondly, the Catholic American is not mechanically present in his pew. He is exercising his piety. The piety of the American Catholic is childlike but not at all childish. It does not rest on profound theology but on deep faith, faith not rationally understood but highly cherished. One might superficially accept the statement that the American Catholics are not convinced Catholics but they are thoroughly persuaded Catholics. The first tie the Catholic feels to the Church is the bond of loyalty. Very many go to Mass not because it involves any religious experience nor because of the excellence of the sermons (which are all too frequently far from excellent), but out of loyalty. This loyalty also explains his readiness to answer the appeals of his pastors and bishops with alacrity and effect. The peculiarly American virtue of "team-spirit" (which is more than *esprit de corps*), can be found in the Catholic even in his religious life and in his piety. In American Catholics there is a strong persuasion that the team must not fail, and if for some reason or other one member of the team falters in his task, another will jump into his place spontaneously. Within the team obedience is always predominant. Orders are not criticized nor analyzed; they are fulfilled. The criticism comes afterwards, especially if the effort was not successful.

There are however two consequences of the American mode of Catholic piety which can be disturbing. Its essential notes are a closed interiority for individual piety and group solidarity for external piety. Inviolable interiority brings with it two bad results. It need not be directed and, in some sense, it should not be directed. Hence fantastic and unsound outlooks can be engendered which can easily vitiate the religious life of the individual. Even when this does not take place, especially in those whose capacity for piety is low, no external manifestation is in theory permitted. This accounts in great part for the indistinguishability of the Catholic in the ordinary activities of life. In the office, in the factory, in the professions, and in social intercourse, the Catholic is rarely distinguished from his non-Catholic fellows. The behavior of both is the same. It is not rare for a Catholic to discover only after years of friendly relations that the man who works next to him is a Catholic also. This is inevitable, for piety should not be manifested and it is impolite to talk about it. What is worse, many Catholics, though quite strict in matters of domestic morality, Catholics who see to it that their children are solidly grounded in ethical matters by giving a splendid example themselves, will in professional life be unscrupulous and sophistic in their evasions of public morality. Not a few Catholic figures in public life have been convicted of highly immoral action, though their sincere and devout adhesion to Catholicism was indisputably evident. The moral shortcomings of the total American community are shared by the Catholics with no notable resistance. The Catholic has striven so hard and so long to be accepted by the American community that he has taken on the color and habits of the general environment, keeping his piety well out of sight. Now that he is unquestionably accepted, he is very loath to do anything which would isolate him from his group, which in its outlook is not Catholic. Piety is invisible and conformity is visible. The American Catholic's attempt at adaptation to his milieu has been successful, perhaps too successful.

Besides the indistinguishability of the Catholic from the non-Catholic, we have the second ambiguity in American Catholicism. The loyal solidarity of the faithful is inspiring, but it entails a lack of sense of responsibility in the formation of programs of activity. The inauguration of projects and their direction are largely left to the clergy. The role of the clergy in American Catholic life is immense. Obviously it should be so in matters of faith, morals and sacramental life. Yet the clergy are dominant beyond these fields. One would imagine such a dominance would arouse anti-clericalism. But it does not. The reasons are many, but all are derived from the American Catholic situation. First of all, the priest is not removed from the people and in his own being and evolution he is rooted in his community. American Catholicism is in general lower middle class tapering upward, and so are the

18 THE CATHOLIC CHURCH, U. S. A.

priests. As an American bishop said publicly, not one American bishop can point to a father who had a college degree. This dictum may not be totally exact, but it certainly is true of the majority of bishops and priests. Priests who come from the laboring class remain loyal to that class and in their priestly activities in the field of labor problems, they represent the laborers' point of view rather than the position of management. Because there is an identity between the priest and the people, he is welcome in all the affairs of his parishioners. His priestly prestige is no obstacle to his sharing in the total life of his congregation. He plays golf, he bowls, he jokes and jests, he sits at the family table. The people are glad to have him around, and youth welcomes him enthusiastically.

The Americans are also strict believers in the distribution of labor. It seems, in consequence, natural that the priest, one of the people, should lead the religious activities of the people. The people expect it and want it so, for, strangely enough, American life in work and play train them for it. Perhaps American play brings this out best. Non-Americans are often amazed to see how mechanical an American sports-event can be. The players are instructed in every detail, and they are expected to obey these instructions. There is little room for spontaneous and personal initiative. The game moves according to a plan fathered and developed not by the players but by the coach. Would it be altogether wrong to say that great sports competitions in this country are struggles between two invisible coaches rather than between two visible teams? One cannot say "no" without reserve, and something of this spirit permeates all American activity.

Hence it is not surprising that it works in American Catholicism as well. The modalities of older, European-born, pastors who successfully ran their parishes like benevolent despots are no longer popular today and they are a sign of the past. But the modern American pastor does something similar but in a genuinely American fashion. He does not order like a king; he orders like a coach. He is of the people but he is a specialist, and as such he has the freely granted right to lead. If he invokes authority, he is lost; if he appeals to his competence as a specialist, he is a success.

No matter how we explain it, it still remains true that the clergy are all too prone to keep the laity out of tasks of planning, and the laity are only too pliant to accept planning and the competent knowledge for it as the reserve of the priests. There is an energetic passivity in American Catholics, but they are weak in initiative.

These three generalizations (for they are not universally valid) will help the reader to understand this book which wishes to give an objective picture of American Catholicism. I repeat the generalizations: first, Catholicism is not induced by American culture but is the exercised choice of the American Catholics; second, the American Catholic is activist rather than contemplative; third, America is propitious to religion and piety so that Catholicism has had a splendid opportunity to develop its own life, which it did in an American way.

In the light of these synthetic generalizations the American Catholic fact can take on significance. The brute fact is obvious enough and quite impressive. In America of a total population of more than 160,000,000, there are 32,000,000 Catholics. This figure is much more realistic than the usual calculations for the countries which culturally are Catholic. The vitality of this church is suggested by its statistics. Within the American Church we have 4 cardinals, 37 archbishops, 173 bishops, 132 dioceses (two of which are of the Byzantine rite), 48,349 priests, 8,868 brothers, 159,545 nuns, 16,193 parishes, 20 universities and 230 university colleges, 505 seminaries, 2,383 secondary schools, 9,569 elementary schools, 931 hospitals, 317 asylums.[1] It is to be remembered that financial resources for the economic maintenance of this vast structure come exclusively from the free-will offerings of the faithful. The government contributes nothing to their support.

---

1. These round numbers are based on the statistics published in *The Official Catholic Directory. A. D. 1956.* New York: Kenedy & Sons, 1954.

We must not fall into the error, pardonable in adolescents and adolescent nations, of considering large numbers as indicators of large significance. Quality is always more meaningful than mere quantity. However, quantity itself is not meaningless. It must be judged in the light of its qualitative significance.

CHAPTER TWO

A History of the Catholic Church
in the United States

———— ◆ ————

BY HENRY J. BROWNE

INASMUCH AS the Catholic Church in the United States
spread outward from the See of Baltimore, we recall
only in passing the Spanish and French missionary activity of
the sixteenth and seventeenth centuries. The Spanish were
active in trying to Christianize the aborigines of Florida in
the Southeast and the natives of what was to become the
states of Arizona, New Mexico and California in the West.
By the eighteenth century, the former missions were virtually
wiped out, and only the Franciscan Friars, who worked out
of Mexico, continued to establish missions along the coast
of California as far as San Francisco by the year 1776 when

---

*Henry J. Browne, a priest of the archdiocese of New York,
is archivist and associate professor of history at the Catholic
University of America. He contributes to* The American
Archivist, *the* Catholic Historical Review, Historical Records
and Studies, *and others. He is currently completing a biogra-
phy of John Hughes, First Archbishop of New York.*

the English colonists on the East coast declared themselves independent of the mother country. Similarly, very little of the French mission work survived among the Indians in the Northeastern states, such as Maine and New York, or in the North Central region of the Great Lakes, or down the Mississippi Valley, where the Jesuits and other missionaries had travelled to missionize the Indians and keep the faith alive among the white settlers.

By the end of the eighteenth century, Catholicism had touched widely but often lightly the great areas of what was to become the United States. The missions to the East of the Mississippi River became the responsibility of the Bishop of Baltimore after the Louisiana purchase made by President Thomas Jefferson from First Counsel Napoleon in 1803. By the middle of the nineteenth century, after victory over Mexico, the ecclesiastical jurisdiction over the Far West also became American. Ecclesiastical continuity of organization was found in a few parishes, such as in Detroit in the Midwest, or in New Orleans, which dated back to 1793, and in the Archdiocese of Oregon City in the Northwest, which dated from 1846 during the Canadian regime. The relics of the Spanish and French colonial Church are found most concretely in the mission churches of the Southwest, some few of which survived, and others have been restored or the style imitated. In the names of pious origin, there is another reminder of that period, although particularly in the East, Protestant Yankee influence changed many of them. Still obvious on the map of the United States there will be found such names as St. Paul and Saulte Ste. Marie in the mid-west, and Los Angeles and Santa Fe in the Far West and many others.

It is necessary, then, to consider Baltimore as the point of origin for the American Church. Its story began in 1634 with the planting of a colony under the proprietorship of the second Baron Baltimore, Cecil Calvert, who was a Catholic. The group of several hundred gentlemen and servants which landed at St. Clement's Island in Chesapeake Bay, south of what is today the capital city of Washington, assisted at Mass on March 25th, the Feast of the Annunciation. The group was numerically more Protestant than Catholic, and Baltimore had given explicit instructions about respecting their consciences and the freedom of their religious observance. Furthermore, he had taken along two Jesuits but only in the same capacity of settlers as the others. This Maryland colony was named after Queen Henrietta Marie and proved by its early history to be the first settlement in the New World where freedom of religion was practiced. There were several occasions when Catholics were fined for infringement of Protestant freedom. With the influx of Protestant Puritans from Virginia it became necessary to embody the tolerant spirit of the founder into a Toleration Act in 1649. This demanded freedom of conscience in religion to all who accepted the Trinity and levied fines for abusive names given to another's religion, such as Jesuit or Papist applied to Catholics. When the Puritan element won political control in 1654 and again in 1689, religious toleration was suspended.

The story of Catholicism in colonial Maryland is a Jesuit one, although technically from 1688 to the Revolution the Vicar Apostolic of the London District presided over the Church in the colonies. The Society of Jesus began to acquire property for support of themselves and in time also the slaves to work those lands. It was made quite clear by the proprietor of the colony that old privileges and special position for clerics which canon law had provided in Europe would have no place in the New World. These priests ministered to Catholics in the area of southern Maryland where their Jesuit descendants still staff the churches of the parishes which are often today those of poor Negroes. They conducted a secondary school at Bohemia Manor near the Pennsylvania border by the middle of the eighteenth century. By 1735 Jesuit missionaries opened the first chapel in Philadelphia, the capital of the colony founded by the Quaker, William Penn, where alone outside of Maryland Catholics were found in any number and with complete legal toleration. Even in Baltimore's colony there were penal periods, reflecting the picture of Catholicism in England and Ireland, during which priests' activity and even their presence in the area were proscribed.

From 1718 to 1776 in Maryland, the Catholic establishment, none of the 10,000 adult Catholics could even cast a vote in an election.

Outside of Maryland, as the eighteenth century progressed, Catholics were found mostly in Penn's colony where in numbers they amounted to about a third of those in the area to the south. The system of colonizing by means of indentured servants or workmen bonded to a master for a period of time resulted in some Catholics finding their way into Protestant colonies. There most of them must have fallen away from their religion from lack of opportunities to practice it. Many of them came mixed in with the non-English element in the thirteen colonies who were Scotch-Irish and Germans. The former were Scotch Presbyterians who had been transplanted to Northern Ireland, and thence many came to America and were called Scotch-Irish. The latter were from the Rhine district and some from Switzerland, but because of the predominant group they became known as Palatines and eventually as the Pennsylvania Dutch, since most of them first settled in the western part of that colony. Besides Lutherans and Moravians and German Reformed, there were Catholics in this wave of early immigration as the chapels at Goshenhoppen and Conewago around Philadelphia illustrated. The Irish element left less concrete traces, for only an infrequent Catholic school master appears on the colonial scene to indicate their presence. Finally there were the 6,000 French Catholic Acadians who were transported for purposes of strategy in 1755 by the British authorities from the region of Nova Scotia on the southeastern coast of Canada to the coastal colonies to the south. They added to the Catholic population in some centers like the city of Baltimore but as often as not they were swallowed up in the Protestant population.

Thus there began the unending process of Catholics in America being overwhelmed by their Protestant environment, very often just from want of priests to work among them. As early as the 1830's their losses in the South were lamented. In the next generation they were feared to be in danger on the priestless frontier of the West, and by the following generation warnings were heard against the losses arising from their position in the crowded Eastern cities. Now this phenomenon is referred to as the "leakage" and ever since Bishop John England of Charleston in the early nineteenth century said over three millions were lost to the Faith, there has been no real agreement on the statistics involved except that England was very wrong. Irish names on many Protestants in the South especially are partially explained by this phenomenon.

Pressures for defection in early America were great, for the position of colonial Catholics was not a pleasant one. In several northern colonies the Congregationalists were the established state religion, and similarly in the South the Anglicans had this position. The restrictions on Catholics limiting their ability to vote or hold office would not be fully eliminated for over twenty-five years after the winning of American independence. So deep was the American distrust of Catholicism that it can be seen as a real inheritance from the English experience of the first settlers passed on to their descendants. During the colonial wars, which in the eighteenth century were the American counterparts of struggle for empire in Europe, Catholics as members of a church to which the French and Spanish gave loyalty were open to suspicion as collaborators within the English settlements. The dreaded papists were linked in plots with warring Indians who raided frontier villages and were viewed as menaces to the security of colonial English Protestants. The fact was that enemies of empire to the North and South were Catholic powers.

The policy that England pursued in Canada when France's American empire fell in 1763 gave occasion for a demonstration of this strong anti-Catholicism. The Quebec Act of 1774 recognized the legal and religious arrangement of French Canada and this was used by the propagandists of revolution in the English colonies. The Romish threat to their very existence now at their borders was used to stir up excitement to the extent that the act has been joined with the "intolerable acts" restricting the American colonies within the imperial framework as a primary cause of the break with the mother country. Catholics, nonetheless, were as loyal as their neighbors to the new cause, which would mean about a third gave active support. The man who had most to lose in terms of property by signing the rebellious Declaration of Independence in 1776 was Charles Carroll of Carrollton. His cousin, Father John Carroll, accompanied a group headed by the leading statesman and outstanding American of his day, even in the salons of Paris, Benjamin Franklin, to try without success to win Canadian assistance in the revolt. Add to this the fact that some of the Commander-in-Chief, George Washington's, aides were Catholic, (Catholic Captain John Barry fathered the navy), and most of all that Catholic France and later Spain gave aid that was indispensable for victory. It is plain why officials of the Continental Congress would join in thanksgiving service at St. Mary's in Philadelphia and why Washington would write publicly and with great kindness of Catholics and their loyalty to the new country.

In 1789, the year that the Federal Government was launched, the American hierarchy was also begun with the consecration of John Carroll in England. Carroll was one of about two dozen ex-Jesuits in the new republic who made up almost the entire priesthood of the country since the order had been suppressed in 1773. He had been superior of the missions, and then by special concession which allowed a vote of the clergy he was elected as first bishop. As he took up his task, he was handicapped by a lack of priests. To face this problem he brought over the French Sulpicians who began at St. Mary's Seminary in Baltimore a long tradition for training a native clergy for American dioceses which continues to this day, but is shared now by seculars, Vincentians, Jesuits and Benedictines.

Another problem was centered in the laity and amounted to unwarranted interference in church administration. This became known as "trusteeism" since the members of the church boards were called "trustees," and it remained a difficulty for over half a century. Due to the laws of the individual American states which were inspired by the needs of Protestants, Catholic churches too had legal status only by the incorporation of a group of members. The laymen so elected often engaged in political maneuvers to keep their positions as trustees and soon were questioning episcopal decisions in the choice of pastors, and in general dividing local Catholic groups into struggling factions. Philadelphia Catholicism in the 1830's witnessed the most infamous of these battles in the Hogan Schism. The spirit of Jacksonian democracy, which was abroad in the land by the 1830's and marked the rise in importance of the common man, also affected this trend which, in threatening the authority of the bishop, ended by centralizing his power and lessening for almost a century afterwards the role of the laity in the work of the Church.

The United States was Francophile after winning its independence and the Church was to profit from this. Emigre clergy who fled the revolution in France made a great contribution to the early development. Some of them like Stephen Badin and Simon Gabriel Brute moved out onto the first frontier of the trans-Allegheny West, at times abandoning seminary desks in the East to link up the old French mission remnants with Baltimore. Two sisterhoods were founded by 1818 to care for this western Catholic growth through their schools, while in the East the Sisters of Charity founded by Elizabeth Seton remained the principal body of religious women for several decades. In both areas of the country and as early as Carroll's time there were nationality problems. Germans in Philadelphia protested their neglect in a foreshadowing of charges that would be made again in the 1880's. The French priests, like Jean Cheverus who went as first bishop to Boston in 1808 (the other three suffragan sees established at that time were New York, Philadelphia and Bardstown, Kentucky), were outstanding for zeal and propriety of life but often an Irishman of undesirable character but with preaching ability would win out in popular favor to the detriment of the French.

The fact remains that in the early national period, the

American Church was probably more socially acceptable than
ever again in its history. Cultured Frenchmen had been
added to the old American stock in the clergy and even the
Irish, both clerical and lay, who were rising in influence, were
well educated, as for example the refugees of the Irish revolutionary attempt of 1798. Bishop John England was Irish
and of this early type. As he rose to a position of leadership
in the 1830's, he showed his appreciation of things American.
He did this in adopting a constitution for the governance of
his diocese in the South and by advocating strongly and with
success by 1829 the first meeting of all the bishops in council.
His promotion of the *Catholic Miscellany* in 1823, the first
real Catholic newspaper in the United States, was thoroughly
American, for the reading of papers was becoming a national
mania. This bishop was even invited to address the Congress
of the United States. As Charleston faded into insignificance
as a port city, so did that episcopal see as a center of leadership after England's day. With his passing in 1842 there went
too the strongest of those who were marked by a deep distrust of the French clergy within the American Church. The
greatest changes of the period of the forties, however, were
to be a result of the flood of Irish and German peasant immigrants that broke on the country.

With this the Catholic minority became gradually more
definitely identified as foreign to the United States. Theological debates in public gatherings had not been uncommon as
when John Hughes, (the leader of the American Church by
mid-century from his position as Archbishop of New York),
argued in 1835 as a young priest with a noted Presbyterian
minister, whether Catholicism was compatible with civil and
religious liberty. Matters went beyond oratory in 1836 when
a convent near Boston was burned to the ground by a mob
inflamed by nativist writing and preaching against Catholics.
The traditional revelations of escaped nuns and other por-
nography had their origin at this time and have never completely died in the repeated expressions of America's most
persistent bias. In 1844 two churches were burned in Philadelphia in riotings that smacked of outburst controlled by

the anti-papist Orange lodges of northern Ireland. The war against Mexico, in which as usual Catholics were heavily enrolled, even by this time in positions of officers, and in which Catholic chaplains were first officially appointed, helped to cool these biased American sentiments. By that time too the Catholic press had bloomed,—the *Catholic Standard* of Philadelphia, *Freeman's Journal* in New York, *Wahrheitsfreund* in Cincinnati, and these were chiefly organs of defense. They increased during the rest of the century and were often conducted by laymen with a personal touch and sense of independence (even of the bishops) which led to battling with one another as well as outside opponents in a spirit that died when bourgeois respectability settled over Catholic journalism in twentieth century America.

A major turning point came in the 1840's when Catholics officially rejected the state supported schools as dangerous to the Faith of their children because of prejudiced text books, non-Catholic versions of the Bible, and the general Protestant tone given to these tax-financed establishments. The brief experience of getting some public funds for schools conducted by religious groups generally speaking came to an end, although there would be local exceptions to this rule even into the next century. Bishops therefore began the struggle, with particular success in the heavily German area of the state of Ohio, to staff the parish schools with religious brothers and sisters usually desperately sought in Europe. Actually the very first parochial schools growing out of instruction classes in catechism were established with lay teachers and for a century this custom had to be at least partially followed for want of religious. Schools began to be built before a church building when parishes were established, and the heavy financial burden was put on the immigrant flocks, the laborers in the national economic picture, particularly the Irish who were expending freely in building first the canals and then the railroads which drew the nation together before the 1860's. Despite these efforts promoted constantly by ecclesiastical legislation, it would not seem that there has ever been more than half of the Catholic

children in the parish elementary schools. A strong tradition
of Catholic distrust for the public schools had its concomitant
origin in the 1840's, although some within the Church who
grew increasingly strong with time insisted that the two types
of schools should cooperate.

By the end of the decade of the 1850's a pattern of Catholicism was emerging. State laws began more to allow the
bishop to hold church property alone or with a select few,
and the way was prepared for heads of dioceses (without
chapters of canons as American legislation developed under
Roman approval) and pastors to become the bearers of the
full burden of temporalities—or business men as well as spir-   ·
itual leaders. Chancery offices were being organized in answer
to more pressing social needs which every diocese faced in
opening orphanages, hospitals, or homes for wayward girls.
The Irish, unhappy with the farming experience which
ended in the scourge of famine and without funds, stayed
mostly in eastern cities near their chapels and taverns and
their friends. In this they were encouraged by episcopal leaders in that section, despite some organized ecclesiastical effort
to settle them in colonies on western farm lands. Another
such effort to remove them from the slums of the east in the
1870's would meet with only very slight success. More of the
Germans (and about a third of their total was Catholic) did
go West but they too helped to build up cities in that area
like Cincinnati, St. Louis, and Milwaukee. The predominantly urban character of American Catholicism was therefore determined a century ago. The western and southwestern
areas, where the last of the Spanish efforts had left nothing
but decay, came under American ecclesiastical jurisdiction,
presenting an Indian problem for missionaries that still en-
dures. The land of the Gold Rush soon gave voice to request
to prelates in the east to send priests among the pioneers, although the first came down from the Northwest in the person
of Jesuits. It was in order to face such problems—although
many of them were also ignored by the assembled bishops—
that the hierarchy met in national council in 1851 and cli-

maxed the series of provincial meetings which had been held under the metropolitan of Baltimore.

The Civil War in 1861 brought havoc and yet some prestige to the Church in the United States. There was real ruin in dioceses like Charleston and Memphis, which stood in line of battle, and distress for the Church throughout the defeated South. Many Catholic boys' colleges closed for want of students at that time. There was no Catholic split on the slavery controversy such as marked organized Protestantism, although strong sentiments were aired on both sides. In the plenary council of 1866, talk of a separate ecclesiastical jurisdiction as a way of giving attention to the freed Negroes never came to fruition. Actually, special work in that field would begin only in the 1890's under the English Mill Hill Fathers who gave origin to the American Josephites. As early as 1903 Rome inquired about discrimination against Negro Catholics in the United States, but the hierarchy's answer was to point to missionary activity among them.

This war also gave a chance for patriotic Catholic service. Sisterhoods sent nurses to battlefields and hospitals. Chaplains were authorized by both governments. Archbishop Hughes acted as an agent of the Union to help convince Napoleon to keep French neutrality, despite the suffering caused in his country by the end of cotton supply from the blockaded southern states. On the other hand, Bishop John Lynch of Charleston was a representative of the Confederate Government abroad, but received no recognition from the Papal Court as anything but a bishop. Catholics fought on both sides but the war left no great fission, although the South continued to be an area into which European immigration did not go. Where once it had been the slave system which kept the Catholic laborer out, later it would be the turbulent reconstruction decade after the war, and then the great allure of the industrial cities and western farms. The South thus became anything but a stronghold of the Church. The section remains the one most given to anti-Catholic prejudice.

The period of the large scale exploitation of America's

natural resources beginning in the 1870's vitally affected the
life of the Church. Since less than ten per cent of those who
might be considered industrial or business leaders would be
Catholic, even in the first decade of the twentieth century,
Catholic proletarians and members of the rising middle class
looked to Protestant Americans with resentment when they
felt their lot heavy. It was Irish Catholics who were hanged
in the anthracite coal fields of Pennsylvania for lawless out-
breaks against harsh mining conditions. They went under
the name of Molly Maguires and, as an episode, it was most
important in turning the Catholic press to an awareness of
the social problem and led to the first major Catholic questioning of the *laissez-faire* philosophy of government. Catholic laborers had already begun to join non-religious unions
of workers, some of which were quasi-masonic in their secrecy, oaths, and rituals. In the prohibition of joining the
dozens of such fraternal and benevolent societies, American
Catholics were further cut off from their fellow citizens, but
when it was a matter of mutual help they did not hesitate to
join unions, although great uneasiness existed for a time in
the consciences of some.

By 1881 Catholic efforts within the national organizations
of labor, the Knights of Labor, resulted in changes leading
toward more practical trade unionism. When this group had
reached a total of 700,000 in 1887, it was estimated that it was
half Catholic in membership and had many Catholic leaders
including its head, Terence V. Powderly. James Cardinal
Gibbons of Baltimore led the overwhelming majority of
bishops who felt Rome should tolerate the Knights of Labor
in the United States in spite of having twice condemned it
on the presentation of the Archbishop of Quebec. The resulting publicity in the United States put the Church on the
side of organized labor with a vehemence greater than the
facts since ascertained would warrant. Mass defections of
workers from a church of the bosses or of the respectable middle class seems thereby to have been curtailed. Furthermore,
this controversy and that over Catholic support of Henry
George's theories on private property called the "Single Tax"

—which Rome condemned, to satisfy both sides of the hierarchy, but *sub secreto*—was an American contribution toward bringing out *Rerum novarum,* the statement of Pope Leo XIII on the social question in 1891.

The period of the 1880's and 1890's was seriously marked by other problems of adjustment of Catholicism to the American environment. All of them were aggravated by the "new immigration," the peoples from southern and southeastern Europe, who added a great deal to the perplexities of the *cura animarum* by their strange languages and frequent lack of priests from their own countries. For example, the Italians were peculiarly priestless and uninstructed in their religion by American standards, the Poles were independent to the point of schism of some (the only large scale break of its kind) into a Polish National Church, and the Oriental Catholics, with a bearded and married clergy, were badly misunderstood. The Germans by the mid 1880's were protesting in Rome their neglect at the hands of a predominantly Irish hierarchy. As early as the 1850's that had been a nativist trend even in the selection of American bishops, but the Germans, and what came to be considered the conservative wing of the hierarchy, led by Michael A. Corrigan, Archbishop of New York, began to find a peculiarly American "liberalism" amongst other members of the episcopate like Gibbons and particularly John Ireland, Archbishop of St. Paul. This was worked up with the help of the writings of some French theologians and observers of American life into the heresy of "Americanism" which was condemned by Rome's *Testem benevolentiae* in 1899. American Catholics united in denying then, as they still do, the existence of heretical notions in their midst and admitted at most to trends along the lines of accusation, such as emphasis on the active over the passive virtues, emphasis on religious vows, and softening of dogma for Protestant ears.

The listing of bishops of the late nineteenth century in two columns according to the speed with which they would have accommodated the Church to America is perhaps an over-simplification, but they did divide time after time. The conservatives, like Bishop Bernard McQuaid of Rochester, were not enthusiastic for the dream of a national and pontifical school for graduate studies in all fields which was to cap the Catholic secondary and collegiate institutions already existing throughout the United States. Nonetheless, it opened with Bishop John H. Keane as rector, under the hierarchy's auspices in 1889 as The Catholic University of America in Washington, the nation's capital. Similarly, when a scheme that had its origins in the 1840's in New England and had been used in New York, too, of getting state support for the parish school by teaching religion after school hours was tried by Archbishop Ireland, he was accused of undermining the parochial school system. Such problems as these and the constant stream of squabbles between pastors and bishops helped to bring the Apostolic Delegate to the United States as a permanent feature of American Catholic life in 1893. With the removal from the supervision of the Congregation of Propaganda in 1908, full maturity was predicated of the American Church. Obviously, its record in the nineteenth century, with imitative copyists for church artists, with much writing but no great literature (the journalist, Orestes Brownson a convert active in mid-century being the nearest to an outstanding thinker and writer), with teachers and scholars dependent on European training and writing—in short the story of a building Church, sacramentarian and essential in its emphasis—would not prove that more than legal maturity had been attained.

The Catholic laity by the 1890's were again moving toward some recognition. Their growth in respectability in American society was an underlying cause for the new anti-Catholicism, that of the American Protective Association. The traditional challenges to Protestant gullibility were paraded with a few new ones, including a bogus papal call to Catholics to arise and take over the country, even as they would be brought out again in 1928 to help defeat a Catholic candidate for the presidency in the person of Al Smith. The nativism of that last period was the work of the Ku Klux Klan. The American Protective Association, however, like its Know-Nothing counterpart of the 1850's, tried strongly to invade the political field, but fell short after some successes on the local level, especially in the mid-west. Signs of improvement were shown before the turn of the century, for the reaction of some Protestant ministers was to condemn the bigotry of some of their fellow religionists. Catholic laymen received another type of notice when they were invited to give papers in 1889 at a Congress marking the centenary of the episcopate in the country, but they remained under close supervision of the bishops even in this. Catholics moved more easily into government positions, and they continued to be found in influential positions in the trade union movement. In the business trade unionism of the American Federation of Labor, which differed from the long-ranged reformist emphasis of the defunct Knights of Labor, they helped to keep the movement non-politicized by the socialists within it. Within the Church itself the laity formed a Federation of Catholic Societies, which amounted mostly to a device for an annual convention at which papers were delivered and resolutions passed. Since the 1850's German Catholics had had their Central Verein, and since the 1870's the Irish their Catholic Benevolent Union, and since the 1880's all had had the Catholic answer to the national urgency for fraternal secret societies, the Knights of Columbus.

Catholics entered the twentieth century being thoroughly American—as even the jingoism of some American bishops about the Spanish American War had shown—and therefore fearful of social upheaval. The sanctity of private property was about their social philosophy and the fear of Modernism their school of thought. A new circle of seminaries came into being in the late nineties, and money for foreign missions began to become something sent from the United States after ten decades of receiving alms from France, Germany, Austria, the British Isles and other parts of Europe. A small voice of social Catholicism began to be heard in John A. Ryan at The Catholic University of America with his study on the *Living Wage* in 1906, and by 1919 the Bishops' Program of Social Reconstruction, which he had authored, was making him heard throughout the land. Its recommendation became the common basis of social legislation in the New Deal period of the early 1930's, although it was widely denounced as socialistic at the time of its publication.

With World War I and American entry into it there came the challenge of mobilizing Catholic efforts, and out of this came the National Catholic War Council, which grew into today's National Catholic Welfare Conference. The old federation gave way and the bishops' organization took its place, centralizing on a national scale, even as in the century before they brought things together in their dioceses. In the 1920's they would further organize diocesan charitable work and do it under clerical supervision. On the national and local levels the laymen were again temporarily set aside and had to await the call to Catholic Action to restore them to a place of dignity. That is a position that history would give them in the Church in the United States, since it was there that for the first time in the Christian era, the faithful preceded the priests and cried for them to come out to them; not to evangelize, but to keep alive their faith.

CHAPTER THREE

The Holy See and the Church in the United States

BY EDWARD A. RYAN, S.J.

THE CATHOLIC CHURCH in the United States is the daughter of the Roman Church in a way that few Churches are. To be sure, Rome is the mother of all the Churches of the West and recourse has always been had to Rome in the *causee majores* and what concerns the state of religion in general. But owing to the circumstances of the times, Rome's surveillance of the American Church has, perhaps, been closer and more effective than was the case of other national churches.

In the Middle Ages time-distances were too great to permit of much control. Moreover, kings and princes frequently took the lead in the organization of new churches and often paid Rome little more than nominal allegiance. In the sixteenth, seventeenth and eighteenth centuries the aristocratic

Edward A. Ryan, S.J., is Professor of Church History, Woodstock College, Woodstock, Maryland since 1936. He holds a title "Docteur en Sciences Historiques" from Louvain.

rulers of the principal countries from which missionaries were sent insisted on such intensive control that Rome's guidance was greatly limited. But in nineteenth century America, because of the absence of ties between State and Church, Rome was in general successful in guiding the development of the Church. Counterbalancing this favorable circumstance was the deep suspicion and even hatred of the Catholic Church entertained by many Protestant Americans. In 1785 the leader of the American Church spoke of "the jealousy of our government towards all jurisdiction of a foreign kind." [1] These sentiments have never ceased to torment large segments of the nation and have influenced unfavorably the development of the Church in the United States.

The principal instrument which the popes used in ruling the American Church was, up to 1908, the Sacred Congregation *De propaganda fide* or Propaganda as it is called. Even questions which normally involved other congregations were referred to Propaganda. The saying that Propaganda *omnes alias congregationes in ventre habet* applied to its relations to the American Church until 1908.[2] From 1808 to 1814, it is true, the Napoleonic oppression of the Papacy brought Propaganda's activities almost to a standstill. During this brief period, the American Church, which had in 1808 been reorganized by the elevation of Baltimore to metropolitan rank and the creation of the suffragan sees of New York, Boston, Philadelphia and Bardstown (Louisville), had to operate under conditions similar to those of earlier centuries. The fall of Napoleon brought back effective control by Propaganda.[3] One of the nineteenth century popes, Gregory XVI, had been Prefect of Propaganda before his election. With the insight gained from that experience, he was able to give the congregation unusually efficient support but all the nineteenth and twentieth century popes have shown great

---

1. P. Guilday, *Life and Times of John Carroll* (New York, 1922) I, 237.
2. B. Ojetti, *De Romana Curia* (Rome, 1910), p. 114.
3. F. Schwager, *Die katholische Heidenmission der Gegenwart* (Steyl, 1907), p. 19.

skill in ruling American ecclesiastical matters. In 1908 St. Pius X withdrew the United States from the tutelage of Propaganda and thenceforth its supervision was conducted in the manner usual in traditionally Catholic countries.

At the time of the peace between England and the revolting colonies (1783), the prospects of the Church in the United States were far from brilliant. The roughly 30,000 Catholics lived for the most part in Maryland and Pennsylvania. They were served by a handful of priests, ex-members of the suppressed Society of Jesus. Among the clergy, John Carroll (1735-1815) stood out as the leader destined to found the American hierarchy. In order to serve the cause of religion in his native land, he had refused the offer of advantageous positions in England at the time of the suppression of the Society of Jesus, to which he had belonged. Rome was watchful and tried to make use of the good offices of France, to which in part the new country owed its independence, to secure freedom for the Catholic religion in the United States. Propaganda also toyed with the idea of entrusting to the French crown the patronage of the nascent Church.[4] Since French diplomats and churchmen were not much interested in this proposal, friends of Carroll were able to secure his appointment as superior of the American missions in 1784. Five years later Pius VI erected at Baltimore the first see in the United States and made it independent of any metropolitan and immediately subject to Rome. The priests laboring in the States were permitted to elect their first bishop. By 24 votes out of 26 they chose Carroll who was consecrated in England in 1790.[5] Thus the founder of the American hierarchy was not only a native son but also the choice of his fellow priests.

Since 1789 there has been a remarkable development of the hierarchy of the United States. Not to mention prefectures and vicariates apostolic, the Holy See has in that period erected in the United States 125 Latin-rite dioceses of which

---

4. J. Baisnée, *France and the Establishment of the American Hierarchy* (Baltimore, 1934), p. 129 ff.

5. D. Shearer, *Pontificia Americana* (New York, 1933), p. 79 f.

23 were later elevated to the rank of archdioceses, 100 continue today and two have been suppressed. In addition there are three archdioceses (Portland, San Francisco and Washington) which were never simple dioceses. Two dioceses for Catholics of Oriental Rites have been established and Belmont Abbey is an *abbatia nullius*.

As we have seen, Pius VI (1775-1799) established the first see at Baltimore. He also erected in 1793 the Diocese of Louisiana and the Two Floridas which later (1826) became the Diocese and ultimately (1850) the Archdiocese of New Orleans. But in 1793 Louisiana and the Two Floridas were not as yet parts of the United States. During his reign (1800-1823) Pius VII raised Baltimore to the metropolitan rank and established seven dioceses. Leo XII (1823-1829) and Pius VIII (1829-1830) each established one diocese in the United States while eleven American dioceses owe their foundation to Gregory XVI (1831-1846).

Pius IX (1846-1878) was the great organizer of the American Church.[6] He erected no less than ten archdioceses (Portland, St. Louis, Cincinnati, New Orleans, New York, San Francisco, Boston, Milwaukee, Philadelphia, and Santa Fé) and 37 dioceses of which two (Allegheny and Walla Walla) were later suppressed. Three archdioceses (Chicago, St. Paul and Dubuque) and twenty-seven dioceses owe their establishment to Leo XIII (1878-1903). St. Pius X (1903-1914) created thirteen Latin Rite dioceses and the Ukrainian Greek Catholic Diocese (at Philadelphia). Benedict XV (1914-1922) erected only one diocese in the United States. Pius XI (1922-1939) erected five archdioceses (San Antonio, Los Angeles, Detroit, Louisville and Newark), ten Latin Rite dioceses and the Ruthenian Diocese (at Pittsburgh). The present Holy Father Pius XII has established seven archdioceses (Denver, Indianapolis, Omaha, Washington, Seattle, Kansas City, Hartford) and fifteen dioceses.[7]

6. When Pius IX was elected, the Archbishop of Baltimore had more than twenty suffragan bishops.

7. In addition to Shearer and the *National Catholic Directory*, cf. P. P. Ciangetti, "A Diocesan Chronology of the Catholic Church in the United States," in *Catholic Historical Review*, 28, 57-70.

The creation of new dioceses was brought about in various ways. Baltimore was erected at the request of the American priests who found that a simple superior lacked the prestige necessary to solve the problems which faced the nascent Church. The elevation of Baltimore to an archbishopric and the creation of the four suffragan sees in 1808 was a result of Carroll's request, made as early as 1792, that his diocese be divided. Propaganda proposed in 1802 that four or five sees be erected. Carroll's proposal of Bardstown (Louisville), Boston, New York and Philadelphia was accepted in Rome. The creation of the Diocese of Charleston in 1820 was in accord with the mind of the American hierarchy, but that of Richmond in the same year was largely the result of intrigue.[8] Thereafter, however, new dioceses and archdioceses were as a rule established by Rome on the recommendation of the provincial and plenary councils which were quite numerous through the century. Since the establishment of the Apostolic Delegation in January, 1893, the Holy Father has consulted the Apostolic Delegate and the ordinary or ordinaries involved in the change. That the advice received has, in general, been pertinent, is indicated by the fact that only two dioceses have had to be suppressed and only about a score of changes of title or transfers from one city to another have been necessary.

The choice of bishops was an important and ever present problem. Bishop Carroll, as we have seen, was elected by the clergy. His coadjutors were chosen by him with the concurrence of the priests. Carroll nominated Cheverus, the first bishop of Boston, Flaget, the first bishop of Bardstown (Louisville), and Egan the first bishop of Philadelphia. Concanen, an Irish Dominican resident in Rome, was appointed first bishop of New York in 1808 without American advice. He died, however, before taking possession of his see.

Carroll, Cheverus, Egan, Flaget and Neale in 1810 "humbly and respectfully suggested to the supreme pastor of the

---

8. *Records of the American Catholic Historical Society*, 38: 297-354, C. F. McCarthy, "The Historical Development of Episcopal Nominations in the Catholic Church of the United States (1784-1884)," p. 331 ff.

Church to allow the nomination for vacant dioceses to proceed solely from the Archbishop and Bishops of this Ecclesiastical Province." [9] In 1814 however, Connolly, another Irish Dominican, long resident in Rome, was appointed second bishop of New York without consultation of the American bishops. And to make matters worse, Connolly was a subject of Great Britain, then at war with the United States. Archbishop Carroll protested against what he considered interference on the part of certain Irish bishops in the affairs of the American Church. On their part, the Irish prelates had been led to believe that the interests of Irish Catholics were being neglected in this country. Carroll and his suffragans moved to have Father John David, a French-born Sulpician, appointed bishop of Philadelphia. This time, also, the Holy See acted contrary to American desires and appointed an Irish priest, Henry Conwell, second Bishop of Philadelphia, David becoming eventually coadjutor of Bardstown.[10]

Through the influence of Bishop Cheverus, Archbishop Neale chose Ambrose Maréchal as his coadjutor. Maréchal succeeded to Baltimore in 1817. In 1820 the Bishop of Quebec, Joseph Octave Plessis was in Rome and he was sent as Apostolic Delegate to learn the facts about certain controversies which had arisen in the Church of the United States and to restore peace. In his report Plessis informed the Prefect of Propaganda that, "the Catholics have in general great respect and affection for their French bishops and that if there are some complaints against those of this nation, they are raised by Irish monks." [11] In that year the dioceses of Charleston and Richmond were filled without consulting the American hierarchy by the appointment of the Irish Priests, Patrick Kelly and John England. The former, who found that Richmond was incapable of supporting a bishop, soon returned to Ireland to fill the see of Waterford whereas the latter became one of the luminaries of the American Church.

This action of Rome in appointing men who knew noth-

---

9. *Ibid.*, p. 323.
10. *Ibid.*, p. 328.
11. *Ibid.*, p. 329.

ing of American conditions, led Maréchal and his suffragans to complain that the Church in the United States was victim of a foreign (Irish) conspiracy. In return Maréchal was informed that "neither the Archbishop of Baltimore nor his suffragans had the right to nominate to vacant sees." [12] Maréchal acquiesced, but nonetheless he pointed out that only men on the spot could nominate capable and worthy subjects. Rome was impressed by Maréchal's pleas and in June, 1822, the American bishops were given the right of recommendation to vacancies in the United States. Moreover, the recommendations of Maréchal and his suffragans led to the appointment of Benedict Fenwick to Boston and John Dubois to New York in 1826 and to the choice of James Whitfield as Coadjutor of Baltimore in 1828. The fact that Bishop Conwell had to be relieved of his responsibilities at Philadelphia served to confirm the new policy.

In 1833 the Second Provincial Council of Baltimore informed Rome that some unified system of episcopal appointment was a necessity. They proposed a method of nomination of candidates by the archbishop and his suffragans which was complicated since it took into account all the likely contingencies. Propaganda approved of the plan the following year but insisted that the names sent from America were not really "elections, nominations or postulations but true recommendations, imposing no obligation on the Holy See to select any of the candidates mentioned." [13] This plan was found to be practical and remained in effect with modifications until 1866.

When Pius IX began to multiply the American archbishoprics, this fact had to be fitted into the system. In 1850 Propaganda decreed that "the archbishop in whose province the vacancy occurs will transmit to the other archbishops of the nation the names proposed." [14] In 1856 this provision was virtually abolished since in many provinces only the archbishop and his suffragans were now to be consulted.

---

12. *Ibid.*, p. 332.
13. Mansi, *Concilia*, t. 39, 320.
14. *Records of the American Catholic Historical Society*, 38, 340.

Three years later, however, a papal rescript granted all the archbishops of the country a deliberative vote in the election of a metropolitan.[15]

In 1861 Rome, which had previously consulted the American hierarchy, made some suggestions which were embodied in the decrees of the Second Plenary Council of Baltimore (1866). Each bishop was to send triennially to his metropolitan and to Propaganda the names of priests considered worthy of elevation to the episcopate. In the case of a vacancy the prelates concerned were to meet and vote on the eligible candidates and the minutes of the meeting were to be forwarded to Propaganda. These regulations were in force for twenty years.[16]

From 1833 on Propaganda had expressed a desire to see cathedral chapters such as existed in England, Ireland and Holland instituted in the United States. One reason for this was the desire of the Holy See that priests might have some active voice in the selection of bishops. The American hierarchy resisted this move. In 1852, however, the fathers of the First Plenary Council of Baltimore urged that distinguished priests should be chosen to aid the bishops as consultors in the administration of their dioceses. The Eighth Provincial Council of Baltimore (1855) advised an increase in the number of consultors and recommended that they be given a share in naming the candidates for the episcopacy. The Second Plenary Council of Baltimore (1866) again urged the appointment of consultors who were gradually becoming a part of diocesan organization in the United States.[17]

During the preliminary meetings held in Rome in the early winter of 1883 in preparation for the Third Plenary Council of Baltimore, Propaganda again urged the institution of chapters. But in the face of objections from the American bishops a system of diocesan consultors was agreed upon in their place. One of the curious consequences of this rejection of chapters is that the American Church is devoid

---

15. *Ibid.*, p. 342.
16. Mansi, 48, 927.
17. Mansi, 44, 674 f.; 47, 147 f.; 48, 919.

of diocesan honors equivalent to the canonries of European dioceses. In their place in almost every American diocese the leading priests receive papal honors as papal chamberlains, domestic prelates, and protonotaries apostolic.

At the Third Plenary Council of Baltimore (1884) detailed legislation for the selection of bishops was adopted. This provided that within thirty days after a vacancy, the consultors and irremovable rectors of the vacant see were to meet under the presidency of the metropolitan or his deputy and select three candidates whose names, the *terna,* would then be submitted to the bishops of the province. When a metropolitan was to be selected, the senior suffragan or his deputy would preside. The bishops of the province were to assemble for discussion of the *terna* within ten days. They had the right to approve or disapprove of any or of all of these candidates. Provisions were likewise made for the selection of coadjutor bishops and bishops of newly erected sees. This legislation is especially significant in that it gave the priests of the dioceses a share in the selection of their bishop.[18]

This continued to be the practice in the United States, with the *terna* forwarded to Rome through the Apostolic Delegation, after January 1893. The system had much to recommend it as a more democratic method of selection, but it proved almost impossible to safeguard the secrecy of the names submitted and long delays often ensued. As a consequence of the not infrequent embarrassment to the Holy See by the publicity given to the candidates, the Consistorial Congregation issued a decree on July 25, 1916, which put the choice of the candidates exclusively in the hands of the bishops.[19] This system has remained operative in the American Church to the present time.

In general it must be said that the various methods of selecting bishops were successful. They gave the American Church able and devoted prelates who met the difficulties attendant on the foundation of a church with energy and competence. The joke attributed to Pius IX expresses in leg-

18. *Records of the American Catholic Historical Society,* 38, 349 ff.
19. T. L. Bouscaren, *The Canon Law Digest* (Milwaukee, 1934), I, 195 ff.

endary form their resourcefulness. According to the story the Holy Father when asked for a certain dispensation replied, "That I cannot grant. You will have to ask an American bishop." It is worth noting, too, that relatively few American bishops have been involved in serious differences with Rome and a still smaller number have had to be removed from office.

Rome, on its part, tried to smooth the path for the American hierarchy. In 1791 Bishop Carroll, who was constantly alert to remove occasions of criticism from his Protestant fellow countrymen, petitioned the Holy See for permission to alter the wording of the customary episcopal oath in so far as it applied to the bishops of the United States. In 1794 Propaganda gave its consent to the deletion of the troublesome promise to "seek out and oppose schismatics, heretics and the enemies" of the Holy See. In this manner the consciences of the American bishops were eased at a time when many of their French colleagues were accepting deposition or exile rather than take the oath to support the Civil Constitution of the Clergy and when, too, the episcopates of the British Isles were agitated by the problem of oaths of civil allegiance.[20]

Forty-five American bishops were present at the Vatican Council (1869-1870). When the debates turned on the use of Roman in the official title of the Church, on what some of them regarded as the too frequent use of the term *anathema sit* for the condemnation of doctrinal errors, or on the far more important question of defining the infallibility of the pope in matters of faith and morals, objections were raised by members of the American delegation which reflected their concern lest these changes should prove to be additional obstacles in winning American Protestants to the Catholic faith, or even give rise to ridicule and abuse from Americans outside the Church. On the central problem of papal infallibility, the American bishops showed themselves, for this and other reasons, as much divided as the hierarchies of other

20. J. G. Shea, *Life and Times of John Carroll* (New York, 1888), pp. 405 f. Cf. P. Hughes, *The Catholic Question* (New York, 1929) and J. Leflon, *La crise révolutionnaire* (Paris, 1949).

countries, and in the sequel five Americans absented themselves from the solemn public session of July 18, 1870 in which the final vote was taken on the question. One American prelate, Edward Fitzgerald, Bishop of Little Rock, was present at the session and was one of the two bishops of the entire Catholic world who voted against the decree.[21]

Since 1870 the charge has sometimes been made that the bishops of the United States are more Roman than American. Doubtless the Vatican decrees did, as they were designed to do, draw the hierarchy of the Church closer to the Holy See than before. But the American Church in its prelates and people had always been distinguished for devotion to Rome. Perhaps the most American of all American prelates up to the present was Cardinal James Gibbons who himself attended the Vatican Council as its youngest bishop and lived to be the last survivor of its members. In addition he received all in the way of honor and affection from his fellow countrymen that an ecclesiastic can aspire to. He is the type of the true bishop, at once American and Roman.

When Father Carroll accepted the appointment as superior of the American Missions in 1785, one of his greatest concerns was the penury of priests. There were only twenty-four in the country and of these five were elderly men while some others were breaking under the hardships their labors imposed on them.[22]

The development from this meager nucleus of a score of active priests to the present-day sacerdotal army of more than two score thousand is due to the generosity of European bishops and religious superiors and to the labors and sacrifices of the builders and faculties of seminaries in the United States. The part of the Holy See in all this has been considerable, not only in pressing for the observance of the laws of the Church on the training of the clergy but also in en-

---

21. R. J. Clancy, "American Prelates in the Vatican Council" in *Historical Records and Studies* 28(1937), 7-135.

22. L. P. McDonald, *The Seminary Movement in the United States; Projects, Foundations and Early Development, (1784-1833)* (Washington, 1927), p. 1 f.

couraging those foreign priests who wished to labor in America and by supporting effectively the actual launching of the seminary movement.

As early as 1783 we find Propaganda writing a letter of encouragement to the Capuchin Father Alexander who had signified his desire to be sent on the American missions.[23] During the 1840's when Catholic immigration reached the figure of 200,000 annually, the American bishops felt that at least 300 new priests from abroad were needed each year and pleaded for them to come. Rome for its part did what it could to encourage the flow of priests. America was not then an attractive field for a priest since it offered nothing but hard work of the most grinding sort. Of those who did come some were useless, or nearly so, because of ill health, ignorance of the English language, or from lack of stability and priestliness. But the majority were devoted and zealous men. Without the immigrant priest the Church in the United States could not have been built.[24]

From the beginning, however, the American hierarchy strove to raise up in America priests trained under their own eyes prepared for the American apostolate, speaking the language of the country and able to assume the responsibilities of the priesthood among their own people.

The difficulties which beset the French Church during the Revolution turned to the advantage of America. Before the actual outbreak of persecution M. Jacques André Emery, superior of the Society of Saint Sulpice, foreseeing the dark days to come turned his thoughts to a foundation in the United States. His Society already had a successful seminary in Montreal but Emery felt the need of further overseas expansion. The papal nuncio in Paris told him that Bishop Carroll needed a seminary. Emery got in touch with Carroll, offering him not only priests for the faculty but also money to erect the Seminary and provide for its needs. Early in 1791 a group of Sulpicians sailed for the United States to begin

---

23. D. Shearer, *op. cit.*, p. 36.
24. W. S. Morris, *The Seminary Movement in the United States; Projects and Early Developments, (1833-1866)*, (Washington, 1932), p. 4.

the first American seminary. The pioneer days were replete with difficulties; so much so that by 1804 Emery and Carroll were at a crisis in their relations and a break seemed inevitable. Fortunately for the Church in the United States Pius VII was in Paris for the coronation of Napoleon and Emery was able to put the case before the pontiff. The pope saved St. Mary's Seminary for the United States. "My son," he said, "let it stand; yes, let that seminary stand: for it will bear fruit in its own time." The words were prophetic. At the present time St. Mary's is not only the largest but one of the best seminaries in the Catholic world. And the contribution of the Sulpicians to the formation of a worthy clergy at St. Mary's and in their other seminaries in the United States has been of inestimable value.[25]

The American Church is also greatly indebted to another Congregation of French origin, the Priests of the Mission of St. Vincent de Paul, in the matter of seminaries. The Vincentians were early in the field and have done invaluable work. It should not be forgotten, however, that the seminary professors were recruited chiefly from among the diocesan clergy whose response to the ever increasing demand is one of the boasts of the American Church.

From the beginning there was also question of the training of American seminarians in Rome. At the time of Carroll's appointment as superior in 1784, Leonardo Cardinal Antonelli invited him to send two young men to Rome to be trained for the priesthood at the expense of Propaganda, offering even to defray the travelling expenses of the candidates. Two young men were sent but they did not persevere.[26]

In 1854 when a number of American bishops were in Rome for the proclamation of the dogma of the Immaculate Conception, the question of the founding of a North American College for the training of students for the priesthood was mooted. Pius IX pushed the project and was strongly supported by Archbishop John Hughes of New York and other influential members of the hierarchy. The College was

25. L. P. McDonald, *op. cit.,* pp. 12 ff.
26. *Ibid.,* p. 9 ff.

formally opened in 1859 and has done much to propagate
and preserve Roman traditions and to cement union with
the See of Peter. Many distinguished members of the American hierarchy, including three of the four living American
Cardinals, were trained in it.[27] In this connection the enthusiastic support given to the project for the foundation of a
Catholic University by Leo XIII should not be forgotten.
The University was launched at Washington in 1889 and has
proved its worth in the field of higher ecclesiastical studies
particularly. It has always been favored by the careful surveillance and continued benevolence of the Roman authorities.[28]

The authority of the Holy See is exercised over its spiritual
subjects in various ways, and one of these is reserving the
right of final approval for laws which are passed in councils
of the bishops. In this respect the Church of the United
States has been no exception. From the time when seven suffragan bishops gathered around Archbishop James Whitfield
for the First Provincial Council of Baltimore in October,
1829, to November, 1884, when Archbishop James Gibbons
welcomed thirteen archbishops and fifty-seven bishops to his
see city for the opening of the Third Plenary Council of the
American hierarchy, the decrees of all the provincial and
plenary councils of Baltimore, as well as those of other ecclesiastical provinces in the country, have been submitted to
Rome's examination before they were formally declared in
force for the American Catholic clergy and laity. In the case
of all the councils the great majority of the laws framed in
the United States received the assent of the Holy See, although from time to time individual decrees were disal-
lowed and modifications were made in the expression of some
of the measures. This legislation touched practically every
phase of the relations of the individual Catholic to his
Church, and it presented a wide variety of subjects from re-
statements of dogmas of the Catholic faith to regulations concerning the administration of the sacraments, laws on the

---

27. *Catholic Encyclopedia* (New York, 1907) I, 423 f.
28. J. T. Ellis, *The Formative Years of the Catholic University of America*,
(Washington, 1946).

proper method of holding ecclesiastical property, and decrees pertaining to Church schools.[29]

By every standard of judgment the most important council ever held in the United States was the plenary gathering of 1884. In this instance the American archbishops were summoned to Rome in advance to counsel with the cardinals of Propaganda about the subjects for legislation. During this Roman conference in November and December, 1883, the American prelates worked out with the officials of the Roman Curia the agenda of the council. In most matters there was substantial agreement, but on some topics the Americans disagreed with the proposals submitted to them and presented their case with such cogency that it prevailed. This is not the place to speak of the differences in detail but they should be mentioned to show that Rome did not arbitrarily impose its will. We have already referred to American opposition to the erection of cathedral chapters. A second difference involved the naming of an Italian prelate to come to the United States as apostolic delegate and preside over the council. This move was also successfully opposed by the Americans, and the Archbishop of Baltimore was appointed by Leo XIII to preside over the sessions.[30]

On the close of the council on December 7, 1884, the decrees were prepared in final form for submission to the Holy See, and after a number of conferences between the bishops delegated by Gibbons to act at Rome in the name of the hierarchy, the Prefect of Propaganda issued a letter on September 21, 1885, declaring that the laws had received the final approbation of the Holy See. So successful, in fact, had the Americans been in their conduct of this important business that not long thereafter their legislation came to be viewed as a model, and the hierarchies of several other countries were instructed by the Holy See to adopt the Baltimore

---

29. On the subject of the conciliar legislation of the American Church cf. P. Guilday, *A History of the Councils of Baltimore* (New York, 1932). In 1828 Bishop England wrote, "In plain practice at present every American diocese is a popedom." *Ibid.*, p. 84.

30. J. T. Ellis, *Life of James Cardinal Gibbons* (Milwaukee, 1952), I, 218.

pattern for their councils. From 1885 to 1918, when the new *Code of Canon Law* went into effect for the universal Church, the legislation of 1884 was the law by which the life of the Church in the United States was regulated, and even after 1918 it remained in force in particulars which were not in conflict with the new code.

The plenary council of 1884 was the last to be held by the American hierarchy. The need for further councils was in part obviated by the fact that at the centennial celebration of the establishment of the hierarchy in November, 1889, a plan was devised to have the metropolitans meet yearly to discuss matters of importance as to the Church of the nation. Thus from July, 1890, when they held their first annual meeting in Boston to April, 1918, when they convened at Washington for the last time without their suffragans, these annual gatherings continued. In September, 1919, virtually the entire hierarchy assembled at the Catholic University of America in the national capital where the bishops have ever since gathered in the autumn of each year to counsel and confer on the business of the American Church.

It was out of the meeting of 1919 that there was born an organization with which all Americans are more or less familiar, namely, the National Catholic Welfare Conference, an outgrowth of the National Catholic War Council which had been brought into existence during World War I to implement the Church's contribution to the nation in wartime. But the National Catholic Welfare Conference was not permanently launched without an episode which relates directly to the subject of Roman authority and the channels through which that authority is communicated to American Catholics. True, the idea of a national organization to co-ordinate the efforts of the Church in fields like education, social welfare, and immigration had been approved by Benedict XV in April, 1919, with generous praise bestowed on the wartime achievements of the National Catholic War Council and the plan of a committee of American bishops to set up facilities for a permanent institution.

In the meantime, however, there had arisen opposition to

the proposed organization from two quarters: first, a few of the bishops in the United States had grown fearful lest the projected organization make inroads on the personal authority they exercised in their dioceses; second, as a result of representations made at Rome from this country, some of the curial officials became suspicious of the N.C.W.C. as having about it the aspect of a permanent canonical council. As a consequence the hitherto friendly atmosphere at Rome changed and a papal brief was prepared suppressing the N.C.W.C. At this juncture Benedict XV died on January 22, 1922. Three weeks after his election, however, Pius XI gave his approval to the document and it was issued on February 25. The N.C.W.C. had been suppressed in the belief that the organization posed a threat to the jurisdiction of the Holy See and that it had in it the germ of a national church in the United States, a development against which, of course, the central government of the Church must always be on guard.

But those American prelates who were most closely associated with the N.C.W.C. were not of a mind to accept the Roman decision without first making an effort to present their side of the case. With this in mind a hurried meeting of the administrative committee of bishops was called for Cleveland on April 6 and there it was determined to prepare a defense of the N.C.W.C. and to send Joseph Schrembs, Bishop of Cleveland, to Rome to press the matter. It was a hard struggle but the strong and reasoned explanations of Schrembs and some colleagues who happened to be at Rome and the fact that eighty-one American bishops signed a memorial in behalf of the organization turned the tide. On July 2 a decree of the Consistorial Congregation was issued which stated that as a result of the new data which had been submitted it had been decided to leave the original organization unchanged, although in its title the word 'conference' was substituted for 'council' as less suggestive of a canonical body. It is noteworthy that what had been considered worthy of condemnation by some members of the Roman Curia early in 1922 has since won unqualified approval and praise of the Holy See, and in recent years the National Catholic Welfare

Conference has been studied as a model by representatives of the hierarchies of other countries.[31]

To trace the action of the Holy See in all the trials and triumphs of the American Church would be an endless task, even if the sources were accessible and the preliminary historical work had been accomplished. Still a word must be said of some of the more important events.

The first great affliction of the Church in the United States arose from the system of lay trustees for ecclesiastical property. Archbishop Carroll had permitted its introduction in the hope that the national spirit and Catholic practice might be reconciled by it. Unfortunately, some of the trustees chosen turned out to be meddlers desirous to use their office as a ladder to prestige and profit. It was, of course, the American clergy and their bishops who had to cope with this threat. The Holy See, however, kept a close watch over the proceedings and as early as 1822 condemned the claims of the trustees in Philadelphia for excessive and undefined powers. When in 1826 Bishop Conwell surrendered to the trustees for the sake of peace, he was deprived of his jurisdiction. Trusteeism was destined to be a plague of the Church in America for a long time. Rome had to make many interventions. We shall have occasion to mention one below. But the firm attitude of the Roman authorities brought about a solution which, although it may have deadened somewhat lay interest in parochial affairs, was the only feasible course at the time.[32]

The Holy See's one important intervention in the slavery issue was well timed. In 1839 Gregory XVI in his apostolic letter *In supremo apostolatus* which was, to be sure, not directed solely to the Church in America, condemned the slave trade. Bishop England of Charleston, who personally considered slavery one of the greatest moral evils, pointed out that the Pope had not condemned the domestic institution of slavery as it existed in the United States. It was fortunate for American Catholics that this papal initiative led to a clari-

31. Cincinnati *Telegraph-Register,* November 16, 1945.
32. D. Shearer, *op. cit.,* pp. 121, 175 f.

fication of principles long before the antagonism within the
States produced the Civil War in 1861. This was one of the
principal reasons, no doubt, why the majority of Catholic
Americans expressed themselves and acted with moderation
during the terrible dispute.[33]

Trusteeism led indirectly to one of the most regrettable
incidents of the anti-Catholic crusade of the 1850's and one
involving a papal representative. The presence of the Catholic Church in predominantly Protestant America had early
produced intense feeling. The great increase of Catholics
during the 1840's and 1850's, due to immigration, led many
Protestants to the conviction that the religious and political
liberty of the Catholics should be curtailed. In the 1850's the
American Party enjoyed a startling success at the polls. Its
phenomenal growth was due partially to the charm of secrecy
in which the order clothed itself. The members were sworn to
secrecy and the universal answer, "I know nothing about it,"
gave the organization its popular name, the Know-Nothings.
All who joined were pledged to vote only for natives, to work
for a twenty-one year probation period preceding naturaliza-
tion, and to combat the Catholic Church. One reason for the
political success of the Know-Nothings was the disruption of
the older parties by the slavery issue. At the same time the
anti-Catholic sentiment long fostered by the churches, societies and the press was reaching its height. Thousands of
Americans sincerely believed that Catholicism and immigration menaced America.

Into this atmosphere of hatred and suspicion Pius IX, in
an effort to show good will to the United States, sent Archbishop Gaetano Bedini. Ostensibly Bedini came to seek a
solution for trustee troubles in Buffalo and Philadelphia, to
report on the condition of the immigrant and to present an
official letter to President Franklin Pierce. Actually the pope
hoped to arrange for the establishment of a permanent apostolic nunciature in Washington and it may well have been
his intention to make Bedini the first nuncio. Bedini was

---

33. *Ibid.*, 201 ff.

tendered a respectful reception in Washington as the representative of a friendly power (the Papal States) with which
the government maintained political and commercial relations. Elsewhere, however, his very life was endangered by
the attacks of the Know-Nothings, who were incited by the
harangues of Alessandro Gavazzi, an apostate Italian priest.
Bedini traveled with as much composure as he could from
place to place, but in the end he left New York precipitously
in January, 1854. Father Theodore Roemer, O.F.M. Cap.,
calls it an ill-timed visit and the Protestant historian, Ray
Allen Billington, lists it among Catholic blunders and comments that few moves could have been more impolitic. Theodore Maynard is somewhat less severe in his judgment, but
he, too, notes that "Bedini had the misfortune to arrive at
the wrong moment." One result was that the project of a
papal representative to the government of the United States
was permanently shelved.[34]

The lack of such representation has, it appears, had no bad
effects. The American government has well maintained its
policy of "hands off" in ecclesiastical matters. In the choice
of John Carroll as the first superior of the American missions
in 1784, it is true, Franklin, the American minister at Paris,
was consulted and warmly recommended Carroll as a man of
fine moral character and a sterling American citizen. But
when Franklin brought the matter to the attention of the
American Congress that body replied in May, 1784, that since
the matter was spiritual, it was not within the jurisdiction
and powers of Congress.[35] Over twenty years later Carroll
himself, perplexed by doubts as to the best way to bring
about order in the distant and troubled Diocese of Louisiana,
inquired of Secretary of State James Madison in November,
1806, if the American government would object to the ap-

---

34. *Historical Records and Studies,* 23(1933), 87-170, has a documented
study of Bedini by Peter Guilday. Cf. T. Roemer, *Catholic Church in the
United States,* (St. Louis 1950), p. 242.
    R. A. Billington, *The Protestant Crusade 1800-1860* (New York, 1938), pp.
300 ff.; T. Maynard, *Story of American Catholicism* (New York, 1941), p. 300.
35. *Journals of the Continental Congress, 3, 493; 27, 368.* (Edited by G.
Hunt.)

pointment of a French-born priest as bishop of that see. After discussing the matter with President Jefferson, the Secretary of State answered that "the scrupulous policy of the Constitution in guarding against political interference with religious affairs," made it necessary to decline an official reply to Carroll's question.[36]

It is true that on several occasions in the history of the American Church, there were rumors of governmental interference in the filling of vacant dioceses. In 1864, for example, during the Civil War the government was alleged to have interposed its views in regard to the candidates for the archdioceses of Baltimore and New York. But no documentary proof to substantiate these rumors was ever adduced.[37] Again in October, 1939, stories circulated that President Franklin D. Roosevelt had intervened to have Bishop Bernard J. Sheil named Archbishop of Chicago on the death of Cardinal George Mundelein.[38] Among the rare instances where an official of the American government was known to have attemped to influence the action of the Holy See in regard to appointments of churchmen in the United States, several involved President Theodore Roosevelt. In 1899, for example, when he was governor of New York, and later as president, Roosevelt expressed the desire to have Archbishop John Ireland of St. Paul elevated to the cardinalate. The Holy See did not agree, however.[39]

The struggle within the American Church on the subject of the Americanization of the immigrant was complex and explosive as well as of considerable moment. Rome was, of course, drawn into the conflict at every turn and it is quite impossible in an article of this length to trace its moderating influence. In the very first decades of its history the American Church felt the stirrings of the nationalities. Archbishop Carroll had at first resisted the demands for the establishment of

---

36. Guilday, *Life and Times of John Carroll* 2, 707 ff.
37. J. L. Spalding, *Life of M. J. Spalding* (New York, 1873), p. 258.
38. *Look* Magazine for December 14, 1954 carries a confirmation of these rumors by a member of Roosevelt's cabinet.
39. Ellis, *op. cit.*, 2, 119, 126.

national (in the instance, German) parishes. But in the face
of charges that he was bishop only of the English-speaking
in the United States, he had been forced to yield.[40]

Rome, however, was never to give way to the demand for
national bishops of the Latin rite. In 1840 the Fourth Provincial Council of Baltimore agreed "that it was not ex-
pedient that the bishop should ordinarily be selected from
those priests who were not citizens of the United States." In
1847 Propaganda admonished the American hierarchy to recommend priests familiar with German for dioceses where
the faithful were predominantly of German origin. In 1854
Archbishop Bedini in a report to the Holy See on his unfortunate mission strongly advised against the appointment as
bishops of foreign-born priests. Doubtless this recommendation had a share in shaping papal policy.[41]

A more important factor was the success of Irish clergymen in at once maintaining Catholic tradition and in adapting themselves to American conditions. With the influx of
immigrants in the second half of the nineteenth century, the
Irish element in the clergy rapidly rose to a position of dominance, notably in the hierarchy. The Irish priests and bishops
undoubtedly were helped by their mastery of English and
their familiarity with the Anglo-Saxon scene. Coming from a
land where the Church of the people had long been persecuted, they were able to adjust themselves to anti-Catholic
atmosphere without sacrificing essentials or quarreling about
non-essentials.

It would be unfair to minimize the importance of the
contribution of priests and bishops of German, French, English, Italian and Polish origin to the building of the Catholic
Church in America. Still it is impossible to deny, although
some regret, that on the clergy of Irish origin and extraction
devolved a greater role than even the large number of Irish
immigrants and clergy would seem to warrant. One striking
proof of this is the fact that leaders of both factions in the

---

40. Guilday, *op. cit.*, I, 292.
41. Mansi 39, 363; Shearer, *op. cit.*, p. 248; *Historical Records and Studies*
23 (1933), p. 166.

acute phase of the nationalist controversy were prelates of Irish antecedents.[42]

Rome's policy varied, substantially, but little on the question of Americanization. While insisting on the proper care of nationals of all countries, Leo XIII showed both in the case of the Abbelen Memorial (1886) and the Lucerne Memorial (1890) that he looked upon the Church in the United States as an American Church and considered that the just claims of all parties had in general been met. It is not pleasant to think of the complications which an anti-Americanizing policy would have occasioned. One of the great services of Cardinal Gibbons to the Church was his quiet determination that this traditional policy should not be reversed.[43]

The action of the Holy See in the school controversy of the 1880's and 1890's was more direct but, owing to the difficulty of the problem less satisfactory. The First Provincial Council of Baltimore (1829) had judged it necessary that schools in America should teach not only letters but faith and morals. Parochial schools already existed at that date and they continued to multiply. In 1851 Pius IX urged the establishment of parochial schools wherever possible and the First Plenary Council, the following year, incorporated this suggestion into its decrees. The Second Provincial Council of Cincinnati (1858) went so far as to maintain that pastors had a grave obligation in conscience to open schools wherever possible. The Second Plenary Council of Baltimore (1866) also urged all parish priests to erect parochial schools.[44]

In 1875 Propaganda admonished all the bishops of the United States to keep Catholic children from schools that endangered the faith and to provide suitable Catholic schools. If a bishop judged that in some instances parents had sufficient reason for sending their children to public schools, arrangements had to be made for their religious instruction. The Third Plenary Council of Baltimore (1884) insisted that

---

42. Ellis, *op. cit.*, 1, 331 ff.
43. Cf. D. F. Reilly, *The School Controversy (1891-1893)* (Washington, 1943) for the acute phase of this controversy.
44. Shearer, *op. cit.*, 367 ff.

where parochial schools were lacking they should be erected within two years. Priests and people were sternly admonished to get behind the program. Nevertheless, the plan was never carried out completely except perhaps in regions where those of German origin predominated. This successful effort on the part of the Germans has been attributed to the desire to preserve the German language and culture but it aimed also at avoiding the dire effects of state control of the schools which were then obvious in Germany.

The principal reason why the decree of the Third Plenary Council was not, and never has been fully implemented, is to be sought in the cost of the parochial school system. Catholics had to contribute to the support of public and Catholic schools. John Ireland, the dynamic Archbishop of St. Paul, made himself the leader of a movement to bring about a compromise so that Catholic schools, too, might benefit by State support. Unfortunately personalities and the bitterness engendered by the controversy on nationalism complicated the issue. In addition some more or less speculative problems were injected into the debate. Rome unquestionably favored some compromise with the State and gave a guarded approval to Ireland's project which in the end did not prove viable. As the controversy continued, the Pope sent Archbishop Francesco Satolli to work for an arrangement whereby the Catholic schools might obtain State support. In the end Leo XIII had to intervene personally to end the dissension. In 1893 he reaffirmed the instruction of Propaganda (1875) and declared that the decrees of the Baltimore councils were still in force. The Pope, seemed to imply, however, that some arrangement with the State should be made if possible.[45]

Leo XIII's decision put an end to the controversy, but the problem of the parochial school in the United States still remains. Unquestionably the policy in vogue puts a heavy burden on the parishes. Some hold that this burden is a distinct advantage because it makes the Catholics realize that their religion is something for which they must be ready to make

---

45. Reilly, *op. cit.*, pp. 223 ff.

great and continued sacrifices. Others hold that it is an injustice to force Catholics to support Catholic schools to which
they send their children and to contribute to the support of
public schools to which in conscience they cannot send them.

The controversies on the schools and nationalism were
not the only ones which swept over the vigorous American
Church. The recurrence of difficulties led Leo XIII in 1893
to institute a permanent Apostolic Delegation, not this time
to the American government, but to the American Church.
Satolli was appointed first Apostolic Delegate. Cardinal Gibbons had just composed a letter to the Holy Father transmit-
ting the all but unanimous opinion of the American archbishops that the Delegation should not be established. They
thought that it would turn non-Catholics still more against
the Church. But since Leo had acted the Cardinal's letter was
never presented.[46]

Time has shown the wisdom of the papal action. The
Apostolic Delegates in Washington, have, without encroach-
ing on the power of the bishops, rendered invaluable service
as liaison officers between Rome and America, in settling dis-
putes and expediting business. Neither did the increase of
bigotry, which the American archbishops foresaw and feared,
prove of long duration. In a few years the voice of criticism
was nearly stilled. Now the Apostolic Delegate has become
an accepted figure on the American Catholic scene. All the
delegates have been distinguished churchmen but none of
them has rendered greater services than the present titulary,
Archbishop Amleto Giovanni Cicognani. He has held office
for more than twenty years, almost twice as long as any of his
predecessors, and his tenure has been stamped with the seals
of charity and prudence. Not an untoward event of moment
has arisen to mar the record of his years of devoted service or
to interrupt his contribution to the cause of religion in the
United States.

The last instance of papal intervention which we shall
consider is quite different in nature from the preceding. In

---

46. Ellis, *op. cit.*, pp. 595 ff.

January, 1899, Leo XIII addressed to Cardinal Gibbons a famous letter *Testem benevolentiae*. In it the Pope expressed his great affection for the American Church and for the United States. He expressly excluded any desire to condemn the spirit, characteristics, political institutions, laws or customs of the American people. He pointed out, however, that certain people, *nonnulli,* were designating as Americanism some dangerous and erroneous ideas. He mentioned especially: (1) the tendency to pass over in silence or to change the traditional explanation of certain Catholic doctrines for the purpose of bringing non-Catholics more easily into the fold; (2) the desire to curb the authority of the Church or even to reject all exterior direction in favor of the interior inspirations of the Holy Spirit; (3) disdain for the vows of religion; (4) contempt for supernatural virtue; and (5) the distinction between active and passive virtues with the slighting of the latter.

Cardinal Gibbons in his response to Pope Leo asserted that he knew of no American Catholic who held such doctrines. Archbishop Ireland, who was considered the leader of the liberals and branded by some as a heresiarch, also emphatically rejected the teaching. Peter Guilday, the distinguished historian of the American Church, called *Testem benevolentiae* the greatest blow to American Catholic pride, but he professed himself unable to give any but the vaguest reasons for the outbreak of the international controversy on Americanism. He stated that at times it seemed that it could be interpreted as a quarrel between liberals and conservatives in the American Church and at other times as the final phase of the nationalist controversy.[47] He was probably right in inclining to see in it an ancillary episode in the Modernist crisis which was then coming to a head in Europe. Not that the Americans involved were Modernists, but modernist leaders abroad made use of some of their opinions to advance their own interests. There was then, a real danger that a misrepresentation of American conditions and of the reasons

---

47. *Catholic Historical Review* 6, 542 ff.

for the success of the Church in the United States would harm the Church in general. That some Americans had wandered a bit beyond the bounds of orthodoxy in matters apologetical, ascetical and dogmatic has never been proved. There was, moreover, a total lack of opposition to the teaching of Leo in America.

We have too rapidly reviewed the papal action in some of the more important problems and controversies of the American Church. A word should be added about the relations between the Holy Father and the American faithful. In a sense this subject has already been treated since the effort of Rome in America was aimed at building up the Church for the benefit of the faithful. American Catholics have always been aware of this and their devotion to the See of Peter has been unquestionable and unquestioned. Gregory XVI (1831-1846) is reported to have said, "Je ne suis pape nulle part autant qu'aux Etats Unis." Whether his successors in the papal office cherished this opinion, we do not know. But certainly they were aware that they had devoted and generous children beyond the Atlantic.

An instance of this is to be found in the career of Alfred E. Smith, poor and uneducated son of Irish immigrants, who rose to be Governor of New York State, a candidate for the presidency of the United States, and probably the most famous Catholic layman of twentieth-century America. Not only the United States but the whole western world rang to his pronouncements among which were frank declarations of his sincere Catholicism. It is doubtful that all Smith's statements on the relations of Church and State would be acceptable to Catholic political philosophers but his loyalty was shown by his acts.[48]

One writer in summing up the action of the popes on the Church in America asserts in the phrase of De Maistre that the "real presence of the sovereign pontiffs was felt in all parts of the nation, was found everywhere, permeated everything, saw everything and was itself seen by everyone."[49]

48. *The Americana Annual* (1945), pp. 648 ff.
49. Shearer, *op. cit.*, p. 2.

Properly toned down, this statement can be accepted. The popes acted unobtrusively but continually, their initiatives were often hidden but generally effective. Leo XIII spoke of his "special care and provision" for the Church in the United States. There is scarcely a pontiff of the nineteenth or twentieth century who could not make the same claim.

CHAPTER FOUR

The Organization of the Church in the United States

—— ◆ ——

BY F. D. COHALAN

THE GROWTH of the American hierarchy reflects the growth of the Church in the United States and also of the country itself. There has been an impressive development since 1789 when the newly erected diocese of Baltimore covered 888,811 square miles, and counted 30,000 Catholics in a population of 3,924,214. Today, the United States, plus Alaska and Hawaii, contains 131 dioceses, and 33,574,017 of an estimated 154,300,474 people are Catholics. These dioceses are divided into 25 provinces. One archdiocese, that of Washington, D. C., established in 1939 and separated from Baltimore in 1947, is immediately subject to the Holy See: it has no suffragans and is not part of a province in the accepted

---

F. D. Cohalan, who studied at Georgetown, Catholic University of America and Harvard before entering the seminary, was ordained in 1938. Since 1941 he has taught history in Cathedral College, the Archdiocesan Minor Seminary in New York.

sense. Two dioceses belong to the Oriental Rites, and one, Alaska, is a Vicariate Apostolic. There are 200 bishops, headed by 4 cardinals, assisted by 29,734 secular priests and 18,615 regulars. There are 16,193 parishes, some of which contain several counties. The clergy are assisted by 8,868 Brothers and 159,545 Sisters. Of the latter, 93,518 are engaged in teaching, and most of the others conduct the 931 Catholic Hospitals that cover much of the country. Impressive as these statistics are, it must be remembered that four-fifths of the people are still outside the Church, and that her strength is very unevenly distributed throughout the country.

Contrary to an impression shared by many, not all American dioceses are large in area, Catholic population, or resources. Before considering the position of the Church in the various regions of the country, a few figures on America as a whole may be cited. The population and area figures for each diocese will be found in an appended chart. The figures for the total population are taken from the Census of 1950. The figures for the Catholic population are estimates supplied to the bishops by the pastors, and to the *Official Catholic Directory* by the bishops. They are universally regarded as too low, whereas the figures for births, marriages, conversions, *etc.* are more easily obtained, and are accepted as correct.

Twenty-three dioceses have fewer than 50,000 Catholics: Baker, Boise, Charleston, Crookston, Cheyenne, Dodge City, Gallup, Grand Island, Juneau, Lafayette-in-Indiana, Lincoln, Little Rock, Owensboro, Raleigh, Rapid City, Reno, Salina, Salt Lake City, Savannah-Atlanta, Spokane, Wilmington, St. Joseph, and Yakima.

Thirty-one dioceses have between 50,000 and 100,000 Catholics: Alexandria, Amarillo, Austin, Belleville, Bismark, Covington, Dallas, Davenport, Des Moines, Duluth, Evansville, Fargo, Great Falls, Helena, Kansas City-in-Kansas, Kansas City (Missouri), Marquette, Mobile, Nashville, Natchez, Oklahoma City, Pueblo, Rockford, St. Cloud, Sioux City, Sioux Falls, Steubenville, Superior, Wheeling, Wichita, Winona.

Forty-one dioceses have between 100,000 and 250,000 Catholics: Altoona, Bridgeport, Burlington, Camden, Columbus,

Denver, Dubuque, El Paso, Erie, Fall River, Fort Wayne, Grand Rapids, Green Bay, Greensburg, Harrisburg, Indianapolis, Joliet, LaCrosse, Lansing, Louisville, Madison, Manchester, Norwich, Ogdensburg, Omaha, Paterson, Peoria, Portland-in-Oregon, Portland (Maine), Richmond, St. Augustine, Springfield-in-Illinois, Saginaw, Seattle, Santa Fe, Sacramento, San Diego, Tucson, Toledo, Washington, Youngstown.

Eighteen dioceses have between 250,000 and 500,000 Catholics: Albany, Baltimore, Cincinnati, Corpus Christi, Galveston, Lafayette, (Louisiana), Milwaukee, Providence, Rochester, St. Paul, St. Louis, Scranton, San Antonio, Springfield (Massachusetts), Syracuse, Trenton, Worcester.

Seven dioceses have between 500,000 and 1,000,000 Catholics: Buffalo, Cleveland, Hartford, Los Angeles, New Orleans, Pittsburgh, San Francisco.

Seven dioceses have more than 1,000,000 Catholics: Boston, Brooklyn, Chicago, Detroit, New York, Newark, and Philadelphia.

The area of the dioceses varies very widely. It has long been the policy of the Church, as her organization and numbers grew, to have the boundaries of the diocese correspond to the boundaries of the States as far as possible. Thus only six dioceses cross State Lines: El Paso, Gallup, Mobile, Richmond, Wheeling, and Wilmington. The States themselves vary in size from Rhode Island (1,214 square miles) to Texas (267,339 square miles), while Alaska has 586,400 square miles. The largest diocese in area, Reno, has 119,542 square miles, with 29,000 Catholics. The smallest in area is Newark with 541 square miles and 1,123,607 Catholics. The Vicariate Apostolic of Alaska has 515,600 square miles, with 10,000 Catholics. Every State has at least one diocese and 16 have only one. These are Alabama, Arkansas, Delaware, Georgia, Idaho, Maine, Oklahoma, Rhode Island, South Carolina, Tennessee, Mississippi, Nevada, New Hampshire, Vermont, Utah, and Wyoming. Twelve of the ecclesiastical provinces contain only one state, because of the large number of Catholics concentrated in those areas. The Province of Kansas is

an exception to this general rule, for it has relatively few
Catholics. The twelve are Dubuque, Cincinnati, Indianapolis, Kansas City-in-Kansas, Newark, New York, Milwaukee,
Chicago, Omaha, Philadelphia, Detroit, and St. Louis. California is the only State which is part of two provinces.

The population of the country is very unevenly distributed, as will appear. It has frequently been pointed out that
American Catholics are concentrated in urban areas; but
many do not realize that almost two-thirds of the total population live in cities. If we recall how much the Church owes
to immigration, this urban concentration will not seem surprising. Between 1820 and 1950, 33,246,330 immigrants arrived from Europe. Of these, 4,619,485 came from Ireland,
4,776,884 from Italy; and 6,248,524—many, if not most, of
whom were Protestants—from Germany. This urban concentration is much greater in some areas than in others, as will
be seen from the following statistics.

New England. The six states of this area are Massachusetts,
Connecticut, Rhode Island, Vermont, New Hampshire, and
Maine. They cover 66,608 square miles, with a Catholic population of 4,438,408, and a total population of 9,485,833.
The Catholics are here nearly half the people; and this is due
almost entirely to immigration. The predominant racial
strain among the Catholics is Irish; but there are substantial
numbers of French Canadians in each State. New England
contains the only state—Rhode Island—in which the Catholics are a majority of the population, and has two dioceses
which contain only a single county: Worcester and Bridgeport, both erected within the past five years. It is in New
England, also that there is found the only diocese, outside
Rhode Island, in which the Catholics are a majority of the
total population: this is Fall River, Massachusetts. If current
trends continue, the Catholics will probably be a majority
in much of New England fairly soon. It is estimated that sixty
per cent of the births and forty per cent of the funerals in
Connecticut in 1954 were Catholic. In the highly industrialized area of New England, the Catholics are weakest in the
rural sections although some of the French Canadians are

moving in as farmers in Vermont, New Hampshire, and Maine. The relatively small area which New England occupies in respect to the whole United States contains 11 dioceses in the provinces of Boston and Hartford, and it is one of the most vigorous centers of Catholic life. In Rhode Island, Italians form the largest single numerical group among Catholics, and in Massachusetts they are the second largest numerical group in the Catholic population.

The Middle Atlantic States. These are New York, New Jersey, and Pennsylvania, with a combined area of 102,745 square miles. They have 9,915,272 Catholics, and a total population of 30,242,860. Here again the great Catholic numbers are due to immigration. The vast industrial resources of this part of the country made it the goal of millions of immigrants in the last century, and even of much of the immigration of the present time, for so many enter the country at New York. This area contains 18 dioceses in the Provinces of New York, Newark, and Philadelphia, and it has the largest single concentration of Catholics in the entire country. The racial strains are very mixed. Both Oriental dioceses have their seats in Pennsylvania, and the Latin dioceses of that State contain very large numbers of Poles and other Eastern Europeans. In the City of New York the Italians are at least a million strong, while the Puerto Rican immigration in recent years has brought approximately 500,000 more people to the dioceses of New York and Brooklyn. The Germans are very strong in the Buffalo area; and there are many French in Ogdensburg, in northern New York.

East North Central States. This section contains Ohio, Illinois, Indiana, Michigan, and Wisconsin, with an area of 248,-283 square miles. It had 7,594,868 Catholics out of a total population of 30,946,418. This is the second largest concentration of Catholics, and it is found in the second largest industrial area in the country. The 26 dioceses are divided among the Provinces of Detroit, Cincinnati, Chicago, Milwaukee, and Indianapolis. There are very large numbers of Germans and Slavs in each of the five States comprising this section. Perhaps it is because of the large body of Catholics in this area that it has been the center of so many militantly Protestant groups.

`The South.` This contains the national capital, Washington, D. C., and the States of Delaware, Georgia, Florida, Maryland, North and South Carolina, Virginia, West Virginia, Kentucky, Alabama, Mississippi, and Tennessee. Its area is 408,496 square miles, and the Catholics number only 1,610,-612 in a population of 33,009,215. All these States make up the Provinces of Baltimore and Louisville, and 14 dioceses including the *Abbatia Nullius* of Belmont, and, in addition, the Archdiocese of Washington (D. C.). This section of the country is that in which Catholics are weakest. This is due mainly to the race problem that overshadows everything else in Southern life, and the hold the Evangelical Protestants have on the rural population of both races, the white and colored alike, in a still predominantly rural area. More than half of America's 16,000,000 Negroes live in the South. It is undergoing a rapid social and economic transformation as the result of growing industrialization and the steadily improving social condition of the Negroes; but it is still the most anti-Catholic section of the country. It was not greatly affected by immigration, because the existence of slavery and, later, the poverty of the newly emancipated Negroes made it impossible for immigrants to make a living. It is interesting to note that the Southern dioceses are among the oldest in the country, and are the ones in which the least progress has been made. Nonetheless, in recent years the rate of increase among the Catholics has risen, and there has been a notable decline in anti-Catholic feeling. It is still a missionary area, and, except for Baltimore and Washington, still has to draw on other places for priests, religious, and financial help. There are 3,070 counties in the entire United States, and 820 of them have no resident priest. Most of the 800 are in the South. However, the total figure represents a marked improvement on the situation in 1938 when there were 1022 priestless counties.

West North Central. This section contains Minnesota, Iowa, Missouri, North Dakota, South Dakota, Nebraska, and

Kansas, which cover 435,957 square miles. It has 2,336,008 Catholics, and a total population of 14,015,626. It has 23 dioceses, which are divided among the Provinces of St. Louis, St. Paul, Dubuque, Omaha, and Kansas City-in-Kansas. Predominantly agricultural in economy, in spite of some big business, it is dominantly Evangelical in religion. Here again the Catholics are concentrated in the cities, as a comparison of the metropolitan see with their suffragans will show. St. Louis is a great Catholic center, and the Irish and the Germans predominate. Milwaukee is mainly German with a large Polish majority.

West South Central States. This zone contains Arkansas, Oklahoma, Louisiana, and Texas, which contains 438,883 square miles. The Catholics number 2,700,762 out of 15,205,-138 inhabitants. The 12 dioceses are divided between the Provinces of New Orleans and San Antonio. The Catholic position in this area is quite uneven. In Arkansas the Catholics number only 40,000 out of almost 2,000,000, though the diocese of Little Rock is over a hundred years old. The State is almost entirely agricultural, and nearly a quarter of the population is Negro. The situation is not notably better in Oklahoma, although in the latter the oil industry has produced a higher living standard than exists in Arkansas. In Louisiana the Catholics are numerous, well organized, and have the prestige belonging in America to those who were first on the scene. The diocese of New Orleans was established before the Louisiana Purchase (1803), and there is still a strong French tradition. Of the 16,000,000 Negroes living in the *Solid South,* only 230,000 are Catholics. They form the major portion of the approximately 420,000 Negro Catholics scattered throughout the entire country. Of those living in the South, 148,000 are within the State of Louisiana. The diocese of Lafayette has the largest number of these, 72,000 Negro Catholics, while those in New Orleans number 60,000. New Orleans is the site of Xavier University, the only Catholic University for Negroes in America. In Texas, there is a strong anti-Catholic tradition. The Catholics are numerous, but many if not most of them are of Mexican descent. As

such they are the victims of racial discrimination on the part
of non-Catholics that makes their position hardly better than
that of the Negro. The vast wealth of Texas is mainly in non-
Catholic hands, and the Church there is really on a missionary footing. It is estimated that in 1950 there were 1,033,768
Mexicans in Texas, which also receives a large number of
the estimated 70,000 immigrants who enter the country illegally every year from Mexico.

The Mountain States. These are Arizona, Colorado, Idaho,
Montana, Nevada, New Mexico, Utah, and Wyoming. They
cover 863,887 square miles. This immense area has a total
population of only 4,952,122, of whom 1,025,272 are Catholics. It contains the Provinces of Denver and Santa Fe, and
parts of the Provinces of Portland, Los Angeles, and San
Francisco. Here again Catholic strength is unevenly divided.
In Utah the Mormons are the dominant group, and the small
Catholic body is scattered over an area larger than England.
In Idaho the Catholics are about as numerous as in Utah, in
approximately the same area, but the opportunities for expansion are more favorable because no single group has the
power in Idaho that the Mormons exercise in Utah. In Arizona and New Mexico—both of which like Texas, California,
and Nevada, once belonged to Mexico—the Mexican problem
is felt acutely. In these two States there are also many Indians. Most Indians live on Reservations where they preserve
their ancient customs and tribal manner of life. Although
counted as part of the general Catholic population, Indians
are regarded as culturally "primitive"; and, ecclesiastically,
they are on a "missionary" basis, for work among them is
supported from outside sources. In Nevada, which is as large
as Italy, the density of population is less than 2 to a square
mile. This State has a national reputation as the center of a
divorce mill and of gambling of all kinds.

The Pacific Coast. This contains California, Oregon, and
Washington, with an area of 323,869 square miles. The Catholics number 3,178,084 out of a total population of 15,763,-
309. California is the only State which has two metropolitan
areas, Los Angeles and San Francisco. The Catholic popula-

tion includes 760,000 Mexicans. The total population of California has increased by about fifty per cent since 1940, and it now ranks second among the States. There has been a very great increase in Catholic strength, too, although there is strong anti-Catholic feeling in California in spite of the general pride in the labors of the Franciscan pioneers who built the California Missions. It is the only State which taxes the Catholic schools. Recently an amendment to the State Constitution removing that provision was passed, but it is still disputed in the Courts, and has not yet been put into effect. In Washington and Oregon the Church is weaker than in any part of the country outside the South. Honolulu is attached to the Province of San Francisco. There the Catholics number nearly a third of the people, and the outlook is favorable, though the Islands have a very acute social problem of their own due to the polyglot character of the population and the uneven distribution of wealth.

The Oriental Dioceses. These are unique in America, for they are not territorial, but embrace the members of their own Rites wherever they are to be found. Both are centered in Pennsylvania. The Ukrainian Greek Catholic Diocese for the Byzantine Rite has 326,949 people, and its 171 parishes are scattered over 25 States and the District of Columbia. The Greek Rite Diocese has 135,261 Catholics. Its 183 parishes are located in 13 States. The major problems facing both are recruiting a sufficient number of priests, and resisting the tendency of many of their younger members to attend Latin Churches or drift away entirely. In both rites celibacy is imposed in the United States.

The Military Ordinariate. Though the first Catholic chaplains to the Armed Forces were appointed in 1845 in spite of a great outburst of Protestant fury, the Military Ordinariate was not erected until 1917. Since the establishment of this ecclesiastical jurisdiction, it has been vested in the Archbishop of New York. Under the spiritual leadership of the Ordinariate are all Catholics in the Military Services of the United States and certain other classes of persons associated with those services. There is a grand total of 1,869 Chaplains under the

charge of the Military Vicar, who is presenty aided by two
auxiliary bishops, the senior of whom is termed the Delegate
of the Military Vicar.

Organization of the Hierarchy. It would not be surprising
if, in a country with so vast an area, in which social, economic, and religious conditions vary so greatly on a national
scale, there would be a diversity of leaders. Actually it is not
so, and one striking aspect of the American Church is the
unity which prevails among its leaders. Although there is no
Primate, the See of Baltimore, because of its historical significance, enjoys, by the decree of the Sacred congregation *de
Propaganda Fide* of July 19, 1858, "Prerogative of Place."
Consequently, the Archbishop of Baltimore ranks immediately after the Cardinals. From 1808 to 1846, when the Province of Portland was erected, followed by that of St. Louis in
1847, there was only one Province in America, Baltimore.
The Bishops met at the Provincial Councils of Baltimore,
seven of which were held between 1829 and 1849. Later there
were three Plenary Councils in Baltimore, in 1852, 1866,
and 1884. Between 1890 and 1918 the Archbishops met annually, always in a different city. Finally, in 1919, the present
arrangement was adopted. The entire Hierarchy meets every
November—after the civil elections, in deference to Protestant prejudice—in Washington. During this meeting they
select the members of the Administrative Board of the
National Catholic Welfare Conference. The members of this
board serve for five years, but the terms are arranged in such
a way that each year some terms expire, thus ensuring a necessary continuity in respect to broad policy and some variety
of view in so far as particular questions are concerned. This
standing committee of the Episcopate supervises Catholic
activities on a national scale in a great number of fields,
e.g., Education, Press, Welfare; and it is an invaluable instrument for effecting unity of action as well as of purpose.

Selection of the Bishops. This is reserved to the Holy See,
and there is no interference of any kind by the Government,
either Federal or State, before or after a selection is made. It

is carried out according to the Decree of the Sacred Consistorial Congregation (July 25, 1916; AAS, 8; 400). Since 1908 this country is no longer under *Propaganda*. The Apostolic Delegation was founded in 1893. As America has no aristocracy, and the wealthier Catholics, still relatively small in number, produce few vocations, the bishops, like nearly all the clergy, are drawn from the lower classes. The Archbishop of Boston pointed out recently that no present member of the hierarchy is the son of a college graduate. It must be remembered that this is also true of a substantial number of the leading figures in public life in the United States, so the Catholic position here reflects the prevailing national condition. Naturally, many of the bishops are chosen from the Curias of the Metropolitan Sees. In some provinces all or nearly all of the bishops at the present time were so chosen. There is also, at the present time, a clearly discernible policy of appointing Ordinaries not only from outside the diocese but, in the case of most Metropolitans, from outside the Province. There is no monopoly enjoyed by any racial group. The Irish and Germans predominate; but that is because they have supplied most of the Catholics. The Poles, and more recently, the Italians, also appear on the lists. At present 7 of 26 archbishoprics have German prelates and 2 bishops are of French descent; 43 of the deceased bishops and 2 bishops were born in France. Only 4 of the present bishops are from religious congregations, although 85 of the deceased prelates were.

The Growth of the Hierarchy. The dean of American Catholic historians, John Gilmary Shea, records the death in Baltimore in 1881, at the age of 95, of a man who was confirmed by Bishop Carroll in 1796 and lived to see the original diocese of Baltimore divided into 61 sees and 6,000 priests. That was a substantial advance, in a life-time, from the 5 dioceses with 92 priests, east of the Mississippi, when Carroll died in 1815. At that time there was no resident priest in any New England state except Massachusetts, which had 3. In the same year, the first resident bishop of New York, John

Connolly, O.P., reported finding 3 churches, 4 priests, and 15,000 Catholics in the present Provinces of Newark and New York, then his diocese. Since 1881 the number of sees has more than doubled and the creation of new sees is a continuous process. Arranged by pontificatism the sees created since 1789 are as follows: Pius VI—1; Pius VII—7; Leo XII—1; Pius VIII—1; Gregory XVI—4; Pius IX—35; Leo XIII—30; Pius X—15; Benedict XV—1; Pius XI—12; and Pius XII—23. Ten new Provinces have been created since 1933.

The Diocesan Structure. The rapid growth of the American population, with its concentration of great numbers in certain centers, has created big administrative problems. Many dioceses are almost unwieldy; but cutting them up would not help. Chicago, for instance, covers only two counties, but has the largest Catholic population in the country. The solution has been to multiply auxiliary bishops, who now number more than 40, with several dioceses having 2 or more. New York has 10, and Chicago 2. Cathedral Chapters, so familiar in Europe, exist nowhere in the United States, and the consultative function of the canons is exercised by the Diocesan Consultors, a group chosen, *ad nutum,* by the American Ordinary, from among the priests of his diocese. Since there are no chapters, no honorary canonies are given; and the custom has arisen of rewarding priests with the Roman Prelature to an extent unknown in Europe. In the United States, this does not imply any reservation of the prelate's benefice to the Holy See. One of the most widespread characteristics of modern society is the tendency to centralize authority, and to extend the authority of the State in matters of health, education, public welfare, etc. Inevitably, this creates the necessity for greater centralization in voluntary organizations that must deal with public officials. It has affected the Church in America by forcing the creation of a number of diocesan-wide organizations in these fields, which have gradually taken over many tasks previously performed on the parish level, if at all. Thus, in our larger dioceses, an increasing number of the clergy are withdrawn from parochial life to serve in various capacities in the diocesan supervisory agencies. The modern chancery of a large diocese reflects the ever more complicated structure of a well organized and progressive ecclesiastical jurisdiction. The change in the public attitude to marriage, which has had its effects on the Catholic minority, has led, too, to a greater number of enquiries into the validity of marriages, so that the matrimonial curia is sure to be operating on a scale undreamed of thirty years ago.

National Parishes. It is impossible to give reliable statistics about national parishes because, although the situation has changed in recent years, there is no indication of it in available statistics. Between 1931 and 1950 only 970,000 immigrants arrived legally from Europe, and naturally not all of them were Catholics. Since the passage of the Immigration Act of 1924, the flow of immigrants has been drastically curtailed, and the need for the national parishes has been correspondingly reduced. Many of these parishes have become territorial, but the same clergy remain in charge. In any case, necessary as they were, they were not intended to be permanent; and as the language problem is solved and new recruits from abroad are cut off, they will be absorbed into the regular parochial structure of the dioceses.

Growth of the Catholic population in recent years. Increases in the Catholic population over a period of ten years may be appreciated after a glance at the following pairs of figures, illustrative respectively of the years 1944 and 1954.

	1944	1954
Bishops	154	199
Priests	37,749	45,451
Parishes	12,791	15,914
Diocesan Seminaries	55	76
Total Seminarians	20,816	33,448
Colleges and Universities	224	250
Elementary Schools (Parochial)	7,436	8,493
General Hospitals	665	790
Baptisms	799,696	1,211,564

Chart A

Dioceses of the United States. (The date following each name indicates the date of erection as diocese (D.) or Archdiocese (A.).

Archdiocese	Area in square miles	Catholic population	Total population
Baltimore	4,801	366,652	1,691,910
(D. 1789; A. 1808)			
Boston	2,465	1,490,229	3,035,168
(D. 1808; A. 1880)			
Chicago	1,411	1,899,357	4,200,000
(D. 1843; A. 1880)			
Cincinnati	8,443	395,000	2,032,106
(D. 1821; A. 1850)			
Denver	54,679	155,730	937,712
(D. 1887; A. 1941)			
Detroit	5,374	1,125,000	3,830,350
(D. 1833; A. 1937)			
Dubuque	17,404	166,619	840,658
(D. 1837; A. 1893)			
Hartford	2,288	641,454	1,323,700
(D. 1843; A. 1953)			
Indianapolis	8,325	160,367	1,505,527
(D. 1834; A. 1944)			
Kansas City-in-Kansas	12,524	101,225	641,479
(D. 1877; A. 1952)			
Los Angeles	9,508	1,075,000	5,427,300
(D. 1840; A. 1935)			
Louisville	10,630	151,435	951,335
(D. 1808; A. 1937)			
Milwaukee	4,758	534,690	1,435,345
(D. 1843; A. 1875)			
Newark	541	1,179,469	2,607,649
(D. 1853; A. 1937)			
New Orleans	1,300	549,371	1,445,260
(D. 1793; A. 1850)			
New York	4,717	1,458,240	4,724,410
(D. 1808; A. 1850)			
Omaha	14,051	138,923	543,656
(D. 1885; A. 1945)			
Philadelphia	5,043	1,325,740	4,025,806
(D. 1808; A. 1875)			
Portland	21,398	119,034	984,894
(A. 1846)			
St. Louis	27,092	475,000	2,133,817
(D. 1826; A. 1888)			
St. Paul	16,050	434,056	1,587,568
(D. 1850; A. 1888)			

Archdiocese	Area in square miles	Catholic population	Total population
San Antonio (D. 1874; A. 1925)	33,025	339,680	899,702
San Francisco (D. 1853)	16,586	870,000	3,540,419
Santa Fe (D. 1850; A. 1875)	74,860	245,000	470,000
Seattle (D. 1850; A. 1951)	24,834	200,863	1,866,036
Washington (A. 1939)	2,104	236,276	1,224,314

Diocese	Area in square miles	Catholic population	Total population
Albany (1847)	10,419	325,675	1,031,747
Alexandria (1853)	22,212	71,760	906,736
Altoona (1901)	6,674	147,443	625,356
Amarillo (1926)	73,000	57,442	700,000
Austin (1948)	25,477	100,272	806,035
Baker (1903)	66,147	17,056	245,992
Belleville (1887)	11,678	101,844	799,594
Bismark (1909)	35,998	61,721	243,794
Boise (1893)	84,290	31,761	588,637
Bridgeport (1953)	663	248,847	504,342
Brooklyn (1853)	1,007	1,497,598	5,201,252
Buffalo (1847)	6,357	725,201	1,446,609
Burlington (1853)	9,135	115,932	375,833
Camden (1937)	2,691	200,337	700,105
Charleston (1820)	30,989	26,313	2,117,027
Cheyenne (1887)	97,548	48,304	288,707
Cleveland (1847)	3,414	659,275	2,400,000
Columbus (1847)	11,310	134,393	1,408,423
Corpus Christi (1912)	22,391	500,000	712,496
Covington (1853)	17,286	72,000	1,353,967
Crookston (1909)	17,210	33,421	238,700
Dallas-Fort Worth (1890)	49,075	97,950	2,697,500
Davenport (1881)	11,438	81,141	628,869
Des Moines (1911)	12,446	56,518	598,541
Dodge City (1951)	23,000	23,818	218,711
Duluth (1889)	22,354	93,569	372,622
El Paso (1914)	30,617	159,139	440,556
Erie (1854)	9,436	186,749	811,651
Evansville (1944)	5,010	65,497	417,327
Fall River (1904)	1,194	240,545	445,060
Fargo (1889)	35,786	84,517	391,107
Fort Wayne (1857)	7,599	248,293	1,240,846
Gallup (1939)	90,749	46,910	150,000
Galveston (1847)	26,847	344,367	1,915,000
Grand Island (1912)	40,000	37,710	287,723
Grand Rapids (1882)	16,540	135,981	1,001,000

Diocese	Area in square miles	Catholic population	Total population
Great Falls (1904)	94,158	55,365	304,287
Green Bay (1868)	10,851	241,261	573,639
Greensburg (1951)	3,334	184,934	661,026
Harrisburg (1868)	7,565	144,049	1,246,815
Honolulu (1941)	6,435	155,000	500,691
Helena (1884)	51,992	81,500	284,992
Juneau (1951)	70,800	11,870	75,000
Joliet (1948)	4,218	137,750	495,281
Kansas City (1880)	23,539	85,000	1,216,239
La Crosse (1868)	15,078	161,845	595,806
Lafayette-in-Indiana (1944)	9,832	52,374	772,494
Lafayette (Louisiana)	11,090	350,000	553,200
Lansing (1937)	8,713	145,363	1,307,650
Lincoln (1887)	23,844	47,114	501,681
Little Rock (1843)	53,102	41,752	1,898,400
Madison (1946)	8,070	117,161	503,313
Manchester (1884)	9,305	206,313	533,242
Marquette (1857)	16,281	99,557	300,407
Mobile (1829)	59,921	90,961	3,256,276
Monterey-Fresno (1922)	43,714	300,788	1,080,348
Nashville (1837)	42,622	60,397	3,129,718
Natchez (1937)	46,340	58,314	2,178,914
Norwich (1953)	1,978	133,127	347,120
Ogdensburg (1872)	12,036	141,728	344,053
Oklahoma City (1905)	69,910	89,029	2,230,253
Owensboro (1937)	12,502	34,906	620,393
Paterson (1937)	1,214	191,316	536,729
Peoria (1877)	16,933	179,031	1,210,591
Pittsburgh (1843)	4,092	757,776	2,225,428
Portland (1853)	33,040	241,982	913,774
Providence (1872)	1,085	480,745	791,896
Pueblo (1941)	51,290	98,469	401,211
Raleigh (1924)	52,349	35,060	4,051,740
Rapid City (1902)	43,000	32,800	158,099
Reno (1931)	110,829	40,050	208,107
Richmond (1820)	35,076	126,098	3,117,822
Rochester (1868)	7,107	357,296	1,044,124
Rockford (1908)	6,457	115,227	610,424
Sacramento (1885)	53,400	209,231	870,270
Saginaw (1938)	10,162	136,531	499,927
St. Augustine (1870)	46,959	173,207	2,743,720
St. Cloud (1889)	12,251	102,380	315,345
St. Joseph (1868)	18,296	37,544	594,558
Salina (1887)	26,685	46,432	337,952
Salt Lake City (1891)	84,990	31,400	686,839
San Diego (1936)	35,879	297,100	1,048,767
Savannah-Atlanta (1850)	58,980	44,070	3,444,578
Scranton (1868)	8,847	344,403	961,137

Diocese	Area in square miles	Catholic population	Total population
Sioux City (1902)	14,518	93,883	543,664
Sioux Falls (1889)	35,091	83,434	491,878
Spokane (1889)	23,456	54,424	403,442
Springfield-in-Illinois (1853)	15,139	134,067	969,006
Springfield (Massachusetts) (1870)	2,822	347,295	641,278
Steubenville (1944)	5,913	46,263	485,735
Superior (1905)	15,716	77,590	291,229
Syracuse (1886)	5,749	319,299	948,963
Toledo (1910)	8,222	241,151	1,125,200
Trenton (1881)	3,777	428,019	1,100,000
Tucson (1937)	52,369	190,783	631,630
Wheeling (1850)	29,172	96,320	2,481,848
Wichita (1887)	20,021	68,025	708,421
Wilmington (1868)	6,211	37,643	535,947
Winona (1889)	12,282	86,309	464,708
Worcester (1950)	1,532	291,939	574,420
Yakima (1951)	17,787	34,588	295,841
Youngstown (1943)	3,404	250,000	935,198
Alaska (Apostolic Vicariate) (1916)	515,600	10,500	60,000

CHART B

The Ecclesiastical Provinces of the United States. (The date in parenthesis, following the name of each Province, is the date of erection.)

BALTIMORE (April 8, 1808). Includes the States of Maryland (except for the five counties in the Archdiocese of Washington), Delaware, Virginia, West Virginia, North Carolina, Georgia, and the eastern part of Florida, as divided into the following dioceses: Archdiocese of Baltimore; Dioceses of: Charleston, S. C.; Raleigh, N. C.; Richmond, Va.; St. Augustine, Fla.; Savannah-Atlanta, Ga.; Wheeling, W. Va.; Wilmington, Del.; and the *Abbatia Nullius* of Belmont, N. C.

BOSTON (1875). Includes the States of Maine, New Hampshire, Vermont, and Massachusetts, as divided into the following dioceses: Archdiocese of Boston; Dioceses of: Burlington, Vt.; Fall River, Mass.; Manchester, N. H.; Portland, Me.; Springfield, Mass.; Worcester, Mass.

CHICAGO (1880). Includes the State of Illinois, as divided into the following dioceses: Archdiocese of Chicago; Dioceses of: Belleville; Joliet; Peoria; Rockford; Springfield-in-Illinois.

CINCINNATI (July 19, 1850). Includes the State of Ohio, as divided into the following dioceses: Archdiocese of Cincinnati; Dioceses of: Cleveland; Columbus; Steubenville; Toledo; Youngstown.

DENVER (November 15, 1941). Includes the States of Colorado and Wyoming, as divided into the following dioceses: Archdiocese of Denver; Dioceses of: Cheyenne, Wyo.; Pueblo, Colo.

DETROIT (August 3, 1937). Includes the State of Michigan, as divided into the following dioceses: Archdiocese of Detroit; Dioceses of: Grand Rapids; Lansing; Marquette; Saginaw.

HARTFORD (August 6, 1953). Includes the States of Connecticut and Rhode Island, as divided into the following dioceses: Archdiocese of Hartford, Conn.; Dioceses of: Bridgeport, Conn.; Norwich, Conn.; Providence, R. I.

INDIANAPOLIS (December 19, 1944). Includes the State of Indiana, as divided into the following dioceses: Archdiocese of Indianapolis; Dioceses of: Evansville; Fort Wayne; Lafayette-in-Indiana.

KANSAS CITY-IN-KANSAS (August 9, 1952). Includes the State of Kansas, as divided into the following dioceses: Archdiocese of Kansas City-in-Kansas; Dioceses of: Dodge City; Salina, Wichita.

LOS ANGELES (July 11, 1936). Includes Southern California, and the State of Arizona (with the exception of the Counties of Coconino, Mohave, Apache, Navajo, and Yavspai), as divided into the following dioceses: Archdiocese of Los Angeles, Calif.; Dioceses of: Monterey-Fresno, Calif.; San Diego, Calif.; Tucson, Ariz.

LOUISVILLE (December 10, 1937). Includes the States of Kentucky and Tennessee, as divided into the following dioceses: Archdiocese of Louisville, Ky.; Dioceses of: Covington, Ky.; Nashville, Tenn.; Owensboro, Ky.

MILWAUKEE (February 12, 1875). Includes the State of Wisconsin, as divided into the following dioceses: Archdiocese of Milwaukee; Dioceses of: Green Bay; La Crosse; Madison, Superior.

NEWARK (December 10, 1937). Includes the State of New Jersey, as divided into the following dioceses: Archdiocese of Newark; Dioceses of: Camden; Paterson; Trenton.

NEW ORLEANS (July 19, 1850). Includes the States of Louisiana, Alabama, Mississippi, Arkansas, and the western part of Florida, as divided into the following dioceses: Archdiocese of New Orleans; Dioceses of: Alexandria, La.; Lafayette, La.; Little Rock, Ark.; Mobile, Ala.; Natchez, Miss.

NEW YORK (July 19, 1850). Includes the State of New York, as divided into the following dioceses: Archdiocese of New York; Dioceses of: Albany; Brooklyn; Buffalo; Ogdensburg; Rochester; Syracuse.

OMAHA (August 7, 1945). Includes the State of Nebraska, as divided into the following dioceses: Archdiocese of Omaha; Dioceses of: Grand Island; Lincoln.

PHILADELPHIA (February 12, 1875). Includes the State of Pennsylvania, as divided into the following dioceses: Archdiocese of Philadelphia; Dioceses of: Altoona; Erie; Greensburg; Harrisburg; Pittsburgh; Scranton.

PORTLAND-IN-OREGON (July 24, 1846, as Oregon City; Name changed by Papal Decree of September 26, 1928). Includes the States of Oregon, Idaho, and Montana, as divided into the following dioceses: Archdiocese of Portland-in-Oregon; Dioceses of: Baker, Oregon; Boise, Idaho; Great Falls, Montana; Helena, Montana.

ST. LOUIS (July 20, 1847). Includes the State of Missouri, as divided into the following dioceses: Archdiocese of St. Louis; Dioceses of: Kansas City (Missouri); St. Joseph, Missouri.

ST. PAUL (May 4, 1888). Includes the States of Minnesota, South Dakota, and North Dakota, as divided into the following dioceses: Archdiocese of St. Paul; Dioceses of: Bismark, N. Dak.; Crookston, Minn.; Sioux Falls, S. Dak.; Winona, Minn.

SAN ANTONIO (August 3, 1926). Includes the States of Texas (except the diocese of El Paso) and Oklahoma, as divided into the following dioceses: Archdiocese of San Antonio; Dioceses of: Amarillo, (Tex.); Austin (Tex.); Corpus Christi (Tex.); Dallas-Fort Worth (Tex.); Galveston (Tex.); Oklahoma City and Tulsa (Oklahoma).

SAN FRANCISCO (July 29, 1853). Includes northern California and the States of Utah and Nevada, the Hawaiian Islands, the

Marianna Islands, and the Ryukyu Islands, as divided into the following dioceses: Archdiocese of San Francisco; Dioceses of: Honolulu, Hawaii; Reno, Nevada; Sacramento, California; Salt Lake City, Utah; and the Vicariate Apostolic of Guam.

SANTA FE (1875). Includes the States of New Mexico, Northern Arizona, and the diocese of El Paso, Texas, as divided into the following dioceses: Archdiocese of Santa Fe; Dioceses of: El Paso; Gallup.

SEATTLE (June 23, 1951). Includes the State of Washington and Alaska, as divided into the following dioceses: Archdiocese of Seattle; Dioceses of: Juneau (Alaska); Spokane; Yakima; and the Vicariate Apostolic of Alaska.

WASHINGTON (July 22, 1939); separated from Baltimore to which, when erected it had been united, November 15, 1947; and archbishopric without suffragan sees; immediately subject to the Holy See. Includes the District of Columbia and five counties in Maryland, viz., Montgomery, Prince George's, Charles, Calvert, and St. Mary's.

In addition, two non-territorial dioceses of Oriental Rite form part of no Province. They are 1) The Byzantine Rite Apostolic Exarchate of Philadelphia (Ukrainian Greek Catholic Diocese of the U.S.A.), embracing certain classes of persons of the Byzantine Rite in lands under the sovereignty of the U.S.A.; and 2) the Diocese of Pittsburgh (Greek Rite), embracing all Greek Catholics of Russian, Hungarian, and Croatian nationalities in the entire United States of America.

CHART C

The Dioceses of the United States arranged according to States

(Figures concerning the area and the population of each diocese are to be found in Chart A, the list of dioceses arranged alphabetically. The date following each state indicates its entry into the Federal Union.)

State and Dioceses within it	Area in sq. miles	Catholic population	Total population
Alabama (1819)	51,609	90,961	3,256,276
Mobile			
Arizona (1912)	113,909	190,783	631,630
Tucson			
Arkansas (1836)	53,102	41,752	1,898,400
Little Rock			

State and Dioceses within it	Area in sq. miles	Catholic population	Total population
California (1850)	158,693	2,752,119	11,967,104
Los Angeles (A)			
San Francisco (A)			
Monterey-Fresno			
Sacramento			
San Diego			
Colorado (1876)	104,247	254,199	1,338,923
Denver (A)			
Pueblo			
Connecticut (1788)	55,000	1,023,428	2,175,162
Hartford (A)			
Bridgeport			
Norwich			
Delaware (1787)	2,057	37,643	535,947
Wilmington			
Florida (1845)	58,666	173,207	2,743,720
St. Augustine			
Georgia (1788)	58,876	44,070	3,444,578
Savannah-Atlanta			
Idaho (1818)	83,557	31,761	588,637
Boise			
Illinois (1818)	56,400	2,567,276	8,284,896
Chicago (A)			
Belleville			
Joliet			
Peoria			
Rockford			
Springfield-in-Illinois			
Indiana (1816)	36,291	526,531	3,936,194
Indianapolis			
Evansville			
Fort Wayne			
Lafayette-in-Indiana			
Iowa (1846)	56,280	398,161	2,611,732
Dubuque (A)			
Davenport			
Des Moines			
Sioux City			
Kansas (1861)	82,276	239,500	1,905,661
Kansas City-in Kansas			
Dodge City			
Salina			
Wichita			
Kentucky (1792)	40,395	258,341	2,925,695
Louisville (A)			
Covington			
Owensboro			

State and Dioceses within it	Area in sq. miles	Catholic population	Total population
Louisiana (1812)	48,523	971,131	2,905,196
New Orleans			
Alexandria			
Lafayette			
Maine (1820)	33,215	241,982	913,774
Portland			
Maryland (1788)	10,557	366,652	1,691,910
Baltimore (A)			
Washington (A)			
Massachusetts (1788)	8,257	2,370,008	4,695,926
Boston (A)			
Fall River			
Springfield			
Worcester			
Michigan (1837)	58,216	1,642,432	6,939,334
Detroit (A)			
Grand Rapids			
Lansing			
Marquette			
Saginaw			
Minnesota (1853)	80,000	749,735	2,978,943
St. Paul (A)			
Crookston			
Duluth			
St. Cloud			
Winona			
Mississippi (1817)	47,715	58,314	2,178,914
Natchez			
Missouri (1824)	69,674	597,544	3,944,614
St. Louis (A)			
Kansas City			
St. Joseph			
Montana (1889)	146,080	136,865	1,282,593
Great Falls			
Helena			
Nebraska (1867)	77,895	214,051	589,279
Omaha (A)			
Grand Island			
Lincoln			
Nevada (1864)	110,540	40,050	208,107
Reno			
New Hampshire (1788)	9,304	206,313	533,242
Manchester			
New Jersey (1787)	7,836	1,991,141	4,944,483
Newark (A)			
Camden			
Paterson			
Trenton			

State and Dioceses within it	Area in sq. miles	Catholic population	Total population
New Mexico (1912)	121,666	291,110	620,000
Santa Fe			
Gallup			
New York (1788)	49,576	4,825,037	14,741,158
New York (A)			
Albany			
Brooklyn			
Buffalo			
Ogdensburg			
Rochester			
Syracuse			
North Carolina (1789)	52,712	36,020	4,162,446
Belmont Abbey (Prel. Nul.)			
Raleigh			
North Dakota (1889)	70,665	146,238	634,901
Bismark			
Fargo			
Ohio (1803)	41,222	1,726,082	8,386,662
Cincinnati (A)			
Cleveland			
Columbus			
Steubenville			
Toledo			
Youngstown			
Oklahoma (1907)	69,919	89,029	2,230,253
Oklahoma City and Tulsa			
Oregon (1859)	96,981	136,090	1,230,886
Portland in Oregon (A)			
Baker			
Pennsylvania (1787)	45,333	3,091,094	10,557,219
Philadelphia (A)			
Altoona			
Erie			
Greensburg			
Harrisburg			
Pittsburgh			
Scranton			
Rhode Island (1709)	1,214	480,745	791,896
Providence			
South Carolina (1788)	30,989	26,313	2,117,027
Charleston			
South Dakota (1788)	78,091	116,234	634,901
Rapid City			
Sioux Falls			
Tennessee (1796)	42,426	60,397	3,129,718
Texas (1845)	267,339	1,598,850	8,171,289
San Antonio (A)			
Amarillo			

State and Dioceses within it	Area in sq. miles	Catholic population	Total population
Texas *(con't.)*			
Austin			
Corpus Christi			
Dallas			
El Paso			
Galveston			
Utah (1896)	84,916	31,400	686,839
Salt Lake City			
Vermont (1791)	9,609	115,932	375,833
Burlington			
Virginia (1788)	40,815	126,098	3,117,822
Richmond			
Washington (1889)	68,182	289,875	2,565,319
Seattle (A)			
Spokane			
Yakima			
West Virginia (1863)	24,181	96,320	2,481,848
Wheeling			
Wisconsin (1848)	56,154	1,132,547	3,399,332
Milwaukee (A)			
Green Bay			
La Crosse			
Madison			
Superior			
Wyoming (1890)	97,914	48,304	288,707
Cheyenne			

	1944	1956
Converts	90,822	139,333
Marriages	289,548	324,907
Deaths	262,291	290,855
Catholic Population	23,419,701	33,574,017
Total Population	133,065,084	154,300,474

Chart D

Certain Statistics, as of 1956, for the various Dioceses of the United States

(The figures following the name of each diocese indicate the numbers, respectively, of clergy, baptisms, marriages, mixed marriages, and children in parochial school. Figures showing the area in square miles, the total population, and the Catholic population of each diocese are given in Chart A.)

Archdioceses:	Clergy	Baptisms	Marriages	Mixed Marriages	Children in Elementary Parochial Schools
Baltimore	669	14,061	3,831	1,689	51,018
Boston	2,132	48,813	13,434	2,569	102,353
Chicago	2,455	59,762	17,632	3,366	237,367
Cincinnati	817	15,788	3,232	1,029	58,520
Denver	270	9,655	1,804	639	16,462
Detroit	1,090	44,088	9,853	2,332	122,326
Dubuque	455	7,359	1,617	345	22,978
Hartford	604	20,251	5,468	1,287	30,535
Indianapolis	470	7,354	1,442	661	27,330
Kansas City-in-Kansas	346	4,681	836	256	14,328
Los Angeles	850	48,775	8,555	2,692	93,899
Louisville	346	6,631	1,536	629	28,364
Milwaukee	913	22,560	5,397	1,386	75,876
Newark	987	34,372	9,747	2,088	104,789
New Orleans	543	20,452	4,863	1,145	58,502
New York	2,312	57,979	16,725	3,198	141,939
Omaha	333	6,036	1,557	421	19,174
Philadelphia	1,865	46,338	12,104	3,133	183,871
Portland in-Oregon	346	5,032	1,251	568	15,155
St. Louis	1,048	20,622	4,595	1,471	76,273
St. Paul	590	20,085	4,122	1,121	66,545
San Antonio	361	17,273	2,497	370	18,820
San Francisco	988	32,596	6,538	2,089	51,009
Santa Fe	245	8,841	1,640	185	12,894
Seattle	349	9,105	1,778	869	20,968
Washington	838	12,441	2,847	1,409	32,642
Dioceses:					
Albany	599	7,575	4,996	1,249	31,808
Alexandria	152	2,860	660	249	9,665
Altoona	246	4,645	1,407	366	13,422
Amarillo	91	4,743	607	123	3,121
Austin	118	4,469	737	213	5,845
Baker	48	1,175	183	84	308
Belleville	198	4,326	970	298	15,442

Dioceses:	Clergy	Baptisms	Marriages	Mixed Marriages	Children in Elementary Parochial Schools
Bismark	148	2,967	710	180	5,559
Boise	93	2,356	428	148	3,172
Bridgeport	245	7,882	1,991	485	17,837
Brooklyn	1,506	70,543	19,980	3,829	197,951
Buffalo	1,056	21,747	5,692	1,469	66,065
Burlington	214	4,811	1,269	421	9,634
Camden	195	8,267	1,908	533	24,762
Charleston	121	1,945	344	210	586
Cheyenne	58	1,964	341	124	3,108
Cleveland	810	24,818	5,799	1,306	93,741
Columbus	284	6,511	1,265	573	19,897
Corpus Christi	186	20,445	2,546	201	12,451
Covington	194	3,160	746	252	13,909
Crookston	86	1,710	347	131	2,766
Dallas-Fort Worth	198	6,378	1,012	382	12,662
Davenport	223	3,868	864	314	9,818
Des Moines	141	2,995	636	188	6,887
Dodge City	73	1,313	241	67	3,055
Duluth	130	3,608	840	361	5,754
El Paso	126	8,552	1,247	187	7,153
Erie	338	7,712	1,239	668	18,499
Evansville	114	3,096	735	261	12,451
Fall River	326	7,234	2,106	369	15,950
Fargo	172	3,845	855	275	4,020
Fort Wayne	503	10,623	2,475	762	36,702
Gallup	78	1,775	360	81	2,141
Galveston	292	10,331	2,026	739	25,424
Grand Island	83	1,957	450	121	2,901
Grand Rapids	245	10,732	1,353	443	20,141
Great Falls	115	3,041	555	236	5,091
Green Bay	424	9,884	2,324	491	34,549
Greensburg	248	5,915	1,774	419	14,602
Harrisburg	210	5,426	1,401	633	19,711
Helena	134	2,734	555	205	6,223
Honolulu	137	5,873	1,154	315	10,726
Joliet	287	5,182	1,088	338	19,293
Juneau	20	571	92	55	353
Kansas City	283	4,569	1,015	306	14,048
La Crosse	360	7,031	1,655	377	24,925
Lafayette-in-Indiana	166	2,535	555	285	7,170
Lafayette (Louisiana)	220	11,484	2,821	480	14,639
Lansing	172	8,409	1,677	543	20,237
Lincoln	156	2,304	559	164	4,889
Little Rock	178	1,683	394	215	6,475
Madison	196	5,582	1,250	321	13,912
Manchester	366	6,904	2,006	606	20,781

Dioceses:	Clergy	Baptisms	Marriages	Mixed Marriages	Children in Elementary Parochial Schools
Marquette	167	3,821	1,019	375	8,314
Mobile	339	4,665	927	593	15,556
Monterey-Fresno	220	10,141	1,844	491	12,122
Nashville	127	3,757	653	366	11,569
Natchez	180	3,152	694	459	9,231
Norwich	189	4,653	1,129	328	9,161
Ogdensburg	248	5,620	1,470	449	7,909
Oklahoma City and Tulsa	234	4,912	828	414	10,900
Owensboro	68	1,679	377	149	7,528
Paterson	292	6,769	1,790	460	17,917
Peoria	377	7,691	1,764	668	21,358
Pittsburgh	739	25,983	6,740	1,910	85,203
Portland	356	8,678	2,327	532	21,525
Providence	531	13,450	4,008	694	35,325
Pueblo	134	4,772	923	184	5,042
Raleigh	165	2,762	511	366	6,449
Rapid City	113	1,534	661	164	2,385
Reno	62	1,329	738	363	1,850
Richmond	262	7,411	1,213	759	22,071
Rochester	522	12,694	3,235	1,078	39,093
Rockford	287	5,224	1,097	394	16,184
Sacramento	179	5,649	994	430	8,580
Saginaw	158	6,312	1,630	486	15,663
St. Augustine	242	10,036	1,955	948	26,050
St. Cloud	291	4,310	1,080	202	10,949
St. Joseph	133	2,057	421	176	5,145
Salina	119	2,289	538	120	5,431
Salt Lake City	79	1,846	277	117	2,087
San Diego	277	17,072	2,118	706	18,932
Savannah-Atlanta	160	3,111	627	426	9,469
Scranton	576	9,623	3,459	733	26,913
Sioux City	196	4,449	1,017	249	12,909
Sioux Falls	202	3,770	920	353	7,789
Spokane	159	2,885	557	219	7,192
Springfield-in-Illinois	364	5,802	1,284	450	18,655
Springfield (Mass.)	458	10,914	2,882	665	22,802
Steubenville	125	2,051	534	216	5,772
Superior	125	3,109	780	275	6,703
Syracuse	397	12,992	3,229	1,015	23,405
Toledo	330	10,602	2,264	698	35,171
Trenton	422	14,654	3,751	1,069	43,728
Tucson	153	9,764	1,592	404	12,405
Wheeling	167	3,958	961	426	9,482
Wichita	190	3,427	693	240	9,283
Wilmington	132	2,761	768	316	10,758

Dioceses:	Clergy	Baptisms	Marriages	Mixed Marriages	Children in Elementary Parochial Schools
Winona	190	4,128	841	218	10,898
Worcester	456	8,813	2,381	479	20,045
Yakima	36	2,128	411	177	2,418
Youngstown	275	7,896	2,021	522	25,473
Byzantine Rite Apostolic Exarchate of Philadelphia	304	5,318	1,637	286	6,426
Greek Rite Diocese of Pittsburgh	204	3,730	1,429	296	2,080
Belmont Abbey	27	50	13	9	377
Military Ordinariate	1,991	33,530	11,639	—	—
Vicariate Apostolic of Alaska	27	558	77	21	600

CHAPTER FIVE

The Financial Structure of the Church in the United States

◆

BY HARRY J. BYRNE

WHEN THE SPANISH founded the city of St. Augustine in September, 1565, a rough primitive shrine to the Blessed Mother of God was constructed. This shrine, at what is now the oldest city in the United States, was among the first temporalities of the Catholic Church in the New World. A visible Church worshipping God, educating its own members and outsiders, and carrying on a multitude of charitable activities has, of necessity, its material side. Churches, school buildings, hospitals and other charitable institutions come into existence as the Church grows. Once the construction has been completed, the problem of maintenance is posed.

Today the Catholic Church in the United States presents a

Harry J. Byrne holds his doctorate in Canon Law from the Catholic University of America. He has been assistant chancellor of the Archdiocese of New York and now is a canonist to the staff of the Tribunal of the Archdiocese of New York. He was ordained in 1945.

startlingly different physical picture from what it presented in the year 1565. Although the strength of the Church lies in human souls and divine graces, her activity is revealed across the continent in physical signs. Villages and towns are marked by the cross-topped steeples of Catholic churches. Those same Catholic steeples are to be found in the great cities, although often dwarfed and hidden by towering skyscrapers. Extended throughout the land is a network of hospitals and other charitable institutions operated by the Catholic Church. The Catholic school is found practically everywhere as an adjunct to the parish church.

Foreign visitors to the United States invariably are impressed by the large-scale development which has taken place in the physical side of the Catholic Church. Since the end of World War II, great building activities of all types have been in progress. New residential communities have developed and older ones have increased in size. The Catholic Church has grown along with the community. New parishes have been founded and new churches have been built in great numbers. Many new Catholic elementary and secondary schools have been constructed.

All of this physical development obviously involved the outlay of great sums of money in construction and maintenance. One Archbishop recently announced in a TV broadcast that $40,000,000 had been spent in new building programs in his jurisdiction in the last nine years. The authorities of two other large dioceses recently disclosed in the public press that under their long-range building programs, each would spend $50,000,000 in the next ten years for the construction of new Catholic schools. It has been reliably estimated that it would cost the City of New York $425,000,000 for buildings alone if the city were to take over the student bodies of the Catholic schools. The Catholic faithful financially support their Catholic school system in addition to paying the governmental taxes from which the public school system is supported.

The figures quoted represent the largest and most populous dioceses in the United States, and they are not therefore typical or representative of the nation as a whole. Yet they are interesting and are indicative of the upper limits reached by the Catholic faithful in the financial support of the activities of their Church in this country. Smaller dioceses and dioceses in more rural areas have generally shown similar physical growth proportionate to their size. It has been reliably estimated that since the termination of hostilities of World War II the Catholic Church has expended the sum of 10 billion dollars in new buildings alone throughout the country.

The marked growth and development of the Catholic Church in its material phase has been made possible and is being continued by the generous financial support of the faithful and by generally efficient and energetic ecclesiastical administration of material affairs. The United States is today and has been in the past a prosperous land. Its Catholic people are generous contributors to the activities of their Church. The United States is a pluralist society, in which government monopoly is shunned and in which preference is shown to the unhampered activities of individuals, families and what are termed "voluntary" groups of persons for the accomplishment of certain purposes. The State in America has no monopoly over education or over charitable and welfare activities, although it does carry these on. Non-governmental groups carry on a large volume of the educational and charitable activities. These activities are not financed from public taxes. Thus Americans, Catholics and non-Catholics alike, are well accustomed to supporting such activities privately and without reliance upon governmental funds. American Catholics are generous in supporting charitable activities carried on by their Church. And in their financial support of the Catholic educational system on the primary and secondary level, there is no comparable non-governmental counterpart to be found.

The present stage of the material condition of the Catholic Church in the United States is the result of a long development. Things are different today from what they were in earlier periods of American history. When the Spanish were attempting to establish colonies on these shores, the Church received revenue through the intervention of the government. Church and State were entwined, and funds were made available to the Church by disposition of the Crown.

In the French colonies of North America the Church labored under great poverty. Unlike the Spanish, the French Government did not leave a record of furnishing money and supplies to the Church. The second Diocesan Synod of Quebec held in 1698 found it necessary to insist strenuously on the obligation of the faithful to support the Church. In Louisiana the intervention of governmental authority dealt a harsh blow to Catholic missionary activity. The Superior Council of Louisiana in 1763, following the lead of the French Parliaments, banned the Jesuits and ordered that everything they owned, except strictly personal property, be sold at auction and that their churches and chapels be razed.

In the English colonies the material side of the Church's activity varies. In New England the Catholic Church was not tolerated and Catholics had no civil rights. In Maryland the Church at times benefited from grants of land under the royal charter. It is interesting to note that the original holdings of the Church in Maryland were considerably increased by the gift of a tract of land from the Indian chief Maquaconen. Thus the Jesuit Fathers in Maryland were able to meet the costs of maintaining their churches and missions on the income from their farms.

The Catholic laity in Maryland generally does not seem to have supported the Church well in those early days. However, this situation changed. In 1785, Father John Carroll, an outstanding leader of the Church in the United States and destined to be made the first American bishop a few years later, wrote in a report to Rome that the priests were supported generally from the income of estates and also from the voluntary offerings of the faithful. From subsequent writings of Bishop Carroll, it is clear that the support of the clergy came to depend largely on the contributions of the faithful, since the numbers of priests had increased to the point where income from estates no longer sufficed.

The first Diocesan Synod of Baltimore held in 1781 set forth the obligation of the faithful to support the Church by their offerings. These offerings of the faithful, the Synod continues, were to be divided into three parts: one to be applied to the maintenance of the pastor, another to the care of the poor, and the third to the procuring of things requisite to divine worship. The Synod stressed the importance of the offerings of the faithful in carrying on the works of the Church in worship of God and in bringing the word of God and the sacraments to the people. The increasing population of Catholics was mentioned and also the fact that they were dispersed throughout the different States, thereby making necessary a greater number of spiritual laborers. It was pointed out that these could not be brought from Europe or maintained unless the faithful were to contribute towards bearing the expense involved.

The subsequent history of the Church in the United States has shown that the faithful caught the spirit expressed in the laws of this first synod and in subsequent synods and councils. It is no reflection on the influence of law to give credit for the long-standing generosity of American Catholics, not so much to the statutes but rather to the vitality of a people's faith and their enthusiastic participation in the life of the Church growing in their new country.

Great waves of immigrants came to America in the nineteenth century from Ireland, Italy, Germany, Poland and other countries. Like most immigrant people they were poor in material things, but as they made their way in the land of their adoption they shared their earthly goods with the Church. There have been Catholics who were possessed of great wealth and who contributed substantially to the work of the Church. But for the most part the Church in America has consisted predominantly of the poor and middle classes.

In the United States today, the Catholic Church relies chiefly upon the continued generosity of its faithful of all economic classes, both for current operating expenses and for capital building funds. There are no government subsidies to support the Church in the United States. The American

principle of "separation of Church and State"—which historically and ideologically is quite a different thing from the
European version of separation of Church and State—prohibits direct financial aid from the government to any religious body. There are no great patrimonies or endowments
from the past to support substantially the work of the
Church.

Some income-producing properties are held by the Church,
but their significance is small by comparison with the importance of the continuous, day-by-day contributions of the
faithful. These contributed funds are generally expended
immediately in one way or another. Perhaps they will be
spent for current operating needs; perhaps they will be
placed in building funds soon to be expended in actual construction; perhaps they will be used to pay interest and
amortization on the money borrowed under mortgage by a
parish or a diocese for some building program. Although invested funds have some role to play, especially in dowries
of religious women and in college and university financing,
the overwhelming emphasis is not upon building up income-
producing properties for future income and support but
rather upon the present and future generosity of American
Catholics.

Far from relying on accumulations from the past, the
Church in America, faced with the continued necessity of
new building, looks rather to the future. Capital building
funds are started with contributions from the faithful, and
then the balance is borrowed under a mortgage taken out on
Church property. Such property is put up as security for the
loan. Thus in the widespread practice of mortgaging property, reliance is placed on the future ability and willingness
of the faithful of a diocese or parish to pay interest on the
money borrowed and to amortize the debt, that is, to pay off
the substance of the loan over a period of time.

It would require a statistical study of vast proportions to
show with any precision the ratio of church funds in the
United States received on the one hand from contributions of
the faithful and on the other hand from income-producing

properties such as securities and real estate. All the indications are that the role of income-producing property in church finance is quite small in comparison to the role played by current contributions of the faithful. One example of this trend is to be found in a recent annual report of a large diocese regarding its budget for charitable activities. Of the annual income received by the central diocesan charities organization, the amount received from investments amounted to only about one per cent of the amount received from the contributions of the faithful.

It is interesting to note that contemporary financing of charitable activities by private, non-religious agencies is also characterized by increasing reliance upon the continued generosity of benefactors rather than upon the accumulating of income-producing holdings. There has been in recent years more widespread use of the "self-liquidating" trust fund in the financing of charitable activities. In this type of plan not only is income from the investments expended but periodically portions of the principal of the fund are themselves expended, so that eventually the entire fund is consumed. For a variety of considerations, financial and otherwise, this procedure is frequently the best way of getting maximum value from funds contributed for charitable purposes.

Americans as a group are consistent contributors to religious, charitable and educational activities. Private agencies, institutions and funds exist in great abundance for the carrying on of such activities, and they are supported by the voluntary contributions of the American public. Contributing to non-governmental groups for the support of religious, charitable and educational activities is very much a part of the American scene today.

American Catholics make their contributions to their Church and its work through their parishes, dioceses, special boards and agencies, and in response to direct mail appeals. On the parish level they contribute financially to the regular Sunday collection, to special monthly collections held in some places, and to other special appeals as, for example, a coal collection to buy fuel to heat the parish buildings during the winter. To meet ordinary operating expenses of church and school or to provide extraordinary building funds some parishes may resort to bazaars and raffles or to parish entertainments.

The bishop must occasionally make special appeals for centralized diocesan activities, such as the maintenance of the diocesan seminary. It seems characteristic of contemporary Catholic life in the United States that many activities are being handled on a centralized diocesan basis. For example, individual parishes might find it impossible to build and maintain high schools. Accordingly centralized diocesan high schools have been built as diocesan projects. They draw their students from many parishes in a particular city or a particular section of the diocese. So, too, in charitable activities the diocese undertakes supervision and administration of hospitals, child-caring institutions, homes for the aged and other similar charitable activities on a diocesan wide basis. Special diocesan-wide appeals are made to support such activities.

Religious orders and communities engaged in foreign mission work make their appeals for support to the Catholic faithful. Many dioceses have a missionary cooperative plan whereby different religious communities are given the opportunity of appealing directly to the faithful of a parish on a particular Sunday. This plan generally provides that such an appeal will be made on one Sunday of the year in every parish. Once a year a special appeal is made through the bishops by the Society for the Propagation of the Faith. Forty per cent of the funds received in this appeal are distributed by the bishops to missionary dioceses in the United States itself and its dependencies. The remainder is sent to Rome for distribution in foreign mission work. "The Catholic Church Extension Society" is a home missionary organization engaged in raising and distributing funds to be used in missionary areas of the United States and its dependencies.

The support of missionary work among the Negroes of the United States is the function of "The Catholic Board for Mission Work among the Colored People." There are boards to raise funds to support missionary activities to the

Indians in the United States and to the Eskimos in Alaska. "The Saint Paul Guild" is primarily engaged in assisting converts to Catholicism who have been Protestant clergymen and Protestant religious. "The Catholic Near East Welfare Association" is a pontifical association whose purpose is to raise funds for the support of the missions in the Near East. Practically all of these societies have their own publications through which they make known the work they are carrying on and through which they make their appeals for financial contributions.

Direct mail appeals are made by various ecclesiastical organizations through the use of the postal service. This is a form of appeal that has developed tremendously in recent years. It is used in the United States by a great variety of organizations ranging from church groups to health and welfare organizations unaffiliated with any church. A person who is known as a contributor to charitable causes can be sure that his name eventually will be included on many of the voluminous mailing lists used in this type of appeal. It is not an uncommon experience for the average person in urban areas to receive several such appeals each week throughout the year. At Christmas time the daily mail brings several such appeals each day. Many of the causes for which money is solicited in this manner are most deserving, as are those sponsored by Catholic Church organizations. However, this type of appeal is being increasingly used by organizations which are not bonafide. There has developed a "charity racket" whereby unscrupulous operators solicit money for various causes and consume most of the money in administrative expenses and in paying their own salaries. There is reason to think that a certain small percentage of charity appeals made by direct mail and in other ways have been grossly abused by organizations of dubious integrity.

While no shadow can be cast on the integrity of appeals made by Catholic organizations under proper ecclesiastical supervision, it nevertheless remains true that the volume of these direct mail appeals has grown so great that it becomes impossible for the average Catholic to respond to the great variety of requests on his generosity. The response to these appeals, however, must be satisfactory to those making the appeals because of the great number of organizations which continue to use this manner of solicitation.

American Catholics are generous in their contributions to their Church. They contribute, not only to their local parish, but support the work of the Church in a larger area—diocesan and worldwide as well. This generosity in voluntary giving seems to be a characteristic of the American person. It is reliably estimated that Americans give each year to religious, educational, health and welfare and other charitable activities the staggering total of 4 billion dollars. This American attribute of generosity is given further emphasis in the case of Catholics by the awareness of and sense of participation in the work of the Church that these American Catholics seem to possess.

The second important factor in the material development of the Church in the United States is the administrative efficiency of the Church authorities and their delegates. The general law of the Church, as contained in the Code of Canon Law, contains various administrative norms and regulations whose purpose is to insure, as far as possible, the conservation and best possible use of the material resources of the Church. The law sets forth certain general principles governing administration of ecclesiastical temporalities. Alienation of church goods is severely restricted and subject to the most careful supervisory controls. So, too, are any transactions which would jeopardize the material goods used by the Church in the fulfillment of its mission. The law provides for the supervision of administrators by superior authorities. Accountings must be rendered to such authorities, and canonical visitations and inspections of properties and financial accounts are provided for.

In addition to the more general norms provided by the universal law of the Church, the Church in the United States has over the years through various synods and councils developed a body of more specific regulations governing the tenure and administration of ecclesiastical goods. For example, diocesan synods frequently legislate that administrators of church goods cannot make an expenditure beyond a certain stated sum without the consent of the Ordinary. Frequently legal statutes will require that the consent of the Ordinary be furnished for the investment of ecclesiastical money, for the purchase of insurance and for other acts of extraordinary administration.

The history of the Church in the United States has been marked by one outstanding legal problem which ecclesiastical authorities have had to meet. It is the problem of the tenure of church property under the law of the civil jurisdiction. In the canon law of the Church title to property is held by various legal, or moral, personalities in the Church, such as a parish or a diocese. The pastor or the bishop do not hold the title to property; they are, according to the canon law, merely the administrators of the property which is held by the "abstract personality" of the parish, the diocese, or other ecclesiastical entity. This abstract or legal person is obviously not a real person, but is an entity recognized by the canon law as being able to hold title to property. However, the law of the civil jurisdictions in the United States belonging to what is known as the "common law" legal tradition provides no way for an abstract legal personality to hold title to property. Only a physical person or persons can hold title. This is one of the significant differences between, on the one hand, the Roman law tradition in which the canon law finds itself, and, on the other hand, the Anglo-American "common law" tradition. The former recognizes the abstract legal entity as capable of holding title to property; the latter does not. Thus the problem arose for the Church in the United States as to who was to hold the title to ecclesiastical property under the laws of the forty-eight States.

Hence the Church had to make some arrangement to meet the problem of holding title to its property in the United States in a way that would afford it all the protection of the civil law. It should be noted that property tenure in the United States is governed by the law of each individual State and not by Federal law. Each of the forty-eight States has its own provision in this regard, all of them in the "common-law" tradition and having many similarities but also being marked by important differences from state to state. Thus the problem had to be met in slightly different ways in the different states.

The Church in the United States addressed itself to the problem and reached various solutions in the different States and over the course of the years. Sometimes the pastor or the bishop held the title to ecclesiastical property. This practice was fraught with many difficulties. A pastor who might rebel against ecclesiastical authority and go into schism might be able to take with him the temporal possessions of his parish, including the church building itself. When a pastor or bishop died intestate, unscrupulous relatives could claim as heirs and actually obtain church property which was held under the civil law in the name of the pastor or the bishop. Even where the pastor or the bishop had a will properly disposing of the ecclesiastical property which they held, many difficulties were encountered. Sometimes contracts had to be made involving property which would be tied up pending the probating of the will.

Where the bishop held civil title to all the church property in his diocese, many difficulties were encountered. If some one parish or other unit in the diocese should incur some great financial liability, all the property of the diocese could be jeopardized.

In view of such difficulties another way of meeting the problem was devised in the "trustee system." Theoretically this appeared as a good solution. Laymen were chosen from the parish and they were made trustees of a parish corporation. As trustees they held the civil title to the property of the parish. This plan of having laymen participate in the material affairs of the parish seemed at first to have much in its favor. It was thought that the priest would be saved from the efforts of fund raising and providing for his support so that he could devote himself more exclusively to his spiritual ministry. However, in actual practice the trustee system showed very serious weaknesses. Many trustees, who were merely holding civil title to property, soon tried to assert the rights of real owners, thus usurping the rights that actually belonged to the Church and decisions that belonged only to pastors and other ecclesiastical authorities. In some cases the lay trustees, using the power that came to them by virtue of the incorporation under the civil law, even defied the authority of the bishops. There are examples of trustees demanding the removal of a particular pastor or appointing a pastor over the objections of the bishop. Because of such inroads upon proper ecclesiastical discipline, the trustee system fell into disfavor.

Practically all of the early synods and councils of the Church in the United States found it necessary to meet the problem of how title to ecclesiastical property was to be held under the law of the civil jurisdiction. Under the pressure of necessity and learning through experience, sometimes bitter, various satisfactory methods were worked out whereby title to Church property could be properly, safely and efficiently held under the law of the civil jurisdiction.

According to authoritative ecclesiastical sources, among the various methods now in use throughout the United States for holding and administering church property, the one known as the "parish corporation" is preferable to others, but only when the conditions and safeguards are involved which are provided for in the law of the State of New York. New York State has a "Religious Corporations Law," providing for the civil incorporation of religious bodies in terms which are congruous and congenial to the structure and discipline of the different religious denominations. It is provided by this New York State law that incorporated Roman Catholic Churches have as trustees the Archbishop or Bishop, the Vicar General, the pastor and two laymen chosen from the parish. It is further provided that no act or proceeding of the trustees shall be valid without the sanction of the Archbishop or Bishop; or, in the case of his absence or inability to act, without the sanction of the Vicar General or administrator of the diocese.

This method of holding and administering church prop-

erty is eminently satisfactory. It provides an interesting example of how in the United States Church and State, while
separate and distinct in their activities, nevertheless can work
together harmoniously to the advantage of both. Under the
civil law of the United States the Church enjoys a full measure of the freedom that rightfully belongs to her. Not only
is this freedom characterized by the absence of interference
by the State in the affairs of the Church, but it is also frequently marked by a spirit of positive cooperation on the
part of the State with various religious bodies.

The Church in the United States has been and is situated
in a growing and expanding country. The construction and
maintenance of churches and schools and other ecclesiastical
edifices have brought up problems both financial and legal
which are not generally encountered where the long passage
of centuries of ecclesiastical life has already established patterns and frameworks within which the holding and administration of temporal resources are carried on. Indeed there
may be some dangers and hazards for ecclesiastics who are
involved in the management and administration of temporalities on so large a scale as is to be found in many places in the
United States. The growth of the Church's material holdings,
however, has many advantages attendant upon it as well.

Among the dangers is the possibility that ecclesiastical administrators might become overly immersed in temporalities
to the detriment of their essentially spiritual mission. The
pastor of a rapidly growing district may see a very real need
to expand the facilities of his parochial school to care for
the many children of the parish. Day after day he may be
faced with the difficult task of telling individual parents
that there is no more room in the present Catholic school
for their children. In order to raise the necessary funds to
initiate a new building program, he may conduct an intensive
drive. Human beings, being what they are, the temporal may
obtrude itself on the spiritual. For example, appeals for funds
for parish building could occupy a disproportionate amount
of time in the pulpit which might better be spent on a directly spiritual matter. The priest might, in some cases, be-

come overly immersed in conducting bazaars, raffles and parish entertainments in connection with fund raising. More immediately priestly duties could suffer as a result.

There can be a shifting of values and emphases on the part of a priest faced with the necessity of raising funds to carry on the work of his parish. A priest could come to the point where he thinks the lay apostolate means dropping money in a collection basket. As in all things, there is the danger of an extreme. Prudence, the moderating virtue, can and generally does exercise its control in preventing the priest from becoming overly engaged in the material side of his parochial ministry.

Under the system of church financing in the United States, as it is now carried on, there appears certain decided advantages. There is quite generally present on the part of the faithful a real sense of participation in the work of the Church. The laity work with the priest and contribute generously for spiritual motives, and yet they can see some of the results of their efforts. A new parish develops great enthusiasm on the part of the people. They are united by a common faith in Christ and through the sacraments and through their loyalty to the Pope. But the actual working with the new pastor, the sight of the parish church or school gradually taking shape amid the welter of concrete and stone and wood, and then the day of the dedication when the bishop comes to bless their new edifice—all of these help to develop a tremendous sense of participation on the part of the faithful. They see what is going on in the church and in the parochial school, and they sense how essential is their own support and cooperation. They become close to their priest and become more alert to the spiritual work of the church which they are assisting.

In some other countries and at different times in history the enemies of the Church have charged that the Church was allied to a particular form of government or to a particular economic system because it drew its financial support from the government or from large income-producing properties held in church ownership. In the United States such charges could hardly be made since the Church is financed practically exclusively from the current contributions of the people. The Church depends almost immediately upon the people for its support. By constitutional provision no governmental funds may be used in support of any religious body in the United States. And there are no great patrimonies of income-producing property from which the Church draws its support. The support which the Church receives is freely given by the people and is a testimony of their own active interest and participation in the work of the hierarchy.

In summary it may be said that the financing of the Church in the contemporary United States looks not to government funds or to reserves accumulated over the years, but rather to the current and future generosity of the faithful. And that generosity today seems to be producing, under generally efficient administration, the parochial schools, the hospitals, the institutions, the churches wherein Catholic faith expresses itself in worship, in charity to others, and in communicating itself to others.

CHAPTER SIX

The Catholic School System in the United States

————— ❖ —————

BY FREDERICK G. HOCHWALT

THE SIZE AND SCOPE of Catholic education in the United States comes as a surprise to most people, including many Catholics, even though they may have had some previous knowledge of parochial schools in their own locality. For the parochial school is only a segment of an educational program that involves literally millions of individuals and ranges from pre-school programs for infants to a complex schedule of education for adults in all walks of life. Why does this system of schooling exist and why do Catholics cherish it and make

---

Frederick G. Hochwalt has been Director of the Department of Education of the National Catholic Welfare Conference since 1944. That same year he was appointed a Papal Chamberlain by Pope Pius XII. He has held directorates in various national educational associations and has served actively on such committees as the Education Committee of the Catholic Association for International Peace and the Catholic Committee on Intellectual and Cultural Affairs.

great sacrifices to protect and expand it? The answer is a very simple one. The Church is engaged in education for one purpose only—to make men saints, that is, to make them holy. The Church is following the divine admonition in helping mankind to achieve a supreme goal— "Be ye perfect as your heavenly Father is perfect." The Church seeks by every educational device to bring men to the knowledge, love and service of God; it seeks to help men live decently and justly in this life so that they may enjoy the presence of God in eternity. Whatever else is done in educational endeavor must remain subordinate to the chief goal of bringing eternal salvation to men.

The purpose of education under Catholic auspices was clearly set down by Pope Pius XI in his encyclical on the Christian Education of Youth: "to cooperate with divine grace in forming Christ in those regenerated by Baptism." It seems appropriate here to point out that the Church is a supernatural society, charged with the mandate of her divine Founder to go forth and teach all nations and to instruct according to His revelation. Monsignor George Johnson once observed that although the Church addresses herself immediately to the individual soul and strives there in cooperation with divine power to make those changes and transformations which are in accordance with the standards of life and living as taught and exemplified by Christ, she is always mindful of the needs of society and of the advancement of human culture in all its phases. Father Gerald Walsh, S.J., speaking to the annual national meeting of the National Catholic Educational Association in 1948 put it this way:

> "Obviously, then, we are conscious as American Catholic educators of our social responsibility in the concrete age in which we live. Without forgetting our responsibility to education *as education,* and to education *as Catholic,* we are remembering our responsibility to education *as contemporary.*
> "But I hope we shall not forget, at any point in our discussions, that, however clearly we *distinguish* the aims, goals, tasks or responsibilities of Catholic education, we must not imagine we can *separate* them. Just as truly as we must distin-

guish without separating body and soul, person and community, tradition and progress, culture and civilization, ethics and economics, morality and legislation, religion and politics, church and society, God and the world, so we must distinguish without separation our threefold responsibility as educators.

"It would be fatal if we should imagine that our job is to give the world *either* scholars *or* citizens *or* saints. Our ideal is to give to our age and still more to the age that is in the womb of history, to the world of tomorrow, citizens who are *both* scholars *and* saints. On the other hand, it would be fatal if we should imagine that merely by making scholars and helping to make saints, we have done our whole task in forming good citizens. Good citizenship, or at any rate, high leadership in society is an autonomous function, and a specific end to be achieved by specific means."

Catholic educators and philosophers generally agree with Father Walsh on the question of the interpenetration of our aims and responsibilities. We cannot separate our responsibility to citizenship from our responsibility to scholarship and holiness. Or as Father Walsh says:

"We shall, in fact, have better citizens and certainly better leaders of society if we have remained true to our ideal of education as education, to our task of disciplining the intelligence, conscience, taste and social sense of our students so that their minds can readily distinguish truth from falsehood; their conscience, right from wrong and justice from injustice; their taste, what is fair from what is foul; their social sense, what they owe to themselves as persons and what they owe to the society in which they live.

"We want our citizens to be scholars in the sense of persons disciplined in the human faculties that give them human dignity. We would like, too, our citizens to be saints in the sense of being always in the state of Grace, of having an habitual claim, in the theological sense, on the life of Eternal Glory, of being always aware of their immortal destiny.

"We want to give to our world of today and tomorrow men and women who think like Athenian philosophers, behave like the best citizens of ancient Rome and love God like those who stood by the Cross and prayed in the upper room in the Jerusalem of Jesus Christ."

It is a matter of historical record that the Church began her educational work in the territory of what is now the United States at the beginning of the Seventeenth Century in the Spanish colonies in the Southwest with a program that was more social and industrial than literary. From that day on she has built schools and colleges and fostered formal education in every possible way. And at the same time she has tried to keep alive the influence of Christian ideals in every phase of our national life.

Philosophers, skilled in the field of education have set down the philosophical bases of the Catholic doctrine of education and the educational bases of the Catholic philosophy of life. They have done this from a conviction that a mutual relationship exists between one's theory of education and one's philosophy of life. For every conception of life involves a theory of education, and every theory of education in turn is based on a philosophy of life. Because the Church has a definite concept of the nature of human beings and their destiny, it is consistent for her to develop definite fundamental principles concerning education. Although certain things may be emphasized at certain times there are common fundamental elements on which all philosophers of Catholic education base their speculations and these are the triple supernatural foundation of Catholic doctrine. The first of these emphasizes that God is the beginning and end of education. It is a fundamental Catholic principle that the soul of all education is the education of the soul. Religion is an essential element in the life of man and his education, therefore, must be essentially religious. Thus God is the cornerstone in the structure of Catholic education.

The second principle rests on the belief that the Living God has revealed Himself in the Living Christ. The Person of Christ who is the Way, the Truth and the Life, is the center of religious education. His educational significance lies first of all in the sublime nature of His Being. "The Word Made Flesh"—the Incarnation of the Son of God—is not only the central dogma of Christianity, it is also the central fact in the Catholic doctrine of education. The God who became

Man in order that He might bring man to God is the life-giving principle of Catholic education. He is the Model for all educators. He is the inspiration and ultimate end of all educational endeavor.

The third principle of Catholic education that is basic is the doctrine that it is only through the Church that man can come to Christ and hence to God. The Church is the Mystical Body of the Savior. To be united with Him, the children of men must, according to His own pronouncement, be incorporated in that Body. Thus the Incarnation, as has been said, is the central dogma of Catholic faith and of Catholic education. But Christ has not ceased to be with man. He continues to live in the Church, not only in the Sacrament of the Altar, but in the teachings of the Church, in its Visible Head, and in every soul that is sanctified by His grace. Thus the Church of Christ becomes a connecting link between man and God, between time and eternity, and between the natural and the supernatural.

The Catholic School System

The history of the beginnings and early development of the parochial schools in the United States has been treated at great length by the Rev. J. A. Burns and Dr. Bernard Kohlbrenner. For our purposes here, however, it is necessary to review certain outstanding happenings that relate directly to modern developments in the Catholic system. Mission schools were established in the Southwest and in Florida as a result of Spanish influence. The foundations of Catholic education in the English-speaking colonies were laid in Maryland. Jesuit priests who accompanied the first settlers developed formal schools and other means of education. Usually a school went hand in hand with a mission development thus laying the foundation for the parish school system which now flourishes in the United States.

The importance of the school for the work of the Church was recognized as early as 1829 when the Bishops of the country met at Baltimore for their first provincial council.

There they said: "We judge it absolutely necessary that schools should be established in which the young may be taught the principles of faith and morality while being instructed in letters." Although schools had been developing at a good pace it was this decision taken by the Bishops that gave impetus to a movement that is still a distinctive feature of Catholic life in America. After 1829 more teachers were needed and there came to America in good numbers from all over Europe the religious orders of men and women who by their dedicated efforts spread the faith and the schools in a magnificent missionary undertaking.

Between 1829 and 1884 when the Third Plenary Council of Baltimore took place the growth of Catholic schools was a steady process especially in large city areas where the Catholic population tended to center. The growth in size, however, did not connote any definite pattern of procedures. It was evident the only uniformity lay in the basic law of the Church that the Bishop is responsible for the conduct of Catholic education in his diocese. In order to establish some uniformity and to insure that Catholic schools would be able to meet current educational standards some dioceses established school boards. The Third Council liked the device and decreed that it should be adopted as a means of supervision. Eventually, however, the school board lost its first importance and became merely an advisory body. The chief task of administration and supervision of education was delegated by the Bishop in most cases to a diocesan school superintendent or a secretary for education. Between 1889 and 1910 more than a dozen dioceses appointed school superintendents including New York, Philadelphia, Omaha, Pittsburgh, Brooklyn, Fort Wayne, Boston, Hartford, Cincinnati, Green Bay and others.

It was no easy task for the early Bishops of the United States to provide at once for the religious and the educational needs of their people. During the period of 1830-1920 hundreds of thousands of Catholic immigrants entered the country. It is estimated that from nine to ten millions would represent the Catholic immigrational increase up to the end of 1920. When this increase, natural growth and conversions throughout the land were combined, the total in 1920 was an estimated twenty million Catholics in a total population of almost 106 million people. It was a notable growth considering the fact that it began in 1830 with an estimated Catholic population of 318,000 souls.

In 1830 there were eleven dioceses and about 232 priests in the country. By 1870, fifty-four dioceses of which seven were metropolitan sees and six vicariates had already been founded. In this same year a total Catholic population of four and one-half millions was cared for by 3,780 priests.

Up to 1840 at least two hundred schools had been erected, more than half of which were located west of the Alleghenies. In 1920 the Catholic school enrollment had risen to 1,970,-507, about 1.8 per cent of the entire population.

The growth of the Catholic schools was intimately related to the office of the school superintendent, usually a priest, especially prepared for his task. Word of the successful operation of the diocesan schools of Philadelphia under a superintendent in the late 1880's got around and did much to encourage other dioceses to imitate a successful pattern. As a professional footnote, one must take note of the influence of the Department of Education of the Catholic University of America which opened in 1905 with the express purpose of training diocesan superintendents. The courses in those early days included: the Science and Art of Study, Psychology of Education, Special Methods, Philosophy of Education and History of Education. Later courses in Administration and Supervision were added.

The work of the superintendent has been made meaningful and professional by the cooperation and collaboration of the various religious communities teaching in the dioceses. These groups appoint supervisors for the schools in which their communities teach and these supervisors work under the direction of the Superintendent.

The early parochial schools like the present ones provided an education in all the secular subjects normally found in the public school curriculum plus special classes in religious instruction that centered around the teaching of a catechism of Christian Doctrine and Bible history. Teaching Christian Doctrine provided likewise an opportunity for instruction in sacred music, hymns, and Christian art, and the liturgy. The instruction in the sacred and religious subjects was of a quality proportionate to the training of the classroom teachers and the zeal and professional background of the supervisors and the superintendent.

Pedagogically speaking, the teaching of the Catechism over the years has been a controversial issue. Conservative educators making much of the value of training the memory have often been at issue with other teachers about the rote learning of Catechism. They felt that with adequate explanations before and after the memorizing process that it was essential to memorize the Catechism in sequence and to be able to respond verbatim to the standard questions with fixed answers. Others insisted that teaching for comprehension was the prime requisite and that the teacher should never require from the student a verbatim repetition of something he could not comprehend. Sometimes, in the dispute the Catechism itself was the loser and the little booklets in graded series fell into disfavor for reasons that had no real connection with the inherent worth of the Catechism itself.

It would be difficult to give the Catechism the praise that it deserves as a teaching medium over the centuries. From an ugly duckling of printed questions and answers the Catechism in America has developed into a beautiful, well-illustrated handbook that no longer causes foreboding to the child or the student with its highly formalized approach. No matter how methods and texts improve or change, it seems safe to say that the Catechism will remain the core of teaching methods in Christian Doctrine.

As catechisms have improved many fine teaching helps have been added to some editions such as graphs and symbolic illustrations, diagnostic tests after the lesson, references from the New Testament, previews before the lesson, an index of words used throughout the study and phoneticized word study before the lesson. In general the new texts are adaptable for use in elementary schools, high schools, parish study clubs, Catholic youth organization programs, released-time classes, and private study.

Until the 1930's the Catechism (with the Bible History) was undoubtedly the most distinctively Catholic text placed in the hands of the child in the parochial school. The other texts, with few exceptions, looked like and for that matter were, the same textbooks found in the nearby public school. There were a few exceptions such as a Catholic reader or history text, or some small supplementary texts of special reading material. But usually the books were public school books with something added or subtracted to make them palatable or at least acceptable to Catholic authorities. Sometimes these books were referred to, in jest, as "baptized versions" and many agreed that the term was appropriate. The lack of good Catholic texts and the absence of a good scientific basic curriculum and course of study led some critics of the parochial schools to refer to them as merely public schools plus the Catechism. The need for making the parochial schools Catholic in the most ideal sense of the term troubled scholars over the years. At the Catholic University of America the problem became one of special concern to Dr. Shields and Dr. Pace. Their discussions and concern were reflected in a brilliant student of theirs, Monsignor George Johnson, who was to serve as the inspiration and first director of the Commission on American Citizenship.

The Commission on American Citizenship

In 1938 Pope Pius XI sent to the American Hierarchy a letter remarkable for its foresight, its wisdom and its results. This Apostolic Letter, written upon the occasion of the Golden Jubilee of the Catholic University, did not merely congratulate the University upon its historic attainments. It called upon the University to assume "greater and more momentous responsibilities" than it had undertaken in the past. The needs of our times, the Holy Father pointed out, require the giving of special attention to the social sciences in order that it might be possible to bring to bear upon the pressing problems of our time Christian principles of justice and charity.

The Holy Father reminded the Bishops and the University that because the University was Catholic, it had the traditional mission of guarding the natural and supernatural heritage of man. It must, then, give special attention to the sciences of civics, sociology and economics. It must evolve, on the basis of study and research, a constructive program of social action, fitting in its details to local needs, which would command the admiration and acceptance of all right-thinking men.

As a result of this request the Hierarchy of the United States called upon the University to establish a program of social education upon all levels. The request said in part:

> "To carry out the injunction of the Holy Father it is necessary that our people, from childhood to mature age, be ever better instructed in the true nature of Christian democracy. A precise definition must be given to them both of democracy in the light of Christian truth and tradition and of the rights and duties of citizens in a representative Republic such as our own. They must be held to the conviction that love of country is a virtue and that disloyalty is a sin.
>
> "To foster this Christian concept of citizenship the Bishops in their annual meeting have charged the Catholic University of America to compile at once a more comprehensive series of graded texts for all educational levels. On the foundation of religious training, which is the distinctive characteristic of our schools, these texts will build an enlightened, conscientious American citizenship."

The Rector of the University accepted the mandate for the institution in these words:

> "The Catholic University of America pledges itself to this great task which the Holy Father declares dear to him. The enemies of God and of right government have known well how to center their efforts and their hopes on the youth of the nation. Shall we be less wise? To train a generation in true Christian democracy means that the elementary school room must begin the task. It must be carried through secondary

schools and keep pace with the developing mind of the future citizen."

Three members of the faculty with Monsignor George Johnson in direct authority over matters pertaining to education organized the Commission on American Citizenship—a structure broad enough, deep enough, and strong enough to fulfill its purpose in the teaching of citizenship. Since it was important that the program meet the highest educational standards, an advisory committee of scholars, distinguished in educational work, particularly in the social sciences was brought together. Cooperating committees were formed of the Diocesan Superintendents of Schools, supervisors of social studies in various dioceses, and the faculty of the school of social science and of the department of education at the University.

The work of the Commission has fallen into three general divisions—an informational service to educators, Catholic and non-Catholic, of its principles, aims and methods; instruction for Catholic school teachers by means of a Curriculum for Guiding Growth in Christian Social Living; and instruction for Catholic school students by means of a series of basal readers and other textbooks.

The Commission at the very start, decided upon two activities to launch the program: The production of a curriculum for the elementary schools whose purpose would be the development in the school child of the understandings, the attitudes, and the habits that are required for Christian living in American society; the writing of a series of basal readers for the grades to accompany and implement the curriculum. Both products were to be closely integrated with religion, with the goal to make the learner aware of all that the dogma and doctrines of the Church require of him in the way of civic and social virtue.

The goals were very practical ones indeed, for the whole project was designed to implement the philosophy of Catholic education (to which reference was made earlier) in such a way that the students in our schools would become more and more aware of the intimate relationship between the love of God and the love of fellowman. Here, at last, was a sound pedagogical approach to help boys and girls put the truth they had learned in their religious classes into their lives at home, in the classroom, on the playground and in the larger community.

Certain basic principles guided the work of the curriculum and the readers. These included:

The dependence of man upon God
The individual dignity of every human person
The social nature of man
The sacredness and integrity of the family
The dignity of the worker and his work
The material and spiritual interdependence of all men
The obligation of all men to use the resources of the earth according to God's plan
The obligation of men to share non-material goods with one another
The obligation of justice and charity that exists between peoples and nations
The unity of all men

The curriculum has been organized into three volumes and published by the Catholic University Press. The material has been graded for three levels, primary, intermediate, and upper grades. Each of the three volumes presents the guided experience of the child under the direction of the school. All of the volumes stress the individual growth of each child toward five goals: physical fitness, economic competency, social virtue, cultural development, moral perfection. All of them take into account the child's basic relationships: God, the Church, fellowman, nature, self.

The curriculum has won the interest and support of educators and is widely used as a basic source in many dioceses; in others it forms the point of departure for local research, experimentation and teacher training. Regional and diocesan studies have been completed or are in progress that take their direct inspiration from the curriculum. Many of the teaching religious communities have set up special committees to associate their normal school training with the basic plan of the curriculum. Hundreds of institutes have been held throughout the nation with the staff of the Commission serving as speakers and discussion leaders. Publishers and authors of textbooks have sought the counsel and guidance of the Commission in the production of materials that are related to the philosophy of the curriculum. It is difficult to weigh the tremendous influence of the curriculum on the American Catholic educational scene. Moreover its influence has reached out to Europe and Latin America and Canada where similar curriculum projects have been launched. The influence of the curriculum designed by the Commission will truly be world-wide.

Just as the Curriculum on *Guiding Growth in Christian Social Living* was designed to help the Catholic elementary school teacher in understanding the social teaching of the Church so, too, the *Faith and Freedom Series* of basal readers were published to implant these principles in the mind of the Catholic student as a guide for use in daily life. Based on the principles integrated in the Curriculum, these Readers were written for the purpose of establishing in the child understandings and attitudes which would determine his behavior both as a student and as an adult. Their construction was based on a plan quite opposite from that of most readers used in Catholic schools, a method which merely added a few Catholic stories, essays and poems to readers already in use in the public schools. The Readers were developed according to the child's growing consciousness, starting with his first impressions of home and family and working outward to the world at large. The titles convey a clear idea of this plan: *This is Our Home, This is Our Family, These are Our Friends, These are Our Neighbors, This is Our Town, This is Our Land, These are Our People, This is Our Heritage, These are Our Freedoms, These are Our Horizons.*

As a corollary to the basal readers the Commission has produced a series of books to present literature at the various grade levels. Manuals, workbooks and various teachers' aid have been developed. Special materials dealing with war relief and famine have been designed for use in school; materials dealing with peace and international understandings have been written.

The staff of the Commission is now at work on a curriculum for the secondary schools which will be a natural sequel to the work that has gone before. Some experimental work on a college curriculum has been launched in the field. All in all work of the Commission has had a most profound influence on the development of Catholic educational procedure in America. The full import of this great undertaking will only be appreciated by the educational historian a half century or so from now, but even in the short years from •1939 until the present it is evident that something wonderful has slowly been accomplished.

The National Catholic Educational Association

In 1954 the National Catholic Educational Association celebrated its fiftieth anniversary. The Association was founded in 1904 and came into being as a result of national meeting of Catholic colleges and seminaries which began in 1897. The Association is a voluntary organization of all who are interested in the welfare of Catholic education. It includes both individual and institutional members.

Its purpose is to keep in the minds of the people the necessity of religious instruction and training as a basis of morality and sound education, to promote the principles and safeguard the interests of Catholic education in all its departments, to encourage a spirit of cooperation and mutual helpfulness among Catholic educators, to promote by study, conference and discussion the thoroughness of Catholic educational work in the United States and to help the cause of Catholic education by the publication and circulation of appropriate materials.

Since 1904 the Association has grown steadily in size and influence. Its original three departments, College, Parish School, and Seminary have expanded to seven which include

Major Seminary, Minor Seminary, College and University, Secondary Schools, School Superintendents, Elementary Schools, Special Education and two sections: Vocations and Newman Chaplains.

With the exception of 1943 and 1945 the Association has held annual meetings in which all the departments take an active part and at which papers are read and perennial problems together with those of prevailing interest are discussed. Each convention produces papers of outstanding merit and the fifty-four volumes that now make up the published proceedings constitute a valuable record of Catholic educational thought since the beginning of the century.

The College and University department has established six regional units: Eastern, Midwest, New England, Northwestern, Southern, and Southwestern. The Secondary School department has five regional units: California, Hawaii, Middle Atlantic, Midwest and Southern. The regional units of these two departments meet separately at regular intervals. This arrangement enables the Association to serve more definitely the interests of its members, and allow likewise for a better discussion and study of local problems.

The official organ of the N.C.E.A. is the quarterly publication, *The National Catholic Educational Association Bulletin*. It appears in February, May, August and November. The August issue contains the proceedings and addresses of the annual meeting. The other issues contain monographs and special papers of general and timely interest. In recent months the subject matter has ranged over a wide educational area including, teaching Catholic history, higher education for women, school discipline, the faculty and the curriculum, teacher accreditation, student exchange, the Fulbright program, international understanding, and reports on international educational conferences.

An N.C.E.A. *News Letter* is sent to all members and a specially designed series of *News Notes* are made available to College presidents and their staffs. The College and University Department issues a *College Newsletter,* the Secondary School Department publishes *The Catholic High School*

Quarterly Bulletin, and the Elementary School Department publishes *The Catholic Educational News Digest.*

The Association has watched closely the formation and continuation of the UNESCO program; it sponsored the initiation of the Catholic Commission on Intellectual and Cultural Affairs; it continues to take an active part in the annual meetings as well as the year around program of the American Council on Education, and the Association of American Colleges. The Association is called upon frequently to work with the staff of the United States Office of Education as well as with the representatives of other government agencies.

Elementary Schools, Secondary Schools, Colleges and Universities

The largest segment in the Catholic school system is, of course, the elementary school. Statistics prepared by the Department of Education of the National Catholic Welfare Conference for its biennial survey for the school year 1953-54 (the most recent figures available) list a total of 9,279 elementary schools with a faculty of 76,833 teachers, 67,477 of whom were religious, that is, members of religious communities. The earliest survey undertaken by this same department showed that in 1920 there were 6,551 Catholic elementary schools. The increase between 1920 and 1954 amounts to 41.6 per cent. It is interesting to note in analyzing these figures that the percentage of increase between 1945 and 1954 was 14.6 per cent, and that between 1952 and 1954 was 4.5 per cent. In 1920 there were 1,970,507 young people in Catholic elementary schools. By 1954 that number had risen to 3,235,251.

Catholic elementary schools are conducted in each of the 126 archdioceses and dioceses in all of the forty-eight states. The number of schools varies from five in the Diocese of Reno to 397 in the Archdiocese of Chicago. New York with 975 has a larger number of Catholic elementary schools than any other state.

In nearly all cases the parochial schools are, as their name implies, parish schools under the immediate control of the pastor and supported by the free will donations of parish members. These schools follow in most cases a course of study worked out by diocesan committees with community supervisors under the direction of the diocesan school superintendent. In this regard, as was mentioned in an earlier section of this report, the influence of the curriculum designed by the Commission on American Citizenship has been increasingly notable since 1942. In many dioceses students in the parish schools are requested to meet periodic examinations prepared either by the diocese or by competent research and testing groups located in Catholic universities, or in special institutes around the country. Textbook adoptions have become uniform through most dioceses. Research in textbook construction has improved greatly among publishers who have done and continue to do special work for the Catholic school system. Among publishers the past ten-year period has discovered new strength and new forces in companies that have been traditional producers of texts for Catholic schools; there has been noted too a marked increase in the number of Catholic departments among companies that produce textbooks. All of these advances have greatly profited the Catholic school system.

It is obvious that the great majority of teachers in the Catholic elementary schools are members of religious communities. It has been advanced that one reason for this is that Catholic schools have to be self-supporting and consequently there are many areas of the country where it would be difficult to furnish adequate compensation for lay teachers, who certainly ought to be paid at the going rate for comparably prepared teachers in the public school system. The members of the religious communities contribute their services asking little more in return than their sustenance. The magnificent growth of the Catholic school system is in large measure the direct result of the willing self-sacrifice of the thousands of men and women who have entered the religious life to give themselves to the dedicated task of teaching our youth.

Today as in the past the preparation of teachers for the schools remains for the most part the duty of the separate religious communities. Dioceses, through the superintendent and the school board, take an increasingly larger interest in the kind and type of teacher training carried on by the various communities. Standards set by state and regional accrediting groups likewise have a large measure of influence in the training program. Considerable influence is exerted by the research carried on by Catholic universities and institutes in the educational field. Our Catholic schools like to regard themselves as self-starters in improving educational content and procedures; they do not want to feel that they are slavishly dependent on state, or other standards, or merely on the current developments in public education.

Although the diocesan authorities in the field of education work closely today with the religious communities there is not observable a trend towards an increase in diocesan teachers colleges. Some years ago it was predicted that such a trend would develop. The pattern, however, remains as described above, a mutual sharing of the responsibility and a cooperative desire on the part of the religious communities to meet the desired standards. Originally the Third Council of Baltimore stipulated that the candidates must take a diocesan examination. Today this is interpreted nearly everywhere to mean that the dioceses will accept the credits and teacher preparation of reputable colleges and universities. It is still a custom in many places to require the school board to pass upon the list of newly assigned teachers in a given diocese.

One of the unsolved problems of the present is the identification and preparation of sufficient teachers to staff a rapidly expanding system. Religious teachers, completely prepared, are not always available to satisfy the need. There are good programs being carried on to encourage vocations to the religious teaching life but admittedly this is a slow process and cannot meet the immediate requirements. The answer seems to lie in the greater use of lay teachers. This solution passes the problem along to the parents who must grow accustomed to the greater use of the laity in schools that have been traditionally staffed by religious teachers, and who must too, pick up a larger tab for school expenses since it will be required of them to pay the lay teacher a stipend comparable to that received by public school teachers of like experience and preparation.

In 1954 there were 2,296 Catholic secondary schools in the United States. About fifty per cent of these are conducted under parish auspices; another approximate thirty-four per cent are academies conducted by religious communities. The balance are central high schools under diocesan direction. Private academies and many parish high schools are maintained by tuition fees, although in many parish high schools part of the cost to the student is provided from parish funds set aside for this purpose. The central high schools receive their support from the diocese in which they are located or from the parishes from which the students attend.

The first survey of Catholic secondary schools was made in 1915 by the Catholic Educational Association, at which time the enrollment was 75,000. In 1938 the enrollment was 300,000, an increase of 290 per cent in twenty-five years. A comprehensive survey of Catholic secondary schools was undertaken in 1947 by Sister Mary Janet, S.C., at the invitation of the Department of Education of the National Catholic Welfare Conference. Sister Janet found that from 1920, when the first N.C.W.C. study was undertaken, until 1947, the number of secondary schools had increased from 1,552 to 2,111, an increase of 36 per cent. The increase in the number of pupils from 129,848 to 467,039 represented a 259.8 per cent rise. The greater growth of the student body is explained by consolidation of schools and by additions made to existing facilities. Of the 2,111 schools 53.6 per cent were coeducational, 33.6 per cent schools for girls, and 12.8 per cent for boys. It is interesting to note the composition of the staff in 1947. Seventy-one and two-tenths per cent were women, and of this number only 7.4 per cent were lay women. Twenty-eight and eight-tenths per cent were men divided in the following way: 7.3 per cent diocesan priests, 7.3 per cent

teaching brothers, 6.6 per cent priests members of religious
orders, 6.4 per cent laymen and 1.2 per cent seminarians.
The total number of teachers in all secondary schools was
27,216 which represented an increase of 10.7 per cent since
the year 1944.

In 1954 the total enrollment in Catholic secondary schools
had rolled past the 500,000 mark to 623,751. This was a trend
clearly indicated by Sister Janet's study.

What goes on in these schools? What is their curriculum
like? Sister Janet's study answered these questions with a careful analysis of the types of program offered: comprehensive,
academic, commercial, technical, agricultural, or vocational.
Schools were asked to label themselves as "academic" only
if they gave credit for nothing except the so called academic
subjects. The term "comprehensive" to be most accurately
applied would be given only to those schools which could
offer programs sufficiently varied to meet the present and
future needs of all classes of students—those preparing for
colleges, professional and technical schools, nursing schools
and the like; those preparing for skilled and unskilled occupations; those preparing for other types of occupations; as
well as providing preparation for home life and leisure pursuits. Although many of the schools do not meet fully the
objectives of the comprehensive school, still, the attempt to
differentiate according to varieties of needs justifies the classification as distinct from the strictly academic or college
preparatory institutions. According to their own classification, then, the schools listed themselves as 64.4 per cent comprehensive, 31.6 per cent academic, 3.8 per cent commercial
and 0.2 per cent vocational. Undoubtedly the cost of maintaining vocational schools is the major factor. It is encouraging to note a wider appeal for students under the heading
"comprehensive," for in the late 1930's the preponderance
would certainly have been on the purely academic side. To
some educators this seems like a retreat from glory, but Sister
Janet made it quite clear which side she was on when she
said:

"The crux of the problem today is found in the program of studies. Here there is urgent need of reorientation, in which the guide will be Christian social principles and in which present needs will exert influence at least commensurate with the importunities of the past. Throughout the year Catholic schools in general have moved slowly in departure from the traditional courses of study. This is explained probably by our firm belief in fundamental unchanging truths, essential to our whole concept of man in his origin and destiny. Catholic educational practice in guarding what is essentially unalterable— belief in God, the spirituality and immortality of the soul, the truth of Faith, fixed principles of morality—may fail to distinguish that certain centuries-old phases of the school curriculum such as the classical tradition to which we have clung for many centuries are not part of the fundamental body of unchangeable truth. Having initiated secondary education in the form of selective schools requiring such a program, we have continued to use it for so long that, in spite of the passing of selectivity, there remain many Catholics who apparently believe that the academic tradition is the very heart and soul of Catholic education. Actually there is nothing of fundamental Christian truth in the study of the classics. There is, however, fundamental Christian truth in the ideal of respecting all types of human abilities, talents, and interests, and in helping to educate youths for Christian family life and Christian occupations in addition to educating the potential scholars.

"This is not to imply in any sense that the classical tradition has no contribution to make. It definitely has. But it is certain that it cannot continue to monopolize the respect of educators, who accordingly, have nothing but condescension for what they consider unworthy materials for educational purposes."

Sister Janet ends her study with a plea for experimental research on a national scale, chiefly by the college and university departments of the National Catholic Educational Association. She feels that another Eight-Year Study is needed, in which Catholic colleges may cooperate with high schools in a real attempt to solve the problem of articulation between the two levels in education. Catholic education needs to be roused to the fact that the power of religion has not been fully used for many years in the compartmentalized curriculums which have resulted from the extremes of electivism. Religion has been correlated throughout, but real integration has not appeared.

Upon the firm foundation of their elementary and secondary schools American Catholics have built a system of college and universities rivaled by no other Catholic group in any country of the world. The 1954 survey of the Department of Education, N.C.W.C., shows 224 institutions of learning of college grade or beyond. Eighty-five of these are conducted for men and 139 for women. In the group of colleges for men are included 30 universities, 53 four-year colleges, and 2 junior colleges. Provisions for women included 1 university, 117 four-year colleges, and 21 junior colleges.

The first Catholic college was established in colonial days at Newton in Maryland in 1677. This institution subsequently became Georgetown University. Today there are more than thirty Catholic universities and colleges that have celebrated their centenary.

In 1954 Catholic colleges and universities for men reported total faculties of 12,839 of which 9,295 were laymen. The lay man has come into his own as a teacher at the college level. The total student population in colleges for men in 1954 was 201,186; in colleges for women there were 80,813 students taught by a faculty of 6,232 of which 2,000 were laymen or lay women.

Although the liberal arts tradition is a strong one in Catholic institutions of higher learning many of these institutions now offer professional or special courses ranging from agriculture to social work, with a wide variety of subject areas such as architecture, business administration, dentistry, engineering, journalism, law, library science, medicine, nursing or nursing education, pharmacy, and physical education. ROTC units are available in many Catholic colleges and universities.

Catholic colleges and universities have been moving slowly but steadily into the graduate level not only in arts and science but in engineering, social work, and other areas. In late years the organization of the colleges and universities has been under close scrutiny with an eye towards better integration with religion, philosophy and theology. The investigations in these areas are basically not too different from those undertaken by the Commission on American Citizenship for the lower levels. There is one basic difference; however, the researchers at the college level have no continuing national focus such as the Commission provides, but depend upon the initiative of the various institutions for their vitality and endurance. Happily the interest in such research is growing and one college after another reports solid progress in seeking the goal of integration of subject matter, philosophy and program.

The picture at the college level would be incomplete without some mention of the work of Diocesan teachers colleges and normal training schools. In all there are 25 such institutions enrolling 6,094 students of whom more than 5,900 are women. It is in these institutions that the young members of the religious communities secure their basic training as teachers.

There is no Catholic accrediting agency for institutions of higher learning; the colleges and universities generally conform to the requirements of regional accrediting agencies.

At the pinnacle of the Catholic educational system stand the major and minor seminaries in which students are trained for the priesthood. In these institutions a very high level of scholarship maintains, and the students may prepare themselves not only for parish and religious life, but for a life of deep learning and scholarship as well. The major and minor seminaries combine to form a total of 294 institutions providing for 29,578 young men seeking theological wisdom and eventual ordination to the priesthood. The major seminary courses are built around the core of dogmatic and moral theology, and scripture. Additional work in graduate philosophy, history, Church history, social sciences, language, liturgy, speech and religious education, especially catechetics, round out a carefully designed program that serves both the scholar and the parish priest. In the minor seminary the basic liberal arts course with a special emphasis on philosophy, introduction to scripture, apologetics and introductory liturgy are the main ingredients in what is generally regarded as a rather stiff course. The faculties of the seminaries are usually priests specially prepared for their assignments in graduate theological schools here and abroad.

The Confraternity of Christian Doctrine

Thus far this overview of Catholic education has dealt with the formal school system as such and has accounted for 4,176,673 students carrying on their educational endeavors under 131,713 teachers. This, of course, does not account for the balance of the educable young people who are Catholics. What of them, this balance, who are not in Catholic schools? They are not neglected. The responsibility for their religious education as well as for that of another large part of the population falls under the care of the Confraternity of Christian Doctrine.

What is this Confraternity? It is a lay apostolate in action under the guidance of the clergy. The Confraternity exists that Catholics may learn more and more about their religion, thus teaching themselves as well as others the knowledge and love of God.

The objectives of the Confraternity have been set down as follows: Religious education of elementary school children not attending Catholic schools, in vacation schools, instruction classes, and correspondence courses; religious instruction of Catholic youth of high school age not attending Catholic schools; religious discussion clubs for adult groups, including students attending secular colleges and universities, and out of school youth; religious education of children by parents in the home; instruction of non-Catholics in the faith; participation as a society, and under the direction of the pastor in function of public worship, such as the annual celebration of Catechetical Day as prescribed by the Bishop of a Diocese.

Although it has not been possible to obtain exact figures on the number of Catholics in public schools some conjectures are in order. Some estimate that there are between 2,500,000 and 3,000,000 Catholic students in public elementary schools and perhaps another 1,000,000 to 1,500,000 in public high schools. It is also estimated that there are 375,000 Catholic students in secular colleges.

It is immediately apparent that the need to supply religious instruction for all Catholics in non-Catholic institutions is a grave one. Moreover, on the adult level there are many thousands of men and women who know little of their faith, or who are inconsistent, or wanting in the practice of it. Some of these, because of the lack of their own religious knowledge, fail to pass on the basic truths of religion to their children. All of these needs represent the work of the Confraternity of Christian Doctrine.

By 1951 the Confraternity was able to report that eight national and fifty-four regional conferences have been held in the United States since 1935. New problems, in addition to the ones mentioned above, are constantly arising and additional personnel as well as new materials, methods and techniques must be found. This is especially true in the field of religious instruction. Because of this, the Confraternity has intensified its activity in the hope of bringing to adults and children of all ages and of all walks of life a better knowledge of their religion.

To accomplish this, the Confraternity has encouraged the establishment in various parts of the country of preparatory courses for lay teachers of religion, fishers (home visitors) helpers, and discussion club leaders. It has also placed emphasis on the preparation of parents for the home religious instruction of their children (parent-educators) and has stimulated progress in the apostolate of good will to non-Catholics.

The regional or provincial congress has been found to be a most effective means of spreading knowledge of the existence of these courses, of acquainting people with materials, methods and techniques which are most effective in learning and teaching religious truth. Since 1939, twenty of the twenty-two ecclesiastical provinces of the United States have held one or more regional conferences; in all fifty-four con-

ferences have convened. At the ten regional conferences held
in 1949, twenty-five thousand four hundred and eighty-nine
official delegates registered. These included members of the
hierarchy, priests, religious and interested laity.

The regional conferences have made a determined effort
to assess the actual conditions of religious instruction which
may handicap or hinder the pastor of souls in carrying out
the teaching of Christian doctrine.

In 1950 the Confraternity of Christian Doctrine carried
out a mid-century survey of its activities in the United States.
Many interesting facts come to light. Ninety-nine dioceses
have organized a program of religious instruction for public
school children as a required activity in each parish. Thirty-
eight dioceses engage in a released or dismissed time program. One hundred and eleven dioceses conduct religious
vacation schools. Forty give preparatory courses to lay teachers of religion. Sixty-four make use of helper and home
visitors. Eighty-three have canonically erected the Confraternity in all parishes. One hundred and twenty have appointed a Diocesan Director for Confraternity work. In the
adult instruction field seventy-eight dioceses have inquiry
classes, ninety-four have religious discussion clubs, and forty-
five have a parent-educator program.

The Confraternity is a vital program carried on by an
interested and dedicated committee of Bishops who have inspired the laity and the religious to do magnificent work in
the field of religious instruction. The program planned for
the future gives every indication of surpassing the great
record made up to this time. Many Catholic colleges encourage students to undertake part time activities in this field
as a part of their own regular religious training.

Department of Education, National
Catholic Welfare Conference

The Department of Education, N.C.W.C., is not an administrative body; it possesses no control over Catholic schools,
and it functions only in the capacity of an advisory agency.

Each diocesan school system is an independent unit. Consequently the word "system" in connection with Catholic education is used only in its widest connotation. Any solidarity of program results from voluntary cooperation among superintendents and stems from programs initiated at their twice-yearly meetings.

The Department does not prepare courses of study nor does it deal in the over-all problem of curriculum. It serves as the medium by which Catholic school systems can exchange points of view, educational materials, and other forms of assistance. The chief reason for its existence continues to be the cooperation with all movements looking to the improvement of Catholic education whether they find their origin in local, state, or national organizations.

The Department of Education has four chief functions: (1) To supply information concerning Catholic education to Catholics and to the general public, (2) to serve as an advisory agency in the development of Catholic schools, (3) to act as a connecting agency between Catholic educational activities and governmental educational agencies, and (4) to safeguard the interests of Catholic schools.

There are four sections in the Department, each devoted to some special phase of education: research and information, statistics, educational liaison with all agencies, and a foreign visitors office. This last activity in recent years has emphasized a program with Germany and Austria including adults as well as secondary and college students.

Other Educational Agencies

The Catholic Commission on Intellectual and Cultural Affairs was founded in 1946. Its purposes were to bring together a broadly representative group of Catholics who are members of the various learned professions, creative artists and writers, and leaders of Catholic opinion, in order to focus attention on Catholic intellectual and cultural life at home. and to promote Catholic intellectual and cultural cooperation in the world at large and by collaborating with similar

groups in other countries to work for a truly Christian life
and for a just and peaceful world order.

The Commission seeks to enlist and to utilize the abilities
of Catholic scholars and leaders particularly among the laity.
Its membership is now 250 members. Besides its national
meeting the Commission has held numerous regional meetings throughout the country. Liaison has been established
with L'Union Catholique d'Etudes Internationales, Centre
Catholique Intellectuels Francais, and Movement International des Intellectuels Catholiques.

Among the publications have been *Catholic Participation
in the Intellectual Movements of Today* and *C.C.I.C.A. at
the Twenty-Second World Congress of Pax Romana, Canada
1952.* A Directory is also available which sets down bio-
graphical sketches of the members, along with their scholarly
classification.

In addition to the C.C.I.C.A. there are many learned societies which publish journals or studies at regular intervals.
These include groups of theologians, philosophers, historians,
economists, sociologists, and the like.

The alumni groups of the various colleges have also proved
to be instruments of education as well as sociability. The
alumnae of Catholic colleges for women have been formed
into the "International Federation of Catholic Alumnae."

The Liturgical Movement is an important phase of Catholic education in the United States. It has stressed the interdependence of the three factors of doctrine, holiness of life
and Christian action in the work of reestablishing all things
in Christ. In seeking above all to restore to the laity an active
participation in the Mass and in the sacramental life of the
Church it has always tried to set down the doctrinal foundations and implications involved and to emphasize the far-
reaching results which such active participation should bring
into the personal and social life of Catholics.

The Liturgical Movement has been said to have come of
age with the publication of the Encyclical *Mediator Dei* in
1947. For the laity it has made most clear the nature and

purpose of the liturgy as well as ways to promote the active participation of the faithful in divine worship.

A Liturgical Conference has sponsored Liturgical Weeks which were originally inaugurated by the Benedictine Liturgical Conference. Valuable periodicals have been launched that deal with the liturgy in general terms, in the home, with reference to music, etc., such as *Altar and Home, The Catholic Choirmaster, Cecilia, Liturgical Arts,* and *Worship.*

Conclusion

These lines have been set down to give a general picture of the Catholic educational apparatus in America. The story is by no means a complete one, and the author offers an apology for his failure to touch upon many important areas. Nothing has been said in praise of the great work done by the Jesuit Educational Association, the Franciscan Educational Conference, the National Benedictine Educational Association, the National Catholic Music Educators Association. The Catholic Art Association, and the hundreds of institutes and conferences conducted by religious communities and lay groups in the United States have not been treated.

Insufficient space has been given to educational research carried on in our Catholic universities. Practically no mention has been made of Catholic books and the Catholic Library Association. For these omissions the author begs the reader's indulgence and hopes that at another time the place of these agencies and their fine contributions to Catholic education may receive adequate attention.

CHAPTER SEVEN

The National Catholic Welfare Conference

———— ◆ ————

BY C. JOSEPH NUESSE

Introduction

A DISTINCTLY American achievement of recent decades in
the history of the Church in the United States, one
which was rapidly given definite form but nevertheless has
an evident prospect of continuing development, is the organ
of the hierarchy known as the National Catholic Welfare
Conference. The name perhaps requires a brief explanation,
for it may at first glance be misleading. It does not signify an
agency of social welfare such as, for example, the French
Secours Catholique or the German *Caritas,* though several
of its departments and agencies undertake social services in
special categories. The National Conference of Catholic
Charities is, however, an independent body. The concern of
the National Catholic Welfare Conference is rather the wel-

---

*C. Joseph Nuesse is associate professor of sociology and dean
of the School of Social Science, The Catholic University of
America, Washington, D.C. He is the author of* The Social
Thought of American Catholics, 1634-1829, *and co-editor of*
The Sociology of the Parish.

fare of Catholic interests in the national society in the whole range of group endeavors. It is constituted as a permanent secretariat for the bishops of the United States through which activities in diverse fields and regions can be unified. In the encyclical letter, *Sertum laetitiae,* addressing the bishops, His Holiness, Pope Pius XII called it "a ready and well-adapted instrument for your episcopal ministry." [1]

Episcopal authority is everywhere exercised by each bishop in his own diocese, unless the bishops meet in formal council. The National Catholic Welfare Conference is a voluntary organization, "a free mutual cooperation," it has been said, "between diocese and diocese, through a common central headquarters." [2] The combination of the traditional ecclesiastical pattern and the characteristically American pattern of voluntary organization is worthy of special note. A future historian will undoubtedly find this a fascinating subject for investigation and even now students of comparative institutions can learn by analytical study of the administrative and organizational problems presented. This brief account must be confined to a review of the founding of the organization and an outline of its administrative structure and activities.

Foundation

The National Catholic Welfare Conference was born directly out of the experience of the National Catholic War Council organized in 1917. Twelve days after the entry of the United States into the First World War, His Eminence, James Cardinal Gibbons presented to President Woodrow Wilson, in the name of the archbishops of the country, a pledge of Catholic service. "Our people, as ever, will rise as one man to serve the nation," the message declared.[3] Among various Catholic efforts—which were then uncoordinated—the Reverend John J.

---

1. Official English text, Par. 14.

2. Most Reverend Austin Dowling, quoted in *National Catholic Welfare Conference* (Washington, D. C.: n.d.), p. 66.

3. Raphael M. Huber, O.F.M. Conv. (comp.), *Our Bishops Speak* (Milwaukee: Bruce Publishing Co., 1952), p. 174.

Burke of the Congregation of St. Paul (an American Foundation directed principally toward conversions), organized the
Chaplain's Aid Association to meet the spiritual needs of
soldiers. Through his urging, after the agreement of the
American cardinals to his plan, a meeting of clerical and lay
delegates from sixty-eight dioceses and representatives of
twenty-seven national Catholic organizations resolved "to de-
vise a plan of organization throughout the United States to
promote the spiritual and material welfare of the United
States troops at home and abroad, and to study, coordinate,
unify and put into operation all Catholic activities incidental
to the war." [4] By November the plan had been sufficiently
developed so that the archbishops of the United States con
stituted themselves as the National Catholic War Council
and appointed four bishops as their Administrative Committee. The Most Reverend Peter J. Muldoon, Bishop of Rockford, Illinois, first chairman of the committee, gave able and
socially conscious leadership to the new association. Father
Burke, who had been president of the preliminary committee, was appointed chairman of the Committee on Special
War Activities, which, with the Knights of Columbus Committee on War Activities, was charged with practical tasks.

The Council's work during the war and the period of reconstruction following the armistice won both official and
popular recognition. In addition to its immediate attention
to needs revealed by the war, the Council provided a matrix
for the development of Catholic initiative in such fields as
education and social service and advanced most significantly
the application of Catholic social teaching to the American
scene. A statement of the Administrative Committee known
as the "Bishops' Program of Social Reconstruction," issued
on February 12, 1919, attracted widespread attention for its
forthright examination of "the social question" and its advanced proposals for social legislation. This statement, which
was drafted by the late Monsignor John A. Ryan, pioneer
American Catholic interpreter of *Rerum novarum,* is a basic

---

4. Quoted in *National Catholic Welfare Conference,* p. 4.

document of American Catholic social action. It is worthy of note that ten of its eleven principal recommendations and proposals—for example, minimum wage laws, social insurance, the elimination of child labor, protection of labor's right to organize and to bargain collectively—have since been enacted either wholly or partially into law.

Also in February, 1919, at the golden jubilee of the consecration of Cardinal Gibbons, the Special Delegate of His Holiness, Pope Benedict XV made known to the hierarchy the Holy Father's wish that there should be an annual meeting of the American bishops with departmental organization to carry out their decisions. In September the bishops assembled in Washington and established the National Catholic Welfare Council. The long pastoral letter which they issued after the conclusion of their meeting summarized Catholic teaching on the widest range of problems. Of the new organization, they wrote:

> In view of the results obtained through the merging of our activities for the time and purpose of war, we determined to maintain, for the ends of peace, the spirit of union and the coordination of our forces. We have accordingly grouped together, under the National Catholic Welfare Council, the various agencies by which the cause of religion is furthered. Each of these, continuing its own special work in its chosen field, will now derive additional support through general cooperation. And all will be brought into closer contact with the hierarchy, which bears the burden alike of authority and of responsibility for the interests of the Catholic Church.[5]

This passage may seem to suggest that the aim of the bishops was centralization. If there was opposition on this ground, there was also pessimism based upon fear that the new association could not be anything but weak. One who was a young bishop at the time recalled later in his life:

> The absolute voluntary element of the Council, which was and is necessary to safeguard every Bishop in his jurisdiction, and which neither imposed nor could impose any obligation on its

---

5. *Our Bishops Speak*, pp. 27-28.

members, was necessarily regarded as an obstacle. On the other hand, there was the desire for united action, for corporate expression and decisions; there was urgent need of information for the Bishops, especially for prelates of poor dioceses, distant from the great centers of population. The period called for constructive movements in which Bishops would unite and carry out the recommendations of the commissions or committees.[6]

Difficulties increased during the early years, so that, in 1922, when a few bishops petitioned His Holiness, Pope Pius XI to suppress the Council, the hierarchy was notified that its annual meetings would be discontinued. The Administrative Committee of the Council immediately petitioned for an opportunity to present its case and sent an episcopal representative to Rome. The Holy Father received the petition and the Sacred Consistorial Congregation revoked the decision for suppression, noting, however, that the term "Council" was open to misunderstanding and could be confused with the canonical provisions for councils with actual jurisdiction. "Conference" was substituted for the objectionable term, and the organization has since 1923 been known by its present name. The crisis served to crystallize episcopal support and at the same time to establish definitively the voluntary character of the organization.

This last point deserves particular emphasis in view of the tendency outside the United States to regard the Conference primarily as a work of centralization. The secretariat does of course provide centralization of services but not of authority. An ordinary who does not share the views embodied in majority decisions of the Administrative Board of the Conference is entirely free not to use the services of the N.C.W.C. departments and to make his own mind known through his public addresses or writings. It is probable that over the years virtually every department has at times received individual episcopal criticism, just as current departmental activities in such fields as educational policy, industrial relations, or international organization sometimes

6. Most Reverend John T. McNicholas, O.P., quoted in *ibid.*, p. xviii.

receive critical reception. In spite of the natural and expected differences in these matters, which of course affect the day-to-day conduct of bureaus, concerted Catholic influence on public affairs is maintained by the pattern of voluntary organization. The N.C.W.C. can thus be an instrument of a "policy of presence." In the American situation, after nearly forty years of experience, it can only be regarded as indispensable. Pope Pius XI in fact once declared it to be "not only useful, but also necessary for you." [7]

Since the establishment of the National Catholic War Council in 1917, numerous statements have been issued by the whole body of bishops, by episcopal committees, and by the Administrative Board of N.C.W.C. Three such statements, after the annual meetings of 1919, 1926, and 1938, were published as pastoral letters. National pastorals had been issued after the seven provincial and three plenary councils of Baltimore between 1792 and 1884, which, with the approval of the Holy See, had legislative jurisdiction. In order to avoid the type of confusion evident in the crisis of 1922, the bishops eventually abandoned use of the term "pastoral letter" for joint statements or resolutions adopted outside formal councils. Since 1941, statements on important problems of concern have been issued after each annual meeting by the Administrative Board of N.C.W.C. in the name of the bishops of the United States. Episcopal committees and the Administrative Board have issued statements, usually on rather specific issues, as occasion warranted.

Organization

There would appear to be no need to review in this chapter the detailed history of the several departments of N.C.W.C. Space would not permit in any case. Instead, an attempt will be made to outline briefly the structure of the Conference as of the present date. There have been no fundamental changes in the original pattern, apart from the addition of departments.

---

7. *Ibid.*, p. xx.

The annual meeting of the hierarchy is now held each November on the grounds of the pontifical Catholic University of America at Washington, D. C. As would be true elsewhere, the presiding officer is the senior ranking prelate— at present, His Eminence, Edward Cardinal Mooney, Archbishop of Detroit. At this meeting there is elected the Administrative Board of the National Catholic Welfare Conference, which consists of ten members in addition to the cardinals, who vote but do not hold portfolios. The Board elects its own officers, viz., Chairman, Vice-Chairman, Secretary, Treasurer, and Chairman for the several departments of the Conference. In addition to these departments there are also episcopal committees for special purposes. All function through a secretariat with a headquarters building in Washington.

There are now eight departments with varying scope and types of activity. Except for the Department of Lay Organizations, each has an episcopal chairman and a director. They are as follows:

Executive Department
Department of Education
Department of Immigration
Department of Lay Organizations
Legal Department
Press Department
Department of Social Action
Department of Youth

The episcopal committees include the following:

American Board of Catholic Missions
Committee on the Propagation of the Faith
Committee on the Confraternity of Christian Doctrine
Catholic Committee for Refugees
Committee on the Shrine of the Immaculate Conception
Bishop's Committee for Polish Relief
Bishop's Committee for the Spanish Speaking
Bishop's Welfare Emergency and Relief Committee
Bishop's Committee for Montezuma Seminary
Committee on Motion Pictures

Committee on the National Organization for Decent Literature
Pontifical Committee for the North American College at Rome
Special Committee to Promote the Pope's Peace Plan

The General Secretary of the National Catholic Welfare Conference is the chief administrative officer for the Administrative Board and its representative in matters affecting Catholic interests and the public welfare. Father John Burke served in this capacity from 1919 until his death in 1936. The present Bishop of Columbus, Ohio, the Most Reverend Michael J. Ready, was, until his episcopal consecration in 1944, Father Burke's successor, and the office has since been held by the Right Reverend Howard J. Carroll, Domestic Prelate of His Holiness.

Ex offico, the Chairman of the Administrative Board is episcopal chairman and the General Secretary the Director of the Executive Department. The General Secretary supervises as well the operations of other departments and coordinates activities of all the agencies established by the Conference. Within the Executive Department itself are administrative offices for Business, Auditing and Finance, and Publications; a Bureau of Information, which serves the Conference principally in its relations with the press; on Office for United Nations Affairs, in New York City, which is in contact with the United Nations and the Specialized Agencies and reports their activities in a monthly newsletter to a selected mailing list; and the National Center of the Confraternity of Christian Doctrine, which is the office of the episcopal committee under this title.

The Legal Department serves as a clearing house for information on problems of a legal nature which concern the Church and maintains liaison with the Congress or governmental agencies in appropriate matters. Since the Church supports a wide range of charitable, educational, religious, and welfare institutions, the attention of the Department must be directed to the legal implications of social trends and it must work in coordination with the N.C.W.C. departments concerned with substantive areas.

The Department of Education has of course no control over Catholic schools and it does not serve as a curriculum planning agency. Its functions are to supply information concerning Catholic education to Catholic educators and the general public, to give advice as requested in the development of Catholic schools, to maintain liaison between Catholic and governmental or private non-Catholic educational agencies, and to safeguard the interests of Catholic education. These functions cover a wide range of activities, illustrated in annual compilations of statistics and directories, the analysis of educational legislation, and the maintenance of an office for international exchange services.

Over the years the principal concerns of the Social Action Department have been industrial relations, international peace, family life and social welfare. Especially in the first field, the long service of Monsignor John A. Ryan as director brought national repute to the Department, since it was associated with his pioneer role in Catholic social action in the United States. While the activities of the Department have sometimes been regarded with suspicion in conservative circles, they have exemplified remarkable consistency of policy. In large part, these activities may be termed educational. Thus, Catholic Conferences on Industrial Problems are sponsored in the various regions of the country; there are held annual Institutes on Industry; national Social Action Conferences have been held in the past; educational materials are prepared for Catholic organizations; a monthly newsletter is published for the clergy; seminars are organized for special purposes, such as the improvement of race relations or the problems of the Spanish-speaking; columns are prepared for the Catholic press. The Department provides secretariats for the Catholic Association for International Peace and the National Catholic Family Life Conference, which hold annual meetings and issue publications, and it provided the original facilities for the National Catholic Rural Life Conference, which has for some years maintained its own offices. Basic to these activities is the study of Catholic social teaching and current social problems required for positive action.

The Youth Department also provides clearing house, liaison, and secretariat services in its own field. It promotes the National Catholic Youth Council, established in 1937 to provide on a voluntary basis, without limitation upon episcopal authority, and on a national scale an instrument for coordinated action on the part of all Catholic youth organizations. The Diocesan Section of the Council includes the voluntarily affiliated Diocesan Youth Councils. The College and University Section includes the National Federation of Catholic College Students and the Newman Club Federation, both of which have secretariats in the Youth Department. The former, as its name suggests, unites student groups from Catholic colleges and universities. Newman Clubs, on the other hand, are comprised of Catholic students attending institutions which are not under Catholic auspices.

The Department of Lay Organizations, while established by the bishops in founding the National Catholic Welfare Conference, was not subsidized by them. The Department was intended to be the seat of federations of lay organizations. The National Council of Catholic Women has 10,184 parish and inter-parochial affiliates throughout the country; its principal activities are organizational and educational, with emphasis upon leadership training and study programs in a variety of fields touching practically every aspect of Catholic life, such as, for example, social action, family and parent education, and international relations. To further this work, N.C.C.W. publishes monthly program suggestions and issues a quarterly bulletin reviewing diocesan council activities and significant studies and reports. During the past ten years N.C.C.W. has made substantial foreign relief contributions through various types of projects. The National Council of Catholic Men, federating Catholic men's organizations on a voluntary basis, sponsors outstanding radio and television programs. Its Catholic Hour, established in 1930, was for many years the radio pulpit of Bishop (then

Monsignor) Fulton J. Sheen. It circulates leaflets and news releases containing Catholic information to continue a work known as the Narberth movement, and publishes a monthly magazine.

Catholic newspapers in the United States and even in other countries can testify to the achievements of the N.C.W.C. Press Department in the development of the American Catholic press. The chief means of development is the provision of news, features, pictures, and special syndicated services. The dispatches of the Department are now sent to publications in fifty-seven countries and dependencies. These include *Noticias Catolicas,* a Spanish-language Catholic news service for countries south of the United States in the Western Hemisphere. Through its headquarter staff and field correspondents, the N.C.W.C. News Service reports from all parts of the world news of specific interest to Catholics which it distributes daily to subscribers. It maintains in addition various special services. The Department has grown appreciably in influence since the foundation of the N.C.W.C., not only through its journalistic activities but through its active participation in the Catholic Press Association of the United States.

Finally, the Department of Immigration represents a special kind of service which has become more rather than less necessary. It was established primarily to serve newly arriving Catholic immigrants and has field offices for this purpose at New York City, and El Paso, Texas. In general, however, many Catholic aliens or even native-born citizens with problems related to immigration and deportation laws or passports consult the Department, which handled cases involving 50,361 persons during its most recent report year.

This incomplete survey of secretariat organization must be supplemented by mention of at least two other large-scale activities. The National Catholic Community Service was organized during the Second World War to perform the functions undertaken by the Knights of Columbus Committee on War Activities some twenty years earlier. As a member of United Service Organizations, N.C.C.S. operates clubs in localities near camps of the armed forces and provides related social services, both at home and overseas. Its staff, with volunteer assistance, served more than 8,800,000 persons during the year previous to this writing.

The Catholic Relief Services (formerly War Relief Services) of N.C.W.C. is well known throughout the world as an agency of the Bishop's Welfare Emergency and Relief Committee. It is supported by voluntary contributions of Catholics of the United States, made largely in an annual collection on Laetare Sunday and, in the form of used clothing, at the Thanksgiving holiday during November. Through these contributions, supplemented by surplus foods distributed for relief purposes by the federal government, Catholic Relief Services has sent to all parts of the world, since its organization in 1943, supplies valued at $367,845,000. During 1954-55 it also helped to find new homes for 10,563 refugees.

This account has not mentioned the Mission Secretariat maintained at N.C.W.C. by the episcopal Committee on the Propagation of the Faith, the Bureau of Health and Hospitals, the secretariat of the National Council of Catholic Nurses, or various other units of the N.C.W.C. organization and the episcopal committees. If nothing else, however, even this cursory presentation must indicate the enormous scope of activities and hence the challenge to the staff of the Conference and to the bishops themselves. The N.C.W.C. must be maintained as a "ready and well-adapted instrument" for the ministry of the hierarchy.

Conclusion

Exposition rather than appraisal is the aim of this chapter. The latter would be difficult in some respects, since counterparts of N.C.W.C. in other countries do not exist. Even within the United States, comparisons with other American voluntary organizations are hazardous because the structure of authority within the Church imposes conditions upon the N.C.W.C. which are different from those in other groups, the

Protestant National Council of Churches of Christ, for example. An impressionistic evaluation can be made only in terms of an ideal model, which is likely to be highly individual and more often implicitly rather than explicitly held. These concluding remarks are therefore presented, not to appraise, but only to advance considerations which appear to be necessary for perspective on the achievements of N.C.W.C.

That these achievements have been of the greatest importance must be evident from even the briefest review of the historical record. Certainly they have long put to rest the fears of some of the bishops at its foundation that the organization could not function. It is virtually impossible to conceive how Catholic achievements on the national plane in recent decades could have been organized without the N.C.W.C.

It has already been explained that these achievements have been attained through the centralization of services without centralization of authority which characterizes N.C.W.C. This distinction is observed most obviously because of the nature of episcopal authority, but also in view of the pattern of voluntary organization in a free society. In many respects the departments of N.C.W.C. function in the same manner as those of secretariats of other national organizations with which they are necessarily in daily contact. The initiative of private voluntary organizations is notable on the American scene. Very probably, the N.C.W.C. organizational pattern would not take root as easily in a society lacking similar traditions.

Problems of bureaucratic organization are inherent and necessarily subject to complications within a structure such as N.C.W.C. The concept of the "friendly conference" basic to N.C.W.C. itself imposes limits upon program development. It is notable, however, that this appears not to have prompted, as in some other organizations, adoption of the "least common denominator" as the criterion of acceptability of program proposals. Departmental services are available to all dioceses, yet they cannot be extended where they are not requested. Budgetary limitations not infrequently seem to rule out what might be considered desirable projects; some of these limitations no doubt inhere in the national tendency of bishops to look first to their diocesan developments. In spite of these and other problems, if they may be called such, a review of the activities of N.C.W.C. departments discloses expansion and improvement, much of it clearly traceable to staff initiative as well as to pressing needs recognized by the bishops.

The relationship of the N.C.W.C. structure to what may be called, for want of a better term and with due respect, the "internal politics" of American Catholicism has not been systematically analyzed. For one thing, N.C.W.C. is of too recent foundation to make its archives freely available and differences of opinion within the Catholic body are not usually given public airing. Occasionally, as in a public controversy over immigration legislation a few years ago, differences between the position of the N.C.W.C. department and that of several other Catholic groups came to light. Less conspicuously, differences of opinion, sometimes rather extreme, have been registered on the work of the individual departments. The public record would indicate, however, that harmony has been the rule and that, since the crisis of the founding period, episcopal support has consistently promoted development and expansion.

One additional point perhaps needs to be mentioned. European observers, after a first visit to N.C.W.C., have been heard to remark that priests are over-represented on its staff. The organization is of course the instrument of the bishops. Moreover, for fairly evident historical reasons, laymen have seldom been appointed in the United States to certain types of positions in ecclesiastical structures which are open to them in Europe. There are nevertheless lay directors of three N.C.W.C. departments—the Immigration, Legal and Press Departments—and the executive secretaries of the two bodies united in the Department of Lay Organizations constitute a fourth. Lay officials are found in greater numbers in various associated bureaus or agencies. The efforts of several departments are, moreover, directed to stimulating lay initiative.

Since this is not the place to undertake an inquiry on this subject, it can only be said that, whatever view is taken of an alleged tendency to "clericalism" in American Catholicism, N.C.W.C. can hardly be represented as a principal instrument of such a tendency.

In summary, it should be evident that N.C.W.C. has developed under the influence of both traditionally Catholic and peculiarly American influences, that it is an instrument of episcopal ministry which has grown steadily in usefulness and importance, and that it has furnished socially-conscious leadership in the application of Catholic teaching to the American scene.

PART II

THE CATHOLIC CHURCH

Her Regional Diversity
in the United States

CHAPTER EIGHT

Nationalities and American Catholicism

———— ❖ ————

BY JOHN L. THOMAS, S.J.

A S THE POET, Walt Whitman, pointed out long ago: "America is a nation of nations." Practically all races and
nationalities of the world have contributed to her population
although the great majority of immigrants have been furnished by Europe. This steady influx of immigrants made
possible the rapid development of her vast territory. Decade
after decade throughout the nineteenth and first quarter of
the twentieth century they came by the hundreds of thousands, sturdy of heart and eager of hand, pushing westward
the stubborn frontier, flooding the industrial centers of the
East and Great Lake regions, clearing the forests and plowing
the plains of the North and Middle-West. It is well to recall
that in 1776, at the time of the Revolutionary War, only a
few colonists were found in the westward boundaries of the

*John L. Thomas, S.J., is a member of the Institute of Social
Order, assistant professor of Sociology, St. Louis University,
and author of* The American Catholic Family. *He has published some fifty articles on industrial relations and problems
related to the family.*

seaboard settlements. At the turn of the century the westward movement gained momentum until it became one of the most amazing mass movements in the history of mankind. Within a century the country was settled from coast to coast —the frontier had ceased to exist.[1]

During the years 1820 to 1920, net immigration totaled approximately 30 million. Three major waves of immigration may be singled out. The first arrived during the years 1830-1860 and drew principally upon the British Isles and north-western Europe. This was the period of heavy Irish and German immigration, although large numbers from these countries continued to arrive throughout the century. The second wave entered the country during the era of industrial expansion which characterized the post-Civil War period. Southern and eastern Europeans started arriving at this time but the major source was still the British Isles and northwest-ern Europe. Finally, beginning in the 1880's and culminating in the enormous influx of 1900-10, a third wave poured in from southern and eastern Europe. Most of these later immi-grants had lived in agricultural areas in their native lands, but poverty, the lack of available land, the barrier of lan-guage, and their lack of knowledge of American agricultural methods caused the majority to settle in the large industrial centers of the East and Great Lakes region. Here their lack of training in the mechanical arts confined them to the low-est economic ranks while their lack of education and inability to speak English left them exposed to every form of exploita-tion.[2]

A summary view of the various countries which have sup-plied immigrants to America during the past century and a quarter can be gained from Table I. The data given in this

---

1. See Frederick Jackson Turner, *The Frontier in American History* (New York: Henry Holt and Company, 1921), pp. 290-359, for the effects of the frontier on American institutions.

2. For the history of American immigration see: Henry P. Fairchild, *Im-migration* (New York: The Macmillan Co., rev. ed., 1925), George M. Stephen-son, *A History of American Immigration, 1820-1924* (Boston: Ginn and Co., 1926), Maurice R. Davie, *World Immigration* (New York: The Macmillan Co., 1926).

table are based on reports of the immigration officials and probably involve some inaccuracy. Furthermore, since they report on the country of origin according to the territorial division of Europe at the time, they do not give an accurate picture of some of the national groups. For example, large

TABLE I

Principal Sources of Immigration to the United States, Total Immigration Therefrom, and Peak Year, During 124 Years Beginning 1820 and Ending June 30, 1943

Country	Total 124 Years	Peak Year
Germany	6,028,377	1882
Italy	4,719,825	1907
Ireland	4,592,595	1851
Great Britain	4,264,728	1888
Austria-Hungary	4,144,366	1907
Russia	3,343,480	1913
Canada and Newfoundland	3,037,561	1924
Sweden	1,218,229	1882
Norway	805,367	1882
Mexico	787,629	1924
France	605,430	1851
West Indies	465,569	1824
Greece	431,279	1907
Poland	415,949	1921
China	383,420	1882
Turkey	361,360	1913
Denmark	335,453	1882
Switzerland	297,763	1883
Japan	277,944	1907
Portugal	257,977	1921
Netherlands	254,798	1882
Spain	170,911	1921
Belgium	160,487	1913
Rumania	157,179	1921
South America	125,200	1924
Czechoslovakia	121,017	1921

Source: Brown and Roucek, *op. cit.*, p. 636.

numbers of Poles entered from Germany, Austria-Hungary, and Russia. In general, it will be noticed that the peak immigration years for the northern and western European nations arrived several decades before those from the southern and eastern nations. This means that the members of the "old" immigration were well-established in the country before the "new" immigration started arriving in large numbers; in fact, the "old" have tended to regard the "new" as "foreigners."

The restrictive laws passed by Congress after World War I drastically curtailed immigration so that for all practical purposes the epoch of American immigration was closed. Since that time, a large proportion of immigrants have come from Canada, Mexico and the Americas. Prior to World War II, a considerable number of refugees arrived from Europe.[3] Since the War, America has been receiving a limited number of displaced persons but their settlement has been accompanied by systematic social planning so that the present immigration resembles the old in few respects.[4]

Although, as Oscar Handlin discovered when preparing to write a history of the immigrants in America, "the immigrants are American history," their entrance into American society has long been a subject of deep concern to "native" Americans.[5] At times, nativist groups have capitalized on religious and racial prejudices to arouse opposition to the immigrants. From 1840 to 1860 the Native American party (the Know-Nothings) stirred up violent opposition to immigrants in general and to Catholics in particular.[6] In the late eighties and early nineties, Know-Nothingness reappeared in the form of the American Protective Association (the A.P.A.).[7] It appeared again after World War I in the

3. See Maurice R. Davie, *Refugees in America* (New York: Harper and Bros., 1947), for most detailed study of their provenance, numbers and adjustment.

4. See William S. Bernard, *American Immigration Policy: A Reappraisal* (New York: Harper and Bros., 1950), and "Reappraising Our Immigration Policy," *The Annals of the American Academy of Political and Social Science,* Vol. 26, (March, 1949).

5. Oscar Handlin, *The Uprooted* (Boston: Little, Brown and Company, 1951), p. 3.

6. See Ray Allen Billington, *The Protestant Crusade 1800-1860* (New York: Rinehart and Company, Inc., 1938), for most comprehensive study of the origins of American nativism.

7. Stephenson, op. cit., pp. 145-47; Carl Wittke, *We Who Built America* (New York: Prentice-Hall, Inc., 1940), pp. 498-505; Joseph L. Cross, "The American Protective Association," *The American Catholic Sociological Review,* X (Oct., 1949), 172-87.

form of the Ku Klux Klan, an organization which took upon itself the promotion, by violence if necessary, of native, white, Protestant supremacy. For two decades the Klan waged a vicious campaign of hatred against Catholics, Jews, Negroes, and immigrants. This powerful, lawless movement declined very rapidly after 1928 when the public grew weary of its mob tactics and the ruthless exploitation of the credulity and ignorance of its vast membership by a corrupt leadership was finally exposed.[8] That anti-Catholic nativism is a hardy perennial can be seen from the fact that the American Protective Association in the late 1890's counted at least a million members and in the 1920's approximately one fourth of the men of the United States eligible to join the Klan were included in its membership.[9]

The American attitude toward the assimilation process of the immigrant has passed through several stages. Throughout the nineteenth century there was little theorizing about the problem, and it was generally assumed that assimilation would take place rapidly and automatically. This assumption of relatively facile Americanization indicated scant knowledge of the nature, origin, development, and survival potential of established cultural patterns. Immigrants coming to the United States tended to cluster together and to foster strong ingroup solidarity. In the first decade of this century, the melting-pot theory gained prominence. In the dramatic words of the playwright, Zangwill, America was "God's Crucible," the great "Melting Pot," where the mighty Alchemist melts and fuses all nations into one with his purging flame! [10]

With the onset of World War I, perceptive Americans became conscious not only that the great Alchemist seemed to be ignoring some of the groups altogether, but many ingredi-

---

8. See Wittke, op. cit., pp. 505-509; Donald Young, *American Minority Peoples* (New York: Harper and Brothers, 1932), pp. 257-261.

9. Willard Johnson, "Religion and Minority Peoples," in *One America*, ed. by Francis J. Brown and Joseph S. Roucek (New York: Prentice-Hall, Inc., 1945), p. 510.

10. See Israel Zangwill, *The Melting Pot* (New York: The Macmillan Company, 1923, rev'd ed.), pp. 184-85.

ents in the Pot appeared highly resistant to the "purging flame." Consequently, a veritable crusade was launched to Americanize the immigrant.[11] The crusaders tried to force the immigrants to divest themselves of their heritages immediately and to take over a highly standardized American pattern for their lives. However well intentioned these Americans may have been, they were working for denationalization and standardization, not assimilation.[12] This desire to enforce conformity has often plagued Americans and some historians look upon it as a carry-over from Puritanism.[13] Fortunately, the crusade was soon recognized as spurious Americanization, and after 1920, social thinkers began to talk in terms of long-range cultural fusion or even of cultural pluralism.[14]

Current theory recognizes the manifold diversity and complexity of the process involved in "becoming an American." [15] Assimilation is viewed as a slow process in which both the host culture and the minorities undergo modification while working toward an eventual cultural unity which implies synthesis, not integral absorption. Consequently, this theory of cultural pluralism does not assume that complete fusion of cultures is a necessary optimum. The nation will be richer in its cultural composition if the best that each national group has brought is conserved. The nature, character, and personality of the minority groups have been molded by a culture different from the American, and the method of effective cultural transmission requires that the

---

11. See Edward G. Hartmann, *The Movement to Americanize the Immigrant* (New York: Columbia University Press, 1948).

12. See Constantine M. Panunzio, *Immigration Crossroads* (New York: The Macmillan Co., 1927).

13. "That was the essence of practical Puritanism—the restriction of others." Marcus L. Hansen, *The Immigrant in American History* (Cambridge: Harvard U. Press, 1948), p. 105.

14. See William C. Smith, *Americans in the Making* (New York: D. Appleton-Century Co., 1939), for a good overall treatment of the assimilation process.

15. See W. Lloyd Warner and Leo Srole, *The Social Systems of American Ethnic Groups* (New Haven: Yale University Press, 1945), for an excellent analysis of the stages and problems involved in assimilation.

fundamentals of their heritages be preserved for generations.

Hence, this theory takes into consideration the time element necessary in processes of assimilation and acknowledges the *de facto* diversity of the American population which has developed out of traditional white-colored demarcations and the variety of cultures associated with the national origins of its immigrant stock. It represents a considerable advance over that traditional American provincialism which saw in all cultural differences the necessary marks of inferiority, and its abandonment of the ethnocentrism characterizing previous theories is commendable. Unfortunately, there is little evidence that this theory of cultural pluralism has been accepted by the traditional nativist elements in American society so that religious and racial prejudice still constitutes a major social problem.[16]

It is against this background of immigration, nativist bigotry, and evolving attitudes toward assimilation that the problem of American Catholicism and its national minorities must be studied. Only in this frame of reference can we analyze some of the unique characteristics of the Church in the United States and arrive at an understanding of the specific problems which she faces in contemporary society. Of course, there are those who argue that since immigration has ceased in the twenties and the second and third generation ethnics are becoming rapidly acculturated, the problem of minorities in the Church is no longer significant.[17] But this is to ignore the facts of history. The Catholic Church in the United States is largely an immigrant Church and it bears the stamp of its origins to this day. Further, there are hundreds of active national parishes existing alongside of, and frequently compet-

---

16. On this point see: George E. Simpson and J. Milton Yinger, *Racial and Cultural Minorities* (New York: Harper and Brothers, 1953); Charles F. Marden, *Minorities in American Society* (New York: American Book Company, 1952); Edward C. McDonagh and Eugene S. Richards, *Ethnic Relations in the United States* (New York: Appleton-Century-Crofts, Inc., 1953).

17. The term "ethnic" as used here refers to those organized groups of immigrants and their progeny who exhibit characteristics of social organization and culture more or less at variance with those of American society.

ing with, the traditional territorial parishes.[18] There are also relatively large subcultural groups such as Mexicans, Puerto Ricans, Indians, and Negroes among whom the work of the Church is hindered by the prevailing racial prejudice. Finally, there are some 670,000 Catholics who belong to the various non-Roman uniate rites. It is obvious that American Catholicism, like American society, is characterized by considerable cultural and racial heterogeneity.

In Table I we saw the overall picture of the American immigration problem. Do we know what percentage of these immigrants were Catholic? Since official government statistics do not report the religious affiliation of the immigrants, we must rely on estimates. Table II presents the findings of one

TABLE II

Catholic Immigration and the Growth of the Church by Decades

Decade	Catholic Population	Catholic Immigration During Preceding Decade
1790	35,000	
1820	195,000	77,000
1830	318,000	54,000
1840	663,000	240,000
1850	1,606,000	700,000
1860	3,103,000	985,000
1870	4,504,000	741,000
1880	6,259,000	604,000
1890	8,909,000	1,250,000
1900	12,041,000	1,225,000
1910	16,363,000	2,316,000
1920	19,828,000	1,202,000

of the most exhaustive attempts to estimate the percentage of Catholics among the immigrants.[19] There is little doubt that both the total Catholic population and the number of Catholic immigrants are somewhat underestimated in this study, but the overall picture remains correct. The Catholic

18. For example, in the Archdiocese of Chicago there are 144 territorial parishes and 140 national parishes. For a brief discussion of the problem, see: Thomas J. Harte, "Racial and National Parishes in the United States," in *The Sociology of the Parish*, ed. by C. J. Nuesse and Thomas J. Harte (Milwaukee: The Bruce Publishing Co., 1952), pp. 154-77.

19. See Gerald Shaughnessy, *Has the Immigrant Kept the Faith?* (New York. The Macmillan Company, 1925), p. 189.

Church in the United States grew from a mere handful of 35,000 scattered throughout the colonies in 1790 to the largest religious group in the country in 1920 and this growth was due chiefly to the heavy influx of Catholic immigrants who arrived at first from the northern and western European countries and later from central and southern Europe.

Several characteristics of American Catholicism closely connected with this growth of the Church through immigration should be noted. First, the Catholic immigrant groups faced the problem of establishing themselves in a society which had been preempted by Anglo-Saxon protestantism. This put the Catholics on the defensive and intensified the minority status of the Catholic immigrants. Second, Catholic immigrants, with the exception of the Irish, encountered a language barrier which slowed down their economic, social and political integration, intensified their dissimilarity with the dominant group, and stimulated them to settle in relatively closed communities clustered around their national parish. As a result, the Irish have been the first of the groups to be assimilated, their clergy have composed the majority of the hierarchy, and in a sense, the Irish have acted as an intermediate group between the dominant Protestant majority and the minority Catholic groups. Of course, this leadership of the Irish has not gone unchallenged. It was strongly contested by the Germans in the latter part of the nineteenth century when Irish-German rivalry aroused considerable animosity. Fortunately, the minority status of both groups in American society forced them to work out an amicable solution.

Third, since the majority of Irish and German Catholic immigrants arrived during the last century, they were well established before the "new" immigrants arrived. Consequently, they tend to look upon themselves as "natives," and to acquire many of the prejudices of the dominant group concerning the later arrivals from central and southern Europe whom they consider "foreigners." This attitude has led to considerable animosity between certain national groups in the Church and has further intensified the tendency of some groups to isolate themselves in an effort to preserve their language and other cultural traits.[20] A manifestation of this was the multiplication of "national" parishes and parochial schools which placed heavy burdens on the parishioners.

Fourth, the majority of Catholic immigrants entered the country through the port centers of the East and tended to settle not far from the point of debarkation. Consequently, Catholics are not evenly distributed throughout the country. Approximately 80 per cent are located in 20 per cent of the territory. Roughly speaking, this is the area north of the Ohio River and east of the Mississippi Valley region. The other 20 per cent of the Catholic population are scattered throughout the remaining territory with rather heavy concentration in Louisiana and those sections of the Southwest where the Spanish-speaking and Mexican population is relatively high. During the last decade there has been a marked movement of population to the western coastal states and this movement will undoubtedly have some effect on the distribution of Catholics in the country.

Fifth, the majority of Catholic immigrants tended to settle in the large industrial centers. Hence, the Catholic Church in America is primarily an urban Church. The uniqueness of the Catholic position in this respect can be seen from the census reports. Using the 1940 reports, since it was on the basis of these that the estimates for Catholics were made, we find that approximately 43 per cent of the population of the country were classified as rural. This includes both the rural-farm (23.2) and rural-nonfarm (20.5) population.[21] Of the

---

20. In some cases, there has been an open break with the Roman Catholic Church over the language question. The best example is the Polish National Church which has drawn some 250,000 Poles out of the Catholic unity and into a fiercely nationalistic dissident sect. See: Theodore Andrews, *The Polish National Church in America* (London: Society for Promoting Christian Knowledge, 1953).

21. By census definition, rural-farm population includes all persons living on farms in rural areas. A farm consists of all the land operated by one person, provided it includes three acres or more or provided it produced a total of agricultural products valued at $250 or more during the year in question. Rural-nonfarm population includes all persons dwelling in rural areas who are not living on farms.

Catholic population, only 19.4 per cent are classified as rural (farm and non-farm) and according to estimates of The Catholic Rural Life Conference, only about 8 per cent of the Catholic population now live on the land as fulltime farmers.[22] Although the secularizing tendencies of urbanization are a commonplace in modern sociological literature, it should be noted that the evil effects of this concentration of Catholic immigrants in large industrial centers have been somewhat mitigated by other important factors. Concentration has made possible the construction of a church and school system without parallel in the world. There is some question that this could have been managed if the Catholic immigrants had been dispersed equally throughout the country on their arrival. Even today in the 9,641 Catholic rural parishes and missions, only 17.9 per cent have Catholic elementary schools and 3.2 per cent have Catholic high schools.[23]

Sixth, since the Catholic immigrants were uniformly poor, unskilled—or possessing skills not readily useful in an industrialized society—they started their lives in America at the bottom of the socio-economic ladder. As Emma Lazarus wrote in the lines inscribed at the base of the Statue of Liberty.

> "Keep, ancient lands, your storied pomp!" Cries she,
> With silent lips. "Give me your tired, your poor,
> Your huddled masses yearning to breathe free,
> The wretched refuse of your teeming shore.
> Send these, the homeless, the tempest-tost, to me!
> I lift my lamp beside the golden door."

Since American society is an open-class system with no clearcut social class barriers and, at the same time offers ample opportunities for education and economic advancement, second and third generation ethnics are characterized by high social mobility. Hence, although the majority of Catholics are still found in the middle and lower socio-economic classes, significantly increasing numbers are seizing educa-

---

22. See: *A Survey of Catholic Weakness* (Des Moines, Iowa: National Catholic Rural Life Conference, 1948), pp. 10-11.

23. *Ibid.*, pp. 12-13.

tional and economic opportunities to alter their status. Two
important consequences follow from this situation. First, the
Church has drawn its strength from the working classes and
has identified herself with their interests so that they have
preserved the faith even under difficult conditions. Second,
the increase of a well-educated laity will require a more intellectual approach to doctrinal and moral teaching in the
Church than has been called for heretofore.[24]

Seventh, it must be emphasized that the process of assimilation requires time, it involves a clash of cultures, and it
produces a generation or two of marginal men. The factor of
time is self-evident. The mature immigrant who arrived in
America could not immediately discard his alien culture even
if he had so desired. Further, a clash of cultures was inevitable.
The immigrant soon learned that his native language limited his facility to learn new ways, inhibited his mobility, and
marked him for discrimination, if not contempt. His ideals
were shattered by crude and merciless exploitation—in construction gangs, stockyards, mines, steelmills, and factories as
well as in housing and general living conditions. Consequently, his first impressions of American culture were dis-
couraging. All too frequently, the natives he encountered
were no models of civic or domestic virtue. It was all very
well for the Americanizers to speak of the "good old American virtues"; what the majority of the immigrants saw,
crowded together as they were in the large industrial centers
at the turn of the century, was widespread and open corrup-
tion in city politics, ruthless exploitation of the worker and
his family in industry, and shocking disregard for morality in

---

24. Fortunately for the Church, the typical Roman Catholic clergyman has
had a better educational preparation for his responsibilities than the Protestant minister. In 1930 it was estimated that over two thirds of the Catholic
clergy had graduated from both college and theological seminary, but only
one third of the clergymen in the 17 white Protestant denominations and
fewer than one out of 12 of the ministers of Negro denominations were
graduates of both college and theological seminary. See C. Luther Fry, *The
United States Looks at Its Churches,* Institute of Social and Religious Research, New York, 1930.

social life. Hence, in the eyes of many immigrants, American-ization came to be synonymous with demoralization. Finally, the process of assimilation produced marginal men. Second and third generation ethnics found themselves partially inte-grated in two cultures. They were neither Americans nor aliens but something of both. Under these circumstances some chose complete rejection of their alien cultural past and became more American than the natives. Others re-treated into cultural ghettoes, seeking security in the preser-vation of the past. Others experienced personal and social disorganization. For all, it involved a period of strain and tension, focusing their attention upon their own problems rather than upon those of the community or the nation.

Finally, the fact that the Church in America is not only an immigrant church in origin but also is composed of relatively large ethnic minorities, has meant that the Church has had limited influence on American culture in general. Even if the Church had been able to present a united front, the late ar-rival of a high percentage of her members in addition to their initially low social and economic position, would have restricted her influence. For all practical purposes, American culture was developed under Puritan Protestant auspices and with the gradual breakdown of this influence, it has become highly secular in character. This does not imply that it is anti-spiritual or pro-materialist. Rather, it is a complex cul-ture tolerating great individual freedom, and, under the in-fluence of its economic system, frankly utilitarian in its general outlook. The consequences of this situation is that while Catholics enjoy a maximum of religious freedom, many institutions such as civil divorce, and practices such as the use of contraceptive birth control lend no support to Catholic ideals. Hence, Catholics must formulate and enforce many of their own moral ideals particularly in the realm of chastity and family life. It was precisely because many ethnic leaders were distressed by the moral ideals and practices which they encountered in the lower ranks of society that they reacted by building strong group solidarity around the national parish and its organizations. In recent times, there is evident a growing awareness among all ethnics of a common solidarity with other Catholic groups. This appears in youth movements, marriage and family organizations, and various diocesan activities.

What are the characteristics of the various national groups within the Church today? In the first place, it should be noted that the large Irish and German aggregates of the "old" immigration have been largely acculturated so that they display few marks of specifically ethnic solidarity. To be sure, there are parishes which are predominantly Irish or German but this is primarily the result of their spatial distribution. The German Catholics struggled valiantly to preserve their language and traditions but the fierce anti-German propaganda campaign of World War I seriously weakened these aspirations. Besides, the inevitable Americanization process had set in among the German immigrants well before that time so that today, even in the relatively isolated German rural parishes of the Middle-West, we find not Catholic "German-Americans," but Catholic Americans of German descent.[25]

There is no way of estimating the number of Catholics of Irish and German descent. Members of both these strains have married rather freely outside their group. The best that can be done is to point out that the total Irish immigration numbered approximately four million. At least two-thirds of these were Catholic and their peak year for arrival was one hundred years ago, so one may conclude they have numerous descendants. Approximately six million Germans immigrated to America. It is estimated that one million and a half of these were Catholic and their peak year for arrival was sev-

---

25. For an excellent treatment of this whole problem, see: Colman J. Barry, *The Catholic Church and German Americans* (Washington: The Catholic University of America Press, 1953); also Emmet H. Rothan, *The German Catholic Immigrant in the United States (1830-1860)* (Washington: The Catholic University of America Press, 1946); and for the non-Catholic German immigrant, see: John A. Hawgood, *The Tragedy of German-America* (New York: G. P. Putnam's Sons, 1940).

enty-five years ago so that they, too, have numerous descendants.[26]

Today the major ethnic minorities in the American Catholic Church may be classified as follows. First, there are the large Catholic aggregates of the "new" immigration who started arriving in large numbers from Europe only after 1880. These people were, for the most part, peasants or semi-skilled workers from central and southern Europe. Since they arrived after the free lands were used up and at a time when the industrial revolution was rapidly transforming America from a rural to an industrialized urban society, they tended to settle in the large industrial centers of the East and Great Lakes region.[27] Second, there are the immigrants from the Americas. This group includes the French Canadians, the Mexicans, and the Spanish-speaking groups from Central and South America, and from the West Indies. The French Canadians settled principally in the New England states, while the Spanish-speaking groups are found mainly in the Southwest with the exception of the Puerto Ricans who have settled in New York City and a few of the major industrial centers of the East and North. Third, there are several distinctive groups such as the American Indians and the Negroes who for various historical and social reasons constitute separate minorities.

A brief description of these groups will be presented in the hope that it will assist us to grasp their significance for the Church in America. Among the Catholic minorities of the first class, those of Polish and Italian background are the most numerous. Polish immigrants and their descendants

---

26. In 1923, Archbishop Joseph Schrembs estimated that Catholics of German descent numbered about four million. This appears to be a rather generous estimate. See, Rt. Rev. Joseph Schrembs, "The Catholic German Immigrant's Contribution," in *Catholic Builders of the Nation,* ed. by C. E. McGuire (Boston: Continental Press, Inc., 1925), p. 63.

27. See Young, *op. cit.,* pp. 34-36 for reasons why "new" immigrants settled in urban areas. However, a small percentage did settle on the land and by sacrifice and hard work became highly successful farmers. See Edmund DeS. Brunner, *Immigrant Farmers and Their Children* (Garden City, New York: Doubleday, Doran and Company, Inc., 1929).

number about 6,000,000 today. Although the Poles are found in practically all parts of the country, their heaviest concentration is in the middle-eastern states and those bordering on the Great Lakes.[28] The great majority of Poles have remained faithful to the Church. They maintain approximately 900 parishes and 600 parochial schools in addition to an active Polish-language press, some 10,000 Polish dramatic, literary, singing, social, religious, and athletic societies, and various national Polish organizations with a membership totaling 800,000.[29] Early studies of the Polish immigrant advanced dire predictions of widespread family disorganization.[30] However, these predictions have not been realized primarily because of the efficiency of the Polish parish organization and the deep religious faith of the immigrant.[31]

It is estimated that the Italian immigrants and their descendants number approximately 6,000,000. These immigrants came largely from the south of Italy.[32] Most of them arrived in the port of New York and many never went further. Those who did, tended to settle in highly congested areas near their compatriots from the home village in Italy thus forming "Little Italys" in almost every major American city.[33] Although the vast majority were professing Catholics, their indifference to the practice of the faith has long con-

---

28. Major concentrations are: Greater New York (650,000), Chicago (600,-000), Detroit (350,000), Buffalo (200,000), Milwaukee (180,000), Cleveland (175,-000). See Arthur L. Waldo, "Poles in the United States," *American-Polish Participation* (New York: New York's World Fair Publication, 1939).

29. See *Rocznik Polonii—Year Book and Directory of Poles Abroad* (London, England: Taurus, Ltd., 1952).

30. See William I. Thomas and Florian Znaniecki, *The Polish Peasant in Europe and America,* rev'd ed., Two Volumes (New York: Alfred A. Knopf, 1927).

31. See John L. Thomas, S.J., "Marriage Prediction in The Polish Peasant," *The American Journal of Sociology,* 55 (May, 1950), pp. 572-78.

32. The heavy immigration from the north of Italy occurred several decades earlier and settled primarily in South America. See the excellent treatise by Robert F. Foerster, *The Italian Immigration of Our Times* (Cambridge: The Harvard University Press, 1919).

33. For example, in 1940, there were 1,095,000 Italian Americans living in New York City. See Brown and Roucek, *op. cit.,* pp. 262-65.

stituted a serious problem for the Church in America.[34] There are many factors in this problem: the immigrants were poor, they were seldom accompanied by their clergy, they were poorly instructed in their faith, they had no tradition of building and supporting church institutions, and their clannishness, further intensified by considerable animosity on the part of other Catholic groups, kept them from affiliating with established parishes. There is general agreement that religious losses have been considerable.[35] Writing in 1939, one eminent authority stated that of the six million Italian Americans, two million are fervent Catholics, one million are lost to the Church, and three million are doubtful. He predicts that this latter group will be lost to the Church within a generation unless adequate steps are taken for their instruction and integration into parish life.[36]

Immigrants and their descendants from Czechoslovakia number about 1,750,000. They are located chiefly in the states of Pennsylvania, Illinois, Ohio, New York, Wisconsin, Nebraska, and Texas. A good percentage of the Czechs settled on the land and have become prosperous farmers. Somewhere between one-half and two-thirds of the Czechs are fervent Catholics. They maintain over 120 parishes, most of which have flourishing parochial schools. A large percentage of the Slovaks are Catholic. They maintain over 200 parishes and are noted for the strength and vigor of their various religious, social, athletic, and cultural organizations.

Immigrants and their descendants from Yugoslavia number approximately 1,000,000. Of these, the Croatians number 500,000, the Slovenes, about 300,000, and the Serbs, about 200,000. Although distributed throughout the Union, their

---

34. See Henry J. Browne, "The 'Italian Problem' in the Catholic Church of the United States, 1880-1900," *Historical Records and Studies, United States Catholic Historical Society,* 35, 1946, pp. 46-75.

35. See evidence offered by Foerster, *op. cit.,* pp. 397-98; Bernard J. Lynch, "The Italians in New York," *The Catholic World,* 47, (April, 1888), pp. 69 ff.; Lawrence Franklin, "Italians in America," *Ibid.,* 71, (April, 1900), pp. 67 ff.

36. See John V. Tolino, "Solving the Italian Problem," *The American Ecclesiastical Review,* 99, (Sept., 1938), pp. 246-56; "The Church in America and the Italian Problem," *ibid.,* 100, (Jan., 1939), pp. 22-32; "The Future of the Italian-American Problem," *ibid.,* 101, (Sept., 1939), pp. 221-32.

chief centers of settlement are the states of Illinois, Minnesota, California, Nebraska, Iowa, and Colorado. The Croatians and Slovenes are Roman Catholics, the Serbs are Eastern Orthodox. At present, the Slovenes maintain some 45 parishes and the Croatians 33, while considerable numbers of both groups are affiliated with other parishes.

The exact number of Magyar (Hungarians) and their descendants is not known but a conservative estimate would be 300,000 to 400,000.[37] Over half of these are Catholic and they maintain 58 active parishes located chiefly in Pennsylvania, Ohio, New Jersey, New York, Connecticut, and Indiana. The Magyars are a mobile group and tend to be acculturated rather rapidly.

Estimates of the number of Lithuanian Americans differ greatly but it seems safe to state that there are at least 500,-000 in the United States today. Research indicates that all but 30 per cent of the Lithuanian immigrants are practical Catholics.[38] There are 120 Lithuanian parishes located primarily in the East and Great Lakes region. The largest Lithuanian center is Chicago which contains about 100,000 of Lithuanian descent.

Finally, there are 632,000 uniate Catholics equally divided between the Ukranian Greek Catholic (Byzantine Rite) diocese of Philadelphia and the Greek Rite diocese of Pittsburgh. The majority of these people are generally classified as Ukranians.[39] Their major settlement is in Pennsylvania, although they are found in most of the principal industrial centers of the East and Great Lakes region and in Los Angeles and San Francisco. They maintain some 350 parishes and numerous schools. The descendants of these immigrants reveal the same tendency toward rapid Americanization as do

---

37. See Brown and Roucek, *op. cit.,* p. 215. Schermerhorn, *op. cit.,* p. 330, states that the safest estimate would be from 1.5 million to 2 million. This estimate appears to be much too high.

38. See Casimir P. Sirvaitis, *Religious Folkways in Lithuania and Their Conservation Among the Lithuanian Immigrants in the United States* (Washington: The Catholic University of America Press, 1952), p. 39.

39. See Wasyl Halich, *Ukrainians in the United States* (Chicago: The University of Chicago Press, 1937).

others of the "new" immigration. This creates a special problem for them, however, since "Americanization" frequently involves a preference for the Latin Rite.

According to our classification, the second category of minorities is made up of immigrants from the Americas. Outstanding among these for their cultural cohesion are the French Canadians. These immigrants and their descendants number between 2.5 million and 3 million.[40] Their principal locus of settlement is adjacent to French Canada in the New England States. Even in the United States, the life of the French Canadian centers chiefly around his parish and his home. On the premise that "qui perd sa langue perd sa foi," the French Canadians have stressed the national parish, French parochial schools, the French-language press, and numerous social and cultural associations.[41] At present the French Canadians constitute a distinct cultural subgroup but there are indications that their efforts to maintain their language will succeed no better than those of other minorities in the United States.

Americans of Mexican ancestry constitute about 3,500,000 persons in the United States.[42] About ninety per cent of the group live in the Southwest and the remainder are settled in or near urban centers in Illinois, Michigan, Minnesota, and Ohio. There are at least four major types to be considered: old native group, new native group, "wetbacks," (Mexican workers who have crossed the frontier illegally), and Mexican Nationals or contract laborers. Although there is some intermarriage with other groups, the Spanish Americans tend to keep their language and their customs. With the exception of the old native group, they are uniformly poor, suffer marked discrimination in education, law, and social life, and are the victims of widespread and flagrant exploitation in the eco-

---

40. See Thorsten V. Kalijarvi, "French Canadians in the United States," *The Annals of the American Academy of Political and Social Science*, 223 (Sept., 1942), pp. 132-33.

41. See D. M. A. Magnan, *Histoire de la Race Francaise aux Etats-Unis* (Paris, 1912) pp. 249-267, 310-333.

42. See McDonagh and Richards, *op. cit.*, p. 174 ff.; Marden, *op. cit.*, pp. 131-33.

nomic sphere.[43] Although most of this group are Catholic, their poverty, the necessity of moving from place to place to find employment, and the difficulty they experience in adapting to a wholly alien culture, tend to produce considerable indifference to religious practice among many.

Somewhat similar in culture to the Mexican group are the Spanish-speaking immigrants from Puerto Rico. They started arriving in large numbers only after 1940. At present they number over 500,000, eighty per cent of which are located in New York City. Although the majority are Catholic, their poverty, their language and cultural diversity, and their overcrowding in industrial slums, raise serious barriers to their facile integration into the American Church.

Our third category of minorities is constituted by Indians and Negroes. It is estimated that there are about 393,600 Indians living within the United States. Approximately two-thirds of the Indians dwell on reservations as wards of the government, the others are distributed throughout the country. According to the latest report there are 104,940 Catholic Indians. The Church maintains 112 mission centers, 404 churches, and 60 mission schools with an enrollment of 8,000 students. There are 217 priests and 700 sisters and male religious devoted exclusively to the Indian missions.

The problem of the Negro minority will be treated in other sections of this book. Suffice it to point out that there are 420,590 Negro Catholics out of a total number of 15 million. There are 461 churches and chapels served by 633 priests, maintained especially for the benefit of the Negroes. In addition there are 325 schools with an enrollment of 71,-810 and staffed by 1,900 sisters and 250 lay teachers. The

---

43. See Pauline R. Kibbe, *Latin Americans in Texas* (Albuquerque: University of New Mexico Press, 1946); for a sensitive study of a Mexican community in California, see Ruth Tuck, *Not with the Fist* (New York: Harcourt, Brace and Company, Inc., 1947); Robert C. Jones, *Mexican War Workers in the United States* (Washington: Pan American Union, 1945); Raymond Bernard, "Runaround for Migrants," *Social Order,* I (Oct., 1951), pp. 353-360; for basic material, see, *Migrant Labor, a Human Problem,* and *Migratory Labor in American Agriculture,* Report of the President's Commission on Migratory Labor (Washington: 1951).

work of the Church among both the Negroes and Indians is hindered by the strong racial prejudice of the dominant white group which results in discrimination, segregation, and the maintenance of cultural patterns little in conformity with Christian ideals.

This brief description gives us some idea of the size and diversity of the Catholic minorities in the American Church. Their presence alone renders suspect most generalizations concerning the Church in the United States. As for the future, the following predictions can be made in the light of present trends. The ethnics of the "new" immigration will continue their trend toward relatively rapid Americanization. This means that third and fourth generation ethnics will become progressively less bilingual, will lose distinctive cultural habits and customs, and will recognize their unity with other Catholics in the country. Around the national parish centers, ethnic solidarity as characterized by high rates of ingroup marriage will probably continue for a long time. This will operate as a strong barrier to mixed marriage and should aid in the preservation of the faith. On the other hand, the existence of relatively large numbers of national parishes, superimposed as they are upon the territorial parishes, will create serious pastoral and jurisdictional problems. Since most of these national parishes are clustered in the heavily populated urban centers and the present tendency of the urban population is to move away from these areas into the suburbs where new churches and schools are established, it will become increasingly difficult to staff and finance the traditional parish centers. Hence, some of these institutions will have to be closed to allow for the rational consolidation of religious resources, but such action will certainly arouse the ethnic sentiments of the group affected. The ethnic sensitivity of the various major minorities is not without its foundation in the past. The continued prevalence of those of Irish and German descent in the hierarchy merely serves to perpetuate a national pluralism within the Church which was inevitable in the past but no longer corresponds to reality.

The Spanish-language minority will continue to face serious problems of adjustment. In many sections they are subjected to extensive and crippling discrimination which shows little signs of abating. The same conditions maintain for the Negro although the past two decades have been characterized by considerable political, economic and educational gains. Particularly in the North, Negroes are being integrated into established parishes and their rate of conversion is encouraging.

To summarize, therefore, the Catholic Church in America had its origins primarily as an immigrant church and is only now developing some semblance of unity. Although there were Catholics here at the time of the Revolution, and the purchase of Louisiana together with the annexations following the Mexican War added several hundred thousand, the major growth of the Church came with the heavy flood of immigrants, first from Ireland and Germany, later from southern and central Europe. Most of these groups have followed rather similar patterns of acculturation except where discrimination and segregation have deprived them of normal opportunities. At present, ethnics from the "new" immigration and those from the Americas are still identifiable entities but they are moving toward an increased consciousness of unity and solidarity with other Catholics in the country. We have indicated some of the problems which result from the present diversity, and have suggested that, although they are not insurmountable, their solution will require considerable understanding and tact.

CHAPTER NINE

The Catholic Church in New England

—— ◆ ——

BY EDWARD G. MURRAY

O F ALL THE REGIONS of the United States, New England was the first to acquire a proper name. It is, likewise, the most geographically distinct and probably the most self-conscious of the regions into which the United States may logically be divided. It is an old name, dating from the first patent of colonization given by the English Crown in 1620. It is, in all the United States, that region which was longest in contention between the original settlers and the native inhabitants. It likewise for the first century and a quarter of its life, knew itself as one of the grounds of disagreement between the English and the French, both of whom claimed it by right of discovery and exploration.

In good measure, too, it may be stated that the cultural beginnings of America are to be found rooted in New England. Most of the enduring literature of the nineteenth cen-

Edward G. Murray, S.T.D., has served as Vice-Chancellor of the Archdiocese of Boston and Rector of St. John's Seminary, Boston. Since 1951, Monsignor Murray has been pastor of the Sacred Heart Church in Roslindale, Mass.

tury derives from New England and has left a lasting impression upon the national consciousness. Our oldest college and university, as well as our oldest public school, date from early seventeenth century New England beginnings, and the passage of years has left New England with academic prestige undimmed.

Politically, the great crisis of the Revolution had its ideological beginnings in New England and here were fought its first battles. In the second great crisis of our national life, the War between the States, it was an intransigent New England public opinion relative to slavery which led to the Emancipation Proclamation and hence added a new dimension to the War, which, in its beginnings, was concerned only with the maintenance of the Union.

These and other reasons have combined to give to New England an importance in the American national consciousness, greater than its relatively small land mass and the approximately six per cent of the population of the United States which lives within its borders.

It is against the background of such a regional importance and self-consciousness that we must assess the impact of Catholicism upon this part of our land and look forward to its future. The original royal grant of November 3, 1620, provided that no Roman Catholic should go to New England unless he first took the oath of the royal supremacy. The first settlement in New England was that of the Pilgrims in 1620 at Plymouth and a later group of Puritans came to Salem and the region about Boston between 1628 and 1630. New England came to be colonized in its first century by dissenters, those who, although of Protestant belief, would not accept the doctrine or practice of the Established Church in England. They had a strong urge toward independence, so far as feasible, from the mother country, and they carried with them, too, a profound distrust and a dislike of the Church of Rome. Their misgivings with regard to the Catholic faith were accentuated by the hostility which within a very few years began to grow between them and the inhabitants of New France (Quebec). One factor of no little importance during these first encounters of the English and French cultures transplanted to new shores, was that the French appeared to have greater success in bringing Christianity to the Indians than did the Puritans. One result of this was to make the Indians the ally of the French in many of the international skirmishes which characterized the uneasy peace between the two domains. It tended, likewise, in the folklore of New England to attribute to the French and to their religion whatever of savagery might have been meted out to the English colonists by the Indians. The reasons for the lack of Puritan success in evangelizing the Indians is probably to be found in their relative lack of interest in the matter. The historic mission of John Eliot among the Indians, which led to the translation of the Bible into the Indian tongue, is outstanding because of its rarity, at least in the early days of New England's foundations.

The first sizeable group of Catholics to come to New England came from French Canada and was ministered to by the first two priests who labored in New England, both of them born in France: one of them, Father Matignon, and the other Bishop Cheverus, who was to end his days as the Cardinal Archbishop of Bordeaux. In these days of Catholicism's beginnings in the early years of the nineteenth century, there was a neighborly welcome extended to the Catholics and to their priests. Even though Congregationalism was maintained as a state Church in Massachusetts for half a century after the Revolution, the pre-Revolutionary anti-Catholicism had died. Few stories of this period are better known in New England than those which surround the person of Bishop Cheverus in the efforts made by the Protestant people of Boston to secure his permanent abode among them when first it was bruited that he would be summoned back to the service of the Church in France. By the end of the second decade of the nineteenth century, it was clear that the Catholic complexion of New England would not be altogether French. In small numbers, but growing ever larger, Catholic migration from Ireland, England, and the

Southern states tended to produce a majority which was non-French.

The great influx of immigrants of Irish stock to New England came during the decade 1846-1856. These were the years of the successive potatoe famines in Ireland, and since Boston and the other New England ports were of all those in the United States closest to Ireland, they received a very great share of those who were fleeing the famine-swept Ireland. The citizenry of Boston prior to this time had been so homogeneous, being composed almost entirely of the genus called then and now "Yankee," that the entry in large numbers of a group of a different culture and a different religious pattern was bound to create shock waves which would not soon diminish in intensity. Today, more than a century later, the largest social and cultural problem of New England is still the relationship between the Yankee and the newer arrivals of Irish, French, Italian, Polish and of Lithuanian origin. It is over-simplification to regard this as a struggle, particularly to regard it as a struggle between Protestant and Catholic in these terms alone. It is not truly to be regarded as a struggle, because now that three and more generations of immigrants have dwelt in New England beside the older inhabitants, all parties have necessarily come to the conclusion that their future is bound up in living together. The question which history poses is how peace rather than victory may be brought to pass.

As in many other parts of the world, the Irish immigrants seem to have served a Providential purpose in that they brought the Catholic faith into New England, as those who spoke English and not as those speaking a foreign tongue. So much that the early Irish immigration represented was new and strange to the New Englander that had they likewise spoken a foreign tongue, one can easily conjecture the many further difficulties which would lie in the path of their acceptance by the New England community. They were, in this way, able to bridge for those of the same faith who were to come later the gap which linguistic difficulties otherwise would have made harder to cross. Catholic New England today is made up in greatest measure of descendants of the races noted above. Most of them are still proudly conscious of their racial origins, even though less and less these tend to erect walls of division within the Catholic community. The phenomenon noted by sociologists that the second generation immigrant tends in some fashion to be vaguely ashamed of the differences which set his parents apart from the rest of the community and that the third generation immigrant tends to be proud of these same differences, is one which has found ample verification in New England.

There have been several recent studies by Professor Oscar Hnadlin of Harvard University, "Boston's Immigrants" and "The Uprooted" which with a great and scholarly detail give the facts of immigration into New England and the reaction on the part of New Englanders to these facts. Perhaps we could set forth the dynamic of this meeting of two cultural strains in terms of what Professor Toynbee has made well-known in his "Study of History" as "challenge and response."

The initial distribution of Catholic immigrants into the six New England states was uneven. Most of them arrived through the Port of Boston and many of these tended to stay in Boston or the immediate vicinity. Others, arriving in New York, made their way to Connecticut and Western Massachusetts. Another group, in great measure French-Canadian from both Quebec and Acadia, came south to form large settlements in Maine, New Hampshire, Vermont and eventually the southernmost tier of states. The industrial revolution which at the mid-century was creating new patterns of economic and industrial life for New England found the new immigrants a boon. The textile mills of New England were in large measure staffed by the newcomers of predominantly Catholic origin. Since, particularly in New England, the soil was inhospitable few of the immigrants took to the land. The only exceptions to this seem to have been the Canadian migrants in Northern New England and the Poles in Western Massachusetts and Connecticut. Since they tended to congregate in urban centers and since one of their first aims was to secure immediate American citizenship, they became a political force of great consequence in every city in New England. They did not always vote for the same party. Indeed, at times their intra-group frictions would almost compel them to vote for opposite parties, at any given time. Yet by the close of the Civil War, when the initial disabilities against the immigrant had disappeared, everyone was conscious of the political force residing in this large number of as yet non-assimilated Americans. In those days before the term "melting pot" had come into use, it was nonetheless taken for granted that each wave of migration would lose itself as it beat upon irrefragable rock of American cultural unity. The politicians therefore were anxious that the immigrant should quickly find his place in society by assimilating the common American ideals and by acquiring the American sense of civic communal responsibility.

We cannot understand the change which has taken part in the thinking of the Catholic immigrant folk and their descendants unless we recognize that these secular influences had a tremendous bearing on them. We must recognize, first of all, the very great natural virtues which the New England Yankee exemplified in his life—virtues of honesty, confidence in his neighbor, thrift, foresight and patriotism. Many of the uprooted came from lands where, for one reason or another, it had been impossible for centuries to erect such standards in public life and where the struggle had been for survival alone. Just as the traces of the struggle gave an appearance of crudity to those who brought with them the Catholic Faith, so the existence of these obvious virtues in the Yankee tended, despite whatever the mutual antagonism, to promote admiration and imitation. In many ways socially and culturally, the standards which the immigrant found in New England a century or more ago, he has adopted as his own. There is none more proud of his New England inheritance than one whose family beginnings here date more than two centuries after the arrival of the Mayflower. This is one of the facts of New England life which needs constantly to be kept in mind, that as the Yankee became less dominant by force of numbers, he was able nonetheless to keep the dominance of the political order which he had painfully evolved and of the society upon which he had set the seal of his approval.

It would not be fair to say that the immigrant or the descendant of the immigrant finds his final satisfaction in a complete acceptance by a dominant Yankee caste. This is an over-simplification of a complex social situation. What has happened, of course, is that as the bonds of acquaintanceship and then of friendship were multiplied among the members of the community, more and more were broken down the cultural enclaves within which the immigrant in his first years would tend to remain. This is part of the pattern of the long-range response of the New Englander and the Catholic to each other.

Much of what would be most striking and, indeed, most interesting in the impact of these diverse cultures upon one another is already in the realm of history. Our concern is in more of the present tense. In another chapter, all too briefly, the history of the Catholic Church in America has been told. We must recognize that perhaps nowhere more than in New England have there been attempts on the part of the immigrants to wall themselves off from the society around them and to preserve as much as possible the likeness of the Fatherland left behind. In this effort, the Church was used as the center around which all the old loyalties could be gathered. Such manifestations are however no longer true of the Catholic people in New England, even in the so-called national parishes, which were erected for the temporary purpose of adjustment to a new language and a new land. There is on the part of most of the clergy a recognition that within several generations at most these parishes will have served their purpose. It is three decades now since the most outstanding example in the history of New England Catholic separatism took place. For several years ecclesiastical sanctions had to be exercised in one diocese against those who sought for an exclusive French indoctrination in the Catholic high schools. Wise counsel prevailed and calm was soon restored and the plans for English teaching were carried out.

As of now, it would seem that in New England the predominant Catholic strain will not much longer continue to be Irish. It will within a few decades become either French or Italian. The much discussed tendency of the Irish to marry late in life or not to marry at all has reflected itself in similar traits in the Irish-American of today with resultant smaller families.

In New England as that part of the United States which has the greatest percentage of Catholics (almost 50%), it is possible to offer, as it were, a showcase of what a Catholic America might mean to those who wonder, or are perhaps apprehensive about such a future. There are in New England at the present time twenty-five Catholic colleges. There are 300,000 children in Catholic schools fully supported by the people themselves. There is a highly organized Curia in each of the 11 dioceses which make up New England. There is a sense of the apostolate which has made good use of press and radio and there has been a very great contribution of vocations to the priesthood and the religious life, which is perhaps in proportion greater than in other parts of the United States. These facts are statistically verifiable but facts not equally verifiable will be of interest to the outside observer. He will find in New England, for example, a very great conservatism on the part of the average Catholic, priest or layman. He will find a sense of patriotism, which is very real and yet which at times will betray something of chauvinism or xenophobia. At the present time, the Catholic population of New England tends by and large to be Democratic in its political allegiance, but in the last Presidential election it gave very many votes, indeed, to the Republican candidate, prompted either by a fear of Communist influence into the camp of his opponent or by more personal reasons concerning the domestic life of his opponent. The alliance between the Democrats of the South and the North, which has governed for most of the past half-century, has within it certain special strains when applied to New England. The tendency toward liberalism found in most of our

Northern cities in the Democratic camp finds not too many adherents in New England. The detached observer tends to impute most of these reactions on the part of our Catholic people to their religious background. There is no question but that at the moment the Catholics of New England are gravely preoccupied with the menace of World Communism. They are thus easily aroused as they were several years ago by any suspicion of a plot within American public life itself to weaken this country vis-a-vis the Soviet Union.

The New England Catholics who are the inheritors of the tradition of the Abolitionists who brought slavery to its end are nonetheless not faced with the problems of large numbers of Negroes in this region. It can be said that acceptance of outgroups is growing and that faced, as they will be in the future with increasing numbers of Negroes, the Catholic people will offer an outstretched hand and a united front to accept them in every way. No mention has been made in this chapter of relations of the Catholic people to the considerable number of Jewish folk resident in New England. There have been episodes of tenseness, particularly during the War years, but the condition of constant working together in business and civic projects has done away with the antagonisms initially present on both sides. The antagonisms, it must be explained, were never so strong as to create the danger of a violent anti-Semitism. At most it would be a species of social anti-Semitism, which would nonetheless be inconsistent with Christian ideals. It is noteworthy that up to the present time, the initiatives of the Holy See relative to Catholic Action and the Apostolate of the Laity has not struck too many sparks on the New England scene. Here again, it may be due to the natural or inbred conservatism of the New England Catholic, it may be his slowness to adapt to that which is new, or it may be due to his state of contentment with things as they are. In all likelihood, the answer is to be found in each of these elements. Within the most recent years, there have been some new centers of Catholic lay action, which show promise of continued growth and extension. There are, however, many other parts of the country with a lesser proportion of Catholics in which Catholic lay action is much better established.

One of the more heartening aspects of the present-day scene is the growing collaboration on the intellectual plane between the Catholic colleges and the great non-Catholic colleges and universities. Not too many years ago, it would be fair to state that their collaboration was minimal if not non-existent. Today, on a very great many planes, there are contacts which are enduring and fruitful. This is something of considerable importance because of the very great esteem in which the things of the mind are held in this part of the United States. Harvard University, for example, the oldest and most prestigious university in the United States, is regarded by many Catholics as a center of Marxist effusion. Ideas such as these tended initially to give a certain air of believability to the assertions made by Father Leonard Feeney, S.J. against Harvard and the whole pattern of its teaching. His condemnation by the Church relieved a situation which was most embarrassing to intellectuals within the Church and within the universities. More and more the professors of the universities are collaborating in the search for truth on a thousand different fronts. Nothing could be a more happy augury than this for a unified society of tomorrow.

In New England, however, perhaps more than in many other sections, the lack of a Catholic intellectual elite is strongly felt. There are many knowledgeable and talented teachers and professors in New England of Catholic origin. However, very few of them do any writing and it is rare to see in the great magazines and periodicals of the country articles written by Catholics or to see new books by Catholic authors of New England derivation. Why this is so, it is difficult to understand. It is something which has however engaged the concern of many leaders of the Church in the past few years, and we may hope that a remedy may soon be found.

One other interesting aspect of New England Catholic life is that of relations with Protestant communions. Father

George Tavard's book, "The Catholic Approach to Protestantism" is one which would seem to have a message for New England Catholics more than to most. In this section, the Protestant Churches are by all means the most sophisticated within their respective denominations in the United States. They are, therefore, considerably removed from the suspicion and bigotry, which in other parts of America, tend to becloud Catholic-Protestant relations. There are in New England many of the great theological schools which have traditionally had their impact upon Protestant thinking. It is, too, the headquarters of several denominations which largely influence Protestant thinking. Here, too, are several of the more prominent Protestant publishing houses. These are reasons which it would seem to make it desirable to initiate that type of rapprochement between Catholics and Protestants on the personal level, which has been commended by the Holy See. It would not be entirely true to say that this has come to pass. Here and there it is being effected on a personal basis but on a much less wide scale than one would expect. The incidence of personal relationships between priests and ministers is perhaps as low as anywhere in the United States. The reason for this is in all likelihood more atavistic than present, more social than religious. While this article has not been explicit in this regard, there is a vast heritage of ancient controversy which tends to be quite clearly remembered at times when friendly cooperation might be most indicated. These would be social in good measure, because the predominant prejudice in New England today could not be truly called religious. With all deference to the Protestant people of New England, it must be said that they do not have an intenseness of religious conviction which could lead to religious bitterness. This is, of course, a general statement and subject to exception. It is on the social level that they tend to remember what were originally religious differences.

For the future, the outlook for Catholicism in New England seems bright, indeed. As I have mentioned above, it is supplying a need for vocations not only for itself but for other parts of the land and other parts of the world. It is growing in a consciousness of Catholic unity rather than ethnic diversity. It is reaching out within its various strains of tradition to conserve those things which are most precious while not bothering to retain those which are harmful and confusing. One of the greatest of New England bishops, Bishop DeGoesbriand of Burlington, set this pattern in the early nineteenth century with the immigrants from Quebec. It is one which has brought blessings to this diocese and to New England. It is one which is finding greater acceptance every day throughout New England. As this sense of unity grows, there will, we may be sure, come to realization a new concept of Catholicism on the march. The relative lack of growth within the past few decades will be succeeded, if present indications are true, by a tremendous intensification of Catholic life, which cannot but lead to a drawing into that Catholic life of those who are now outside the fold. The Catholic hierarchy of New England is a dynamic one and in spite of the conservatism mentioned above, it is constantly trying new methods for the new day. This is particularly true of the renowned Archbishop Cushing of Boston, who already within his lifetime has become a legend throughout the United States and who has accomplished much that would in previous days have seemed impossible by a total identification of himself with his flock.

New England, which in the past has meant so much to the United States by way of leadership and example, may have its greatest contribution yet to give in the sphere of religion. Here there has been tested out for America an issue which has been such a troubled one to many non-Catholics—the problem of a Catholic majority and its impact on freedom of the individual conscience. New England has had the Catholic majority but has not imposed a theocracy. Its people are concerned rather with bringing themselves and their neighbors into the Kingdom of God. For all this their past is a happy prologue and their present a great promise.

CHAPTER TEN

The Catholic Church in the
Middle Atlantic Region

BY JOSEPH N. MOODY

ALTHOUGH AMERICAN CULTURE is profoundly European in its origins, we can nevertheless speak broadly of an American type of Western man who has been molded by a common language, fundamental law and political institutions; by a more or less common attitude towards life and society; by the unifying effect of a highly integrated economy and by the pervasive influence of mechanized communication and popular entertainment; and by the considerable mobility of the American population. These unifying factors, however, have not obliterated the powerful regional characteristics which still play their differentiating role in American society. Accordingly, this study of the Catholic Church

Joseph N. Moody has taught history at Cathedral College, New York City, Notre Dame College, Staten Island, the College of New Rochelle, and the Catholic University of America. He is presently chairman of the New York region of the Religious Education Association.

in America wisely considers the situation of Catholics in various important sections of this vast continental nation.

In this chapter we shall deal with the area known as the Middle Atlantic States—from the Potomac River to the Canadian border, excluding New England, and from the Atlantic Ocean to the Western slopes of the Appalachian mountains. It embraces the states of New York, New Jersey, Pennsylvania, Delaware, Maryland, West Virginia, and the District of Columbia. This grouping, which has the approval of geographers and sociologists, is not entirely satisfactory from the viewpoint of regional characteristics. The Southern fringe of the area, particularly Southern Maryland where Catholicism has played a considerable role, belongs culturally to the "South"; while the area around Pittsburgh and the state of West Virginia belongs economically to the great industrial complex of the Middle West. But basically, the designation "Middle Atlantic" can be accepted as a working concept.

The classic study, *American Regionalism,* by Howard W. Odum and Henry E. Moore (Henry Holt, New York, 1938), makes the following generalizations in regard to this region. It is the wealthiest in the United States, containing the financial center and the greatest concentration of capital, as well as the highest ratio of retail sales. Its mineral wealth made it an early center of manufacturing and the first home of the coal-steel industry. It is important in education and culture, and leads in publishing, music, theater, the arts, and literature. It has the highest density of population. As the gateway to America, it has a high proportion of foreign born, with the greatest ethnic mixture. Hence, it has been considered the most typically American in the specific sense of an illustration of the operation of the "melting pot." This was true even in colonial days. Colonial New York had English, Germans, Dutch,—the Roosevelts are descendants of this strain—Swedes, Scotch, Irish, French, Spanish, and West Indian. Pennsylvania was the only colony, except Maryland in its earlier history, which granted toleration to Roman Catholics. Thus with "all phases of the Christian religion, and all branches of the Teutonic and Celtic races, Pennsylvania set the original type to which all America has conformed: that of racial inter-mixture on the basis of religious and political equality." Today, of course, the variety is more bewildering with "men of every nation under heaven." To give but one example, the region is the cradle of American Jewry and contains more Jews than the whole population of Jefferson's America.

The region is overwhelmingly urban (over 75%), with 40% industrial workers and 15% farmers, the latter being specialized in dairy products, fruits, and vegetables. The region has the highest expenditures for health, charity, and correction, with accompanying high taxation. It has progressive social legislation in most of its states.

For the specific purpose of this study, we may go beyond this list and hazard the following:

1. This region is the seed-ground of American Catholicism. During the period of the exploration of the New World, Catholic missionaries played an heroic pioneering role. French priests, predominantly Jesuits, established Catholic centers among the Indians in northern New England, and made considerable progress among the aborigines despite the hostility of the English settlers. The record of Père Isaac Jogues and his companions in Northern and Central New York is one of the most inspiring in the missionary annals of the Church. Other priests pushed down the Great Lakes with the explorers and trappers, and visited most of the great Mississippi watershed. From the other direction, Spanish padres worked along the Gulf Coast, in the South-West, and ultimately strung that beautiful chain of missions along the Pacific Coast as far as San Francisco. These efforts have had great inspirational value for American Catholicism, but the Church in America today is almost exclusively a development of the tiny cell of colonial Catholicism in Maryland and Pennsylvania, reinforced by successive waves of immigrants. Immediately following the War of Independence this Catholic minority of about 25,000 with 24 priests, all of them Jesuits before the suppression of the Society, was given

a bishop who set up the primatial see at Baltimore in Maryland. The existence of this organized Catholic Church in the vital seaboard area, with an attitude of loyalty to American institutions, provided the mold into which the raw material of European immigration was poured. It also provided the missionary impulse for the first permanent Catholic efforts on the expanding frontier. This region, consequently, has been the root from which American Catholicism has grown.

2. It provided the first contact with the Church for the bulk of arriving immigrants, the majority of whom came to America through the port of New York. Consequently, it was the center of whatever agencies came to be established to facilitate the placement of various national groups. These organizations, financed by European Catholics, were of considerable assistance to the new immigrants, both materially and spiritually.

3. It has a rather high density of Catholic population. For at least a century Catholics have played an increasing role in the political and social life of this area.

4. It is still the area best known to visitors from abroad, and impressions of American Catholicism are generally drawn from contact with the large cities of the Northeast. This is unfortunate in that one cannot derive a balanced picture of the Church in America from a visit to this area. But it is inevitable that the attitude of American Catholicism to current problems would be judged in large part by the statements of Catholic leaders in the commercial capital of New York and the political capital of Washington. The importance of the former city in radio and television broadcasting gives an added dimension to Catholic activity in New York.

It is extremely difficult to fix regional traits with any exactitude. It would be generally agreed that the Northeast would be more conservative than the inland regions and more interested in international and European questions. Do these flow over into the religious field and affect Catholics? It does seem that Catholics in the Northeast are more reluctant to change established patterns than their coreligionists in the Mid-west. The recent decree of the new Easter liturgy met with slight response in this area, while it was adopted in many dioceses in the West. Generally, the Mid-west has taken the lead in the liturgical movement with Chicago, Saint Louis, and Saint John, Minnesota, as recognized centers. The same area has been more active in the successful Cana Conferences and Christian Family Movement to promote a spiritual approach to marriage. A recent survey on the teaching of papal social doctrine in Catholic colleges showed that there was a higher proportion of such teaching in the West than in the Northeast. In the whole field of Catholic Action, while there would be nuances rather than sharp distinctions, one would discover more conservative tendencies in the East, and greater experimentation in the West.

Unquestionably, Catholics in this area share with their non-Catholic fellow-citizens a preoccupation with European affairs. There is great sympathy for the work of the Church both in the free and dominated countries. News of Catholic activity in any European nation is eagerly received and lectures from visitors or Americans on these subjects is assured of a favorable response. Catholics in this region have taken the initiative in providing material aid for their brothers abroad. Similarly, the leading American foreign mission society was founded at Maryknoll, near New York, where it still maintains its headquarters, while its first junior seminary is located in Pennsylvania.

This interest does not necessarily involve sympathy for European political problems nor for international movements. The cleavage between "internationalists" and "isolationists" seriously affects Catholics in the Middle Atlantic region. Some diocesan newspapers, such as the Brooklyn *Tablet*, take a highly nationalist position and are critical of the UN, UNESCO, foreign aid, etc.; while the influential Jesuit weekly *America* and the lay-directed *Commonweal* defend the diametrically opposite positions. The craving of a suspect Catholic minority to refute the charge that they are not "fully American" because of their international religious connections may account for this phenomenon. The ethnic background of some immigrants may also be a factor. Whatever the cause, a considerable proportion of the seaboard Catholics is not conspicuously international-minded.

The Middle Atlantic region illustrates all the problems that have faced American Catholics, and generally in a more acute form:

1. Historically, the basic Catholic problem in America has been the immigrant. The overwhelming problem from the beginning was to provide vast groups of newcomers, almost all poor and illiterate, with churches, clergy, schools and other basic necessities to prevent wholesale defection from the faith. Inevitably, there has been tremendous leakage, but the miracle has been the relative success. In the Spring of each year Fifth Avenue in New York witnesses the Saint Patrick's Day parade; in the Fall the same thoroughfare sees the observance of Pilsudski Day. While the former in recent years has become multi-national and even has a sprinkling of Negro Catholics, to see the massed thousands of immigrant's sons—110,000 this spring—march in serried ranks under national and religious banners is to grasp the dimensions of the achievement. One can visit the mining and manufacturing regions of Pennsylvania and find in a single town a half-dozen Catholic churches, several with their own schools, each caring for a different national group. Behind each is an amazing story of sacrifice to provide buildings and personnel under the most difficult conditions.

Closely related to the above is the problem of absorbing these many linguistic and cultural groups into a unified Church. With very few exceptions, this has been effected, not without stress, but with remarkable success. The process has unquestionably been assisted by the climate of political democracy and the strong cultural pressure toward uniformity, but the absence of important schisms on a nationality basis in a region that is a mosaic of many Catholic minorities is a real achievement. An exception is a Polish National Church, originating in Scranton, Pennsylvania, toward the end of the nineteenth century, and now claiming 250,000 adherents.

The slackening of European immigration has not diminished this problem. In more recent decades, northern New York has shared in the French-Canadian migration that has its origin in population pressure in the rural Saint Lawrence Valley. This group, coming from an area of strong Catholic culture and practice, from homogeneous centers in rural counties and mill towns, and preserve their own way of life and their Catholic faith with remarkable tenacity. They provide their own clergy and religious institutions and are not deterred by the vigorous social disapproval to which they are often subjected.

An entirely different problem is presented by the recent flood of immigrants from Puerto Rico, and to a lesser extent from other Latin American countries. The bulk of this enormous influx remain in concentrated districts in New York City, although they are beginning to fan out and establish secondary centers as far as the Mid-west. They come from a weak Catholic background,—there are only eleven native Puerto Rican secular priests on an island of 2,300,000 (1950) nominal Catholics—are usually nearly totally uninstructed in the faith, with Catholicism merely a "memory trace." They are unable to provide their own clergy and are generally uninterested in the sacrifices necessary for establishing the material substructure of the faith. Their strong group consciousness and their desire to retain their cultural heritage—a desire strengthened by the fact that many of them are of mixed blood and do not wish to be identified with the American Negro,—coupled with the fact that few American priests speak Spanish creates an almost insuperable obstacle to missionary work among them. Fortunately they move into areas, vacated by earlier immigrants, where churches already exist. Increasing efforts are being made by clergy and lay Catholics to reach them. Coordinated efforts are now being made by Catholic religious and social agencies with some success. Two newly ordained New York priests are working this year in Puerto Rico to familiarize themselves with the people. Nearly a dozen New York seminarians spent last summer doing catechetical work on the island. Spanish is being taught in the Seminary in New York. But there is formidable competition: 200 Protestant chapels and churches, generally well-endowed, have been established in New York City to appeal to the Puerto Ricans and non-Catholic social agencies are equally active.

The present Puerto Rican population of New York City is estimated at 455,000; 350,000 of whom were born in Puerto Rico; 210,000 of these were added from April 1, 1950 to December 31, 1953: 172,000 immigrants, 44,000 births less 6,000 deaths. This group had a crude birth rate of 49.1 per thousand because the immigrant is usually healthy and young and the feeling for family life is very strong (the average age of the Puerto Rican in New York is 20-21, with only 10% over 45). Already they form over 8% of the elementary school population.

These immigrants have a low level of education and technical skill. Hence they usually fill unskilled or semi-skilled vacancies not desired by the native whites. Their median earnings are $1,700 per year as against $2,400 for the city as a whole; but as this is more than twice as much as can be earned in Puerto Rico and as there is no barrier to their entry as they are full citizens, the tide will continue as long as economic conditions warrant.

A third recent immigration has been the Negro from the South or from the West Indies. Of the five American cities with the largest Negro concentration, none is in the South, while four are in the Middle Atlantic region: New York, Philadelphia, Baltimore and Washington (Chicago is the fifth). In this area the Negro has made his greatest advance and many of his leaders have been recruited from this relatively advanced segment. The overwhelming majority of Negroes are Protestant, but Catholics have done well in retaining the occasional Catholic and in winning new converts. There are flourishing Catholic parishes in Negro urban centers in this region, with Negroes found in many churches and in all Catholic activities.

These recent immigrations merely repeat the pattern of the past under new conditions. Generally, the first impact is upon the Middle Atlantic region.

2. A related problem, gathering momentum since World War II, is the large exodus of Catholics from the urban centers to the suburban areas, which have grown prodigiously. Recent statistics show that 55% of American families own their own homes. To make this possible hundreds of thousands of new houses have mushroomed around the larger cities. The rapidity of this development has taxed existing Catholic churches and schools. While new building has progressed rapidly, there is a lag which may be spiritually dangerous to young couples with children. In Hyattsville, Maryland, a suburb of Washington, a pastor recently completed a large parochial school. He had 500 applicants for the first grade class alone. Similar conditions exist in Nassau County, Long Island, in northern New Jersey, and along the Delaware River near Philadelphia.

3. Another problem stems from the fact that the Catholic population in this area is overwhelmingly urban. Hence the Church in the past had to provide for these large concentrations in the cities and at the same time reach out to the scattered Catholics in the rural regions. In thinly settled areas, the Church even in the Northeast is often a missionary organization with considerable difficulty providing for the maintenance of clergy and churches. In several dioceses with this problem such as Albany, New York, the Bishop imposes a tax on the larger parishes to aid the struggling congregations in the countryside. The generosity of the Catholic population has met the need but rural pastors often must struggle to make ends meet. Even in areas such as this, the "wealth" of the American Church is largely urban. It does not include endowments of other accumulations from the past, but depends on the continuing contributions of large bodies of middle and working class Catholics.

4. A favorable factor in this area, as in America generally, has been the ease with which Catholics of diverse lands have adjusted to the climate of political democracy. The example

of the early Catholic core set the precedent. The minority position of Catholics and the desire of the immigrants to gain the protection of citizenship facilitated the process. As early as the 1830's, Alexis de Toqueville in *Democracy in America* noted that Catholics were the most democratic and most republican segment of the population. This has not changed substantially and Catholics in this region, as elsewhere, have avoided the conflict with the enveloping political institutions which have plagued their brethren in several European countries.

5. More difficult has been the adjustment to a cultural climate that was predominantly Protestant and generally hostile. While Catholics never have suffered active persecution, the new immigrants were generally subjected to social and economic pressure and were denied access to prestige positions as long as they remained attached to their national and religious heritage. This was particularly true as long as the immigrants remained concentrated in "little Dublins," "little Italys" and "little Polands." Discrimination of various forms persisted throughout most of the history of this region. The author of this chapter remembers that in his youth in a town near New York he was denied membership in a neighborhood football team because of his religion. While this has largely disappeared as far as the older immigration is concerned, the appearance of secularist tendencies in United States education and cultural life has retarded the rise of Catholics to prominence in these fields. Catholics were able to gain recognition in politics where they could count on a bloc of their fellow nationals; and they slowly won their way in business, sports, entertainment, and the professions. But even in regions of heavy Catholic concentration such as the Middle Atlantic, they are still poorly represented in school administration, boards of foundations, leadership in civic organizations, literature and science. Basically it was the immigrant's struggle for survival which accounts for the cultural poverty of American Catholicism even in the East; but social hostility was a contributing factor.

6. This accounts for a certain feeling of inferiority among

Catholics even in regions of heavy concentration. There is a certain survival of the "we" and "they" attitude toward non-Catholics that is generally not warranted by present conditions, but is a consequence of historic memory.

7. Historically the Church in this region was a proletarian Church. The immigrants sought shelter in urban slums, moved on to factory or mining towns, or became laborers on the canals or railroads. The Catholic expansion in New York State as elsewhere can largely be traced along the routes of the transportation systems where the immigrants provided the cheap labor and where they ultimately established communities and churches. The town of Auburn, New York, (population 37,000) on a branch of the old Erie Canal, is still 75% Catholic, a most unusual proportion anywhere in the United States.

The Catholic clergy have been drawn overwhelmingly from the working class. Even today where the social composition of the Catholic population has radically changed, more than half of the seminarians in the New York Archdiocese are sons of workers.

It was natural that Catholics should provide a large share of the labor movement which developed in response to the rapid industrialization of the country after 1865. Pennsylvania was the center of the serious class conflict of this burgeoning industrial society. The embryonic trade unions from the Molly Maguires and Knights of Labor to the AFL, the United Mine Workers and the modern C.I.O. have had a high proportion of Catholic leadership.

One might have imagined that the clergy would have been nearly unanimous in the support of their working class flocks. It was not always so. The fear of radicalism and the desire not to add fuel to the hostility of the "better elements" frequently led the clergy to conservative positions. The conflict of Archbishop Corrigan of New York in the 1880's with one of his prominent pastors, Father McGlynn, divided his diocese for several years. It largely concerned the priest's support of Henry George's *Single Tax* plan which the clergyman felt would help his miserably poor parishioners. But this hesitation and indifference of some did not create a gulf between the working class and the Church in the industrial Northeast. The cause of labor found a powerful champion in the best-known prelate of the post-Civil War period, John Cardinal Gibbons of Baltimore, who carried the fight for the Knights of Labor to Rome and occasioned a reversal of the prohibition against Catholic membership. Other distinguished episcopal and clerical champions of the labor cause prevented any identification of the Church with an anti-union position and Catholicism in this area has generally retained the loyalty of the bulk of the workers.

8. Generally, the Catholics in this region have had a good record in the other major social question—the status of the Negro. Except in Maryland, only an infinitesimal proportion of the Negroes was Catholic. With the same exception, the constitutions of these states had prohibited slavery from the beginning, but even in the free states the Negro long labored under severe social handicaps. Throughout the nineteenth century, the concentration of the immigrant on his own condition left him little time for the luxury of humane sympathy. The fact that he met the Negro as a competitor for jobs and housing did not tend to develop active support for rights of this minority. The tendency of the immigrant to accept the prevailing cultural standards was another factor. But since the great surge of Negro migration to the North during and after World War I, the conscience of Catholics has been aroused. Pioneer organizations such as the Catholic Interracial Councils have appeared. Catholic schools and institutions were opened to Negroes and they were accepted in seminaries and religious congregations of men and women. Today, practically complete non-segregation in all Catholic activities exists in this area, and informed Negroes have responded with gratitude. Most noteworthy is the situation in the National Capital which geographically and in sentiment belongs to the "South." Although segregation is still practiced in the public schools and in civic facilities, Archbishop O'Boyle has made every Catholic parish and agency completely non-segregated. Thus Catholics have the only non-segregated school system in the District of Columbia, open

to all from the elementary level to the University, the only non-segregated hospitals, orphan homes, etc.

Catholics in the heavily populated Middle Atlantic States can look with pride on the record of their achievements. But there is much left undone. The responsibility of so numerous a body toward the intellectual defense of the Church, so generally neglected during the decades of construction, can no longer be ignored. With this goes the need of educating their people to the deeper implications of Catholicism and to the world-wide responsibilities of Catholics in the present crisis. Catholics in the large Eastern centers must shed their defensive mentality and consider their obligation to penetrate their environment and take their rightful place in the community. To do this they must develop greater flexibility in handling the problems of a pluralistic society. They must develop a more independent lay leadership and so retain the loyalty of their more energetic and able young members. They must prepare a more competently trained clergy to meet the challenge of the time. Briefly, the Church in these older areas of American Catholicism must come of age.

The record offers some hope that they may succeed. The Catholic Universities, particularly those operated by the Jesuits, have made striking gains in the field of scholarship. To meet the needs of Catholic schools in the Archdiocese of New York, newly ordained priests have been sent to various graduate facilities for higher studies. There are apostolic stirrings in the growing body of articulate university-trained Catholic laymen. But there are formidable obstacles. The support and encouragement of Catholics of other lands would be of inestimable assistance. We still draw heavily on the intellectual contributions of European Catholics. But their active sympathy in the tasks ahead is equally valuable. We recall that anti-Americanism originated in the religious field, in that curious excrescence of nineteenth century French politics known as *Americanism*. There are similarities as well as differences between the Abbé Maignen and Mlle. Simone de Beauvoir. Perhaps the cooperation of Catholics on both sides of the Atlantic might have a healing effect in the political crisis of our time.

CHAPTER ELEVEN

The Catholic Church in the
Rural Mid-west

◆

BY EDWARD W. O'ROURKE

Tʀᴀᴅɪᴛɪᴏɴᴀʟʟʏ, the Midwest has been considered synonymous with corn and wheat and cattle. In no other place
in the world is there so large an area of land so fertile.
Fertile soil, a temperate climate, adequate rainfall and an
unusually efficient argiculture make this the garden spot
of the world. In this chapter we shall define the boundaries
of the Mid-west rather broadly including the States of Illinois, Indiana, Iowa, Kansas, Kentucky, Michigan, Minnesota, Missouri, Nebraska, North Dakota, Ohio, South Dakota
and Wisconsin. All of these states except Kentucky are described as "North Central States" by the United States

---

*Edward W. O'Rourke has served for twelve years as an assist-
ant chaplain at the Newman Foundation at the University
of Illinois. He is a member of the Executive Committee of
the National Catholic Rural Life Conference. He has helped
resettle over 1200 Displaced Persons and Refugees in the
Peoria Diocese.*

Bureau of Census. This area is bordered by the Great Lakes on the north, the Ohio River valley on the east and south and on the west by the Missouri River Valley and the Rocky Mountain states.

In spite of the huge expanse of this area there are many ties which bind its peoples together and warrant their being considered as an economic and sociological unit. From an agricultural point of view, this is the great corn and wheat belt of America. The people of this area speak with their own idiom and accent. Most of them are conservative in their political views. This is sometimes referred to as the "Bible Belt," a stronghold of Fundamentalist Protestantism.

In order to form an accurate picture of the Mid-west today we must attend to far reaching changes which are taking place in this area—changes which vitally affect the Church. During the past century the population of the Midwest has changed from one that was dominantly rural to one that is dominantly urban. In 1850, 91 per cent of the population was rural, in 1950 only 42 per cent. Although this is still a great agricultural area, it now has extensive industrial developments. There are rural industries such as meat packing in Kansas City and Chicago and corn and soy bean processing plants in Decatur. There are also heavy industries—the steel mills on the South Shore of Lake Michigan, the automobile factories in Detroit, the Caterpillar Tractor Works in Peoria and the Farm Implement industry in Rock Island and Moline.

Even the rural population has undergone significant changes. Farms in this area are larger and fewer than in 1940 (an 11 per cent decrease in the number of farms in the decade from 1940 to 1950). Yet the value of the products sold off these farms increased by 25.9 per cent even after adjustments were made for price changes. During the same decade there was a 44 per cent increase in the level of living indexes of farm operator families. The number of tractors used increased 101 per cent while there was a 22 per cent decline in the amount spent for hired farm labor. In brief, Mid-west

farms are fewer, more prosperous, and more highly mechanized than they were in 1940.

Even more significant for the Church is the rapid growth
of a rural non-farm population in the Mid-west. Fifty-two per
cent of those listed as "rural" in the 1950 census do not depend upon farming directly for their livelihood. This
increase in rural non-farm population is due in part to the
establishing of factories in the country and small towns. Still
more significant is the growing movement of professional
people and industrial workers out of the cities to make their
homes in rural areas.

The presence of many non-farm families in a country community will affect its attitudes and activities. This new blood
may give rise to personality clashes, but it can lead to a
better community life. If the newcomers are absorbed into
the parishes and other organizations of the community, they
will bring with them new ideas and more vitality. Isolated
from other segments of the population, rural people tend to
be narrow minded and unprogressive.

In spite of these changes among rural people of the Mid-
west, there is a feature of farm life in America which remains and which makes it very much different from farm
life in most of Europe. We refer to the fact that most American farm families do not live in villages as do many European
farm families. In America the farmer and his family live on
a homestead separated from his nearest neighbor by a half
mile or more. This isolation from other families was once a
handicap. Better means of travel and communication has removed almost all the disadvantages of this arrangement.
Many real advantages remain. The American farm family is
sufficiently apart from other families to enable it to work
and pray and recreate as a unit. A close-knit wholesome
family life is one of the best features of rural life in America.
Farming here is a family enterprise. The farm boy or girl is
usually given work commensurate with his age and ability.
Hence, he feels wanted and develops a sense of responsibility.
Today in America it can be truly said that the country is the
natural habitat of the family.

This quick survey of agriculture and industry in the Mid-west provides us with the context which will enable us to better understand the position of the Church in this area. The following data taken from *The Official Catholic Directory for 1956* reflects the Church's position more directly. In the Mid-west there are 10,066,022 Catholics or 22.4 per cent of the total population. These Catholics are served by 17,413 priests, one priest for every 569 persons. There is an enrollment of 1,316,956 in Catholic elementary schools and 252,-171 in Catholic high schools. There are 6,525 parishes and 1,364 missions. Baptisms in 1954 totaled 414,672; 13,598 seminarians are preparing for the priesthood in this area.

It is difficult to prove the extent to which these statistics are applicable to the rural communities of the Mid-west. However, through the efforts of the Reverend Father Irvin R. Will, Rural Life Director of the Diocese of Springfield in Illinois, we have statistics which will throw considerable light on the question. The Springfield Diocese is a typical non-metropolitan area of the Mid-west.

In the Springfield Diocese 70 per cent of the Catholic families are urban and 30 per cent rural. Among the rural families 16 per cent operate farms and 14 per cent are rural non-farm. 14,162 children attend the Catholic elementary schools, representing 76 per cent of all Catholic children in the Diocese; 20 per cent of these 14,162 children are rural, 80 per cent urban; 46 per cent of the Catholics in high school are in Catholic schools. It is interesting to note that among the 417 nuns teaching in Grade Schools of the Diocese, 48 per cent were reared in rural areas.

These statistics help to confirm our opinion that the Church is vigorous and growing in the rural communities of the Mid-west. Very little immorality is found among rural Catholic families of this area. The location of some families makes it impossible for some children to attend Catholic schools. In most of these instances, religious instruction in the home and classes conducted under the auspices of the Confraternity of Christian Doctrine help keep the Faith strong and pure among these people.

At the turn of the century there were 200,000 school districts in the United States. Many of these were tiny rural districts with one room elementary schools serving as attendance units. Today only 63,000 districts remain. Most of the one room schools have been replaced by consolidated schools in villages and towns. This consolidation has increased attendance at Catholic schools. Children formerly attending one room public schools in the open country now go to the parochial schools. In many states public bus transportation is made available to parochial school children.

Protestant churches in rural America have suffered greatly from small membership and poor attendance at their services. This is due in part to a decrease in population in some rural areas and in part to the fact that Protestant churches in America have been splintered into more than 300 sects. The Catholic Church here has not been greatly troubled by problems of this sort, because of the unity of the Church and the high rate of church attendance found among American Catholics. In a nation wide poll conducted by an independent opinion-research firm, it was discovered that 99 per cent of the American people believe in God. However 32 per cent of the Protestants and 18 per cent of the Catholics don't attend Church service. Only 25 per cent of the Protestants and 62 per cent of the Catholics attend church services every Sunday.[1]

In America there is a very close bond of understanding between the clergy and laity, particularly in the rural Midwest. Visitors from Europe invariably comment on the ease with which Catholic rural people approach their priests and feel at home with them. The small size of rural parishes facilitates this interchange and makes it possible for rural priests to visit frequently at the homes of their parishioners. Today, almost all of the recently ordained priests in the Mid-west are natives of the dioceses in which they labor. This eliminates conflicts which formerly occurred when priests of different nationalities and tongues were made pastors of American congregations.

---

1. The Catholic Digest. Jan. 1953, pp. 2-8.

A number of circumstances, therefore, are nurturing a very excellent religious life among rural Catholics in the Mid-west. These circumstances include the religious and civil liberties guaranteed by the Constitution of the United States, the growing number of parishes and parochial schools in rural communities, the challenge which a minority religious group experiences when surrounded by persons of other faiths, the close-knit home life which we described above and the wholesome impact which contact with nature and farm work has traditionally had upon the faith and morals of rural people.

Catholics in rural communities of the Mid-west have numerous contacts with their Protestant neighbors. Rural communities involve a relatively small number of families in the community. Hay making, harvesting and other farm jobs require the help of neighbors. In most communities Catholics and non-Catholics exchange help indiscriminately.

Catholics work and recreate with persons of other faiths in farm organizations such as the Farm Bureau, Farmers Union and the Grange. Catholic boys and girls participate in the same 4-H Clubs, Future Farmer and Future Homemaker Clubs to which Protestant boys and girls belong. These farm organizations and rural youth clubs are not affiliated with any particular church, but do inculcate respect for God and country and encourage members to be active in the religious programs of their churches.

The bigotry once prevalent in some dominantly Protestant communities has nearly disappeared. Incidental manifestations of anti-Catholic feeling occur occasionally, especially when there is a question of employing a Catholic teacher in a public school or electing a Catholic to a position on a school board. Some Mid-west Protestants still feel that the public school should be a mouthpiece for their beliefs and policies.

Disagreement over the extent to which Church and State should be separated is a source of conflict among the people of the rural Mid-west as well as those of other parts of the United States. The First Amendment of the Constitution

certainly rules out the establishment of a state religion or
the granting of special advantages to a particular church. A
Supreme Court ruling handed down in 1948 declared that
this Amendment prohibits government aid to any and all
religious sects.[2] This decision has a bearing upon religious
education since it prohibits the use of public school facilities
for instruction in religion. Representatives of the Catholic,
Protestant and Jewish faiths still conduct religious instruction for children attending public schools. However, this instruction must be arranged in rooms not a part of the school
itself.

Debate over Church-State relationships brings out many
basic differences between Catholic and non-Catholic religious
convictions. Some Protestant leaders have overtly joined
forces with anti-religious organizations in their effort to
"keep high the wall of separation of Church and State." The
result is an organization entitled "Protestants and Other
Americans United for Separation of Church and State"
(POAU). The chief bond which unites its members is a
common hatred for the Catholic Church.

One of the tasks confronting the Church in the rural Mid-
west is that of developing more and better lay leadership.
Some leadership training is obtained by the officers and committee chairmen of organizations such as the Holy Name
Society, St. Vincent de Paul Society, Council of Catholic
Men, Altar and Rosary Society, and Council of Catholic
Women. However, in most parishes the officers of these
organizations tend to lean heavily on the pastor for all plans
and decisions. The programs of most of these organizations
are confined chiefly to fund raising, recreational events and
encouraging certain devotional practices. The impact of
these organizations on the general environment is not great.

The Legion of Mary and the Christian Family Movement
are more specifically apostolic in their objectives and techniques. The Knights of Columbus promote and finance many
excellent charitable projects. They have also accomplished an

---

2. The McCullom Case. 333 U. S. 203.

outstanding apostolic work through their Religious Information Bureau. This Bureau purchases advertising space from many magazines and newspapers to acquaint non-Catholics with the Church and her teachings and to dispel some of the bigotry and misinformation which still plague many such persons. Pamphlets about the Faith and a comprehensive correspondence course in Catholic Doctrine are among the services of the Bureau. This program is especially valuable in the Mid-west where Catholics are a minority and many non-Catholics have never met a priest.

There should be an increase in the number of converts to the Church in the Mid-west during the next decade. The present rate of conversion is not impressive. In 1954 there were 51,988 converts in the Mid-west which is only one convert per 190 Catholics and 7.7 per parish. The lessening of bigotry and more widespread knowledge of the Faith described earlier in this chapter should prepare the way for many new members of the Church. The large number of seminarians preparing for the priesthood in the Mid-west (13,598) should assure an adequate number of priests to contact and instruct prospective converts.

Rural parishes will thrive or regress in proportion to their accommodation to the two features of rural community life mentioned above; namely, the advent of many new non-farm families in the countryside and the close knit family life made possible by the location of farms distinct from each other and the division of farm work among members of the family.

The National Catholic Rural Life Conference persistently reminds rural pastors and lay people of these features of rural life and suggests ways of utilizing them for the betterment of parish life. Parish devotional and recreational programs should never be put into competition with family activities. For example, a pastor would be foolish to urge large rural families to leave their homes on a winter night to come to the church to recite the Rosary. It would be much more realistic to encourage each family to recite the Rosary in their homes.

New members of a rural community should identify themselves with the local parish, school, clubs, etc. Homesteading will be in no way advantageous to them if they commute to the city for their liturgical and recreational activities as well as their work.

We have reason to hope that in the rural Mid-west a way of life is developing which is thoroughly Catholic, in keeping with the best traditions of America and preserving those ideals found among rural people in all parts of the world.

CHAPTER TWELVE

The Catholic Church in the Deep South

———— ◆ ————

BY DALE FRANCIS

THERE IS A STORY that is told of a northern Catholic, passing through a southern city on a Sunday. A colored boy was playing along the side of the street and the motorist stopped to ask directions to the nearest Catholic Church.

The little boy smiled, gave precise directions to the lone church on the other side of town. The motorist surprised at such clear directions, thanked the boy and asked, "Are you a Catholic, Son?"

"No, Sir," the boy said, shaking his head vigorously, "bad enough to be colored down here."

This story is appropriate precisely because it is dated. There was a day it was difficult to be a Catholic in the south,

---

Dale Francis, upon his conversion to Catholicism, has been editor of the North Carolina Catholic paper, Publications Director at the University of Notre Dame, and director of a Catholic Information Center in Charlotte, N.C., where he continued his missionary work over local radio stations. He is now in Cuba studying the approach to the Latin American mind to counteract Marxist and Protestant propaganda.

211

a day when the Ku Klux Klan told Catholics to get out of the city, when priests were spat upon, when worldly wise Catholics kept quiet about their faith.

That day has passed. Now priests are respected citizens, the Catholic Church is growing rapidly and Catholics exert an influence on the south out of proportion to their still small numbers.

Of course, there have always been Catholic centers in the south. New Orleans is a strongly Catholic city. There have been considerable numbers Catholics in such cities as Savannah, Charleston and scatterings of Catholic concentration in varied areas from Texas to Florida.

But most of the south has been and still is strongly Protestant. Those Catholics who settled in small southern cities soon lost their faith because of the lack of priests and it is not uncommon to find Baptists with French or Irish names.

Typical among the southern states is North Carolina, which combines four types of southerners within its borders. North Carolina is slightly larger than England in area, stretches from the Smoky Mountains in the west to the Atlantic Ocean on the east. In the west, the mountain people live in their seclusion. The central portion of the state is industrial, textiles, cigarettes, hosiery. The eastern area is largely argricultural, cotton and tobacco, and on the coast there are the fishermen.

There are more than four million people in North Carolina; less than one per cent of these are Catholics. Ten years ago there were only 12,000 Catholics in the state but since that time there have been more than 6,000 converts from Protestantism and this, added to Catholics who have come from the north and the natural growth of Catholic families already there, have increased the Catholic population by 300% since 1945.

Even more significant than the increase in numbers is the attitude of non-Catholics toward the Catholic Church. A generation ago, inflamed by the mouthings of bigots and ignorant of the truth about the Church, the people hated the Catholic Church. One priest told of his first visit in a small rural community. As he walked down the street, the people stared at him in hatred. One man came up to him and spat on him. There is a Catholic Church in that city now and, except for the little children, all of the members are converts. The priest who serves them from a nearby city is highly respected in the community.

The state university once had an unwritten rule that no Catholics could sit on the faculty. Now there are many Catholics teaching there and one of the highest officials of the university is a Catholic. One of the oldest colleges in the state—Woodrow Wilson was a graduate—had a regulation that banned Catholics from the student body. A few years ago a small group of students became Catholics, the old rule was abandoned and one of the graduates of this college is now studying for the priesthood.

This change in attitude did not come overnight. It came after years of hard work on the part of zealous priests and lay people. Today under the guidance of the Most Reverend Vincent S. Waters, Bishop of Raleigh, the Catholic Church is moving ahead.

When Bishop Waters arrived in North Carolina in 1945 he measured the problems of the state. Catholics are widely scattered. A priest may have a parish that is larger in area than the whole of Belgium and the Netherlands combined. Some Catholics must go 40 miles or more to Mass—and they do it.

Bishop Waters met this problem by uniting all of the Catholics in the state into a single laymen's organization. Once a year the Catholics of the state meet together to discuss common problems, plan projects to help the faith. The organization has given a sense of unity to the scattered Catholics in the state.

They are further bound together by the Catholic newspaper in the state. This 12 page weekly has more than 6,000 subscribers, brings not only international and national Catholic news but the news of other North Carolina parishes.

It was through the laymen's association and the newspaper that Bishop Waters and his auxiliary, Bishop James Navagh,

were able to carry out one of the most ambitious projects
attempted by the Catholics in the state.

During the month of October for the last two years, the
Catholics of North Carolina knock on the doors of their non-
Catholic neighbors to ask them to take instructions in the
Catholic faith. Hundreds of thousands of non-Catholics are
given personal invitations and with the invitation a pamphlet
explaining the beliefs of Catholics. The result has been that
thousands of people have learned about the church for the
first time and last year nearly 800 of them became Catholics.

Two fully equipped automobile trailers carry the truths of
the Catholic Church to smaller communities where there are
no Catholics. These trailers are fully equipped chapels and
the back platforms are arranged so that sound motion pictures may be shown. When the trailer arrives in a community
a vacant lot is chosen. Cartoons are shown on the screen, then
a priest appears, introduces himself, speaks briefly about the
Church. A film on the Mass is then shown, a sermon is given
and the open air audience has learned for the first time something about the Catholic Church.

Radio and television are used, too. One radio program,
conducted by a Catholic layman, allowed non-Catholics to
phone the broadcaster while he was on the air to ask him
questions about the Catholic Church. An estimated half
million people listened to this program every week and once
more than 200 Protestants pledged to say the rosary daily
when the broadcaster asked they do so.

There are two full scale Catholic information centers
in the state—both of them located in the heart of the business
districts of the two largest cities in the state. Nearly 300
Protestant ministers have come in to the center in one city
to take away Catholic literature.

Parish organizations often take on special tasks connected
with the minority position of the Church in the state. In one
city parish, a group of 40 young men have formed an organization to study the teachings of the Church and to practice
talks that explain the faith. Bishop Navagh is currently training dozens of lay people to act as lay catechists.

Catholic schools are highly respected in North Carolina. Protestants often send their children to Catholic schools, knowing they'll get a better education there than they could in public schools. In some North Carolina communities well over half the students in Catholic schools are non-Catholics.

Four Catholic hospitals in North Carolina serve non-Catholics as well as Catholics. They have done much to increase the prestige of the Church in the state. Like the Catholic schools, the Catholic hospitals are integrated racially.

The Catholic Church in North Carolina has never recognized any color bar but in the last few years the Church has been vigilant in the battle for integration. When Bishop Waters closed a Catholic Church that was serving colored Catholics exclusively and ordered them to merge with a nearby parish serving the white people, secular newspapers managed a rebellion by their overplay of the event. Some white Catholics boycotted the parish church, drove many miles to another church in another state. But Bishop Waters' pastoral letter on the question gained widespread attention all over the nation and became one of the most widely quoted documents of the year.

Except for this one flurry, which was largely brought about by the interference of non-Catholics, there has been no unpleasant reactions to integration. The laymen's association was from its origin an inter-social organization and there have always been Negroes among the officers of the organization. When the Supreme Court ruled state segregation laws were unconstitutional, the Church in North Carolina, moved quickly to integrate the schools. In North Carolina, only Catholic schools are integrated. The Catholic Church in the south has clearly led the entire south in this important matter.

Where the Catholic Church has the opportunity to lead in integration, there are less possibilities of leadership in other social problems. The very smallness of numbers makes it impossible for the Church to give the leadership in all things.

Yet when in southern states a rash of anti-labor feeling

brought so-called right-to-work laws, which banned union shops and placed other hardships on labor unions, it was the Catholic Church that struck out most boldly against these restrictions.

The Catholic Committee of the South has long been a leader in the fight for social justice and it has an importance far beyond what might be expected. In Louisiana, almost the entire battle against the right-to-work bills was carried by Catholic priests and laymen.

There are some observers who say the Catholic Church in the south is the hope of the Church in the United States. It is certainly true that in the south there are the greatest opportunities for growth. It is true, too, that bishops, priests and lay people in the south are zealous for the Church and her growth. This zeal is already bringing results, it may bring even greater results in the future.

CHAPTER THIRTEEN

The Catholic Church in Louisiana

———— ❖ ————

BY JOSEPH B. GREMILLION

"A CATHOLIC SAHARA" best describes the southeastern quarter of the United States.

In 1861 the ten states extending from Louisiana and Arkansas along the Mississippi River in the west, to Virginia and Georgia along the Atlantic Coast to the east, formed, with Texas, the ill-fated Confederate Army in defense of states' rights and slavery, becoming a battleground for the fratricidal four-year "War Between the States" which officially freed the Negro.

Only 1,367,000 Catholics, a mere 4.8 per cent of the region's inhabitants, reside as a diaspora in a population of 28,768,000 in an area of 485,214 square miles. In this heavily

———————————————————————————

Joseph B. Gremillion is pastor of St. Joseph's Church, Shreveport, Louisiana. He has conducted a survey of Relief-Refugee conditions in Germany, Austria, Trieste and Italy for War Relief Services of the National Catholic Welfare Conference. A frequent contributor to Catholic publications, Father Gremillion will publish his first book this year, The Journal of a Southern Pastor, *Fides Publishers.*

rural quadrant, we find Catholics grouped as small minorities in the larger cities. Most outstanding demographically is the fact that we find 59 per cent of the Church's few southern adherents concentrated in one oasis, one sector of the single state of Louisiana.

In an arc fanning out 150 miles north and westward from the city of New Orleans live 808,690 Catholics, the majority of whom bear French names like Lemoine and Mouton, live in cities like Baton Rouge and Lafayette, in farming communities like Napoleonville and Grosse Tete, or along silted delta streams like Bayou La Fourche and Riviere Rouge. The Archdiocese of New Orleans and the Diocese of Lafayette, with 500,690 and 308,000 Catholics respectively, preside over this Catholic oasis. The state's third diocese, that of Alexandria, is more typical of the whole U. S. Southland— heavily Protestant, with a predominance of the Baptist and Methodist sects, in a population made up of native-born Anglo-Saxons and slave-scarred Negroes.

This "French" Louisiana differs from her neighbors, differs in origin and history, in nomenclature and *mode de vie,* in its civil code Napoleon, customs and cuisine, in culture and religion. Today, these differences are disappearing. Louisiana has been a part of the United States since 1803, and the melting pot has been boiling here also. The daily journals and national magazines, the cinema, radio and TV accelerate the process of assimilation.

You can still hear French spoken in the village square and along the levees—with an *accent douce* and a vocabulary harking back to Louis Quatorze, a reminder that we have been culturally isolated from the Mother country since 1763, when the Treaty of Paris divided the vast Mississippi Valley wilderness between Spain and Great Britain. The French so loved their own native soil that colonists never departed for New France in numbers sufficient to assure allegiance to the *fleur-de-lys.* Consequently, Louisiana has become anglicized, or better yet, americanized, in due degree.

In perhaps fifty or sixty rural churches you may still hear a French sermon each Sunday and the sixty-year-old confesses his sins in that boyhood tongue because he has never learned the formula and prayers in his more lately acquired English, which he usually employs in transacting his Monday morning business. His forty-year-old son may speak both languages (often in the same sentence and both with a French accent!), but do not ask him to write French, because he has learned it by oral tradition, at the knees of his parents, at the family hearth and supper table. In all probability he has never seen a French newspaper, never read French literature, would not even recognize the names of Corneille and Moliere. Since New Orleans has become the nation's door to Latin America, Spanish has replaced French as a second language in the schools. Today's youth cannot converse in grandpere's tongue. He will, however, spice his well-dictioned English with an occasional French expression; in anger he is likely to explode into genteel epithets like *diable! tonnere m'ecrase!* and *cochon!*

So in Louisiana the language is dying. We make no organized effort to preserve it. Nothing exists here comparable to the tooth-and-nail struggle of French Canada, where the battle-cry rings out: "Preserve the language to preserve the Faith!" We in Louisiana have reached a point in history where knowing *only* French would be a barrier to Faith and livelihood. Remaining bi-lingual has become in practice difficult if not impossible. A more realistic slogan might read: "Perfect your English to propagate the Faith!"

Willy-nilly Louisiana is a part of the whole country, and Catholic Louisiana is a part of the Church in America. We will retain our distinctive characteristics for generations to come. These will become more finely shaded within the national whole. Perhaps the passage of the centuries will relate us to the other diverse sectors of our vast land as Provence relates to Burgundy and Bretagne.

The Church in Louisiana shares most of the strengths and weaknesses of the Church in the nation as a whole. Hollywood's hedonism, the breakdown of family life, divorce and birth control, "keeping up with the Joneses," alcoholism (unfortunately, Louisianians also drink whiskey instead of wine), are numbered among the national moral faults as typical of Louisiana as elsewhere. Beyond religious motives the close family tie and tradition might, however, condition our people to resist birth control and divorce with greater constancy. One weakness distinctive of our era is the crippling dearth of native vocations. After 240 years we only now begin to obtain a bare sufficiency of clergy and religious from the local faithful.

Like the rest of the Church in America we in Louisiana have experienced no doctrinal heresies, despite our French heritage. Schisms or excommunications *nominatim* never seem to occur. Lay trusteeism and Jansenism brought in by the colonizers 200 years ago disappeared with the past generation. Anyway Jansenism would have hard going in America's relaxed moral climate. As we shall shortly see, we have perhaps tended by a careful selection of social doctrines and official papal teaching to underemphasize certain dogmas which may rile tempers, reflect upon rooted customs however un-christly, or startle a convenient complacency.

And we have shared in the strong points of the Church in America as a whole: our growing school system (we lag somewhat behind the East and Mid-West here: Voltaire made himself felt); a real closeness between priest and people (truer today that heretofore, although the relatively new native-born clergy could lose touch with our people by "high-living" and "office hours"); personal sacrifice by the faithful for financial support of Church and School; a recent increase of priestly vocations (though vocations to the teaching and nursing Sisterhoods while still constant are inadequate to meet the heavy demands of our booming educational and charitable works); some manifestations of a growing intellectual and spiritual maturity as indicated by a developing literature and interest in contemplative life; frequent Communions and regular Mass attendance; vigorous public demonstrations.

In all these ways we are representative of the Church of the nation as a whole. Our truly great Archbishop of New

Orleans, the Most Reverend Joseph Francis Rummel, has been for two decades a leading figure in the National Catholic Welfare Conference, that centralizing cause and symbol of "unity within diversity" so unique to the Church in America.

However, we do have our peculiar problems.

The first and greatest of these is the integration of the Negro on an equal status into the total life of our society.

Until World War I the Negro was concentrated heavily in the Southeastern states. Some 95 per cent of the colored population resided in this formerly slave-holding area until recent migration into the industrial North and East. Even today, some states like Mississippi are 50 per cent colored. Living in this dominantly Protestant area, the U. S. Negro took to himself the religion of his white masters, the Baptist and Methodist sects dominating. Louisiana's population is 30 per cent Negro. Of these, 160,000 are Catholics, residing in the Catholic oasis of "French" Louisiana. In fact, these Louisianians make up 40 per cent of the mere 400,000 Negro members of the Church in the United States.

During the past decade our 16 million Negroes have made astounding strides towards full equality. The great milestone in this saga of the race's progress came through the U. S. Supreme Court decision of May 1954 which declared that Negroes by constitutional right can attend the same public schools as their white neighbors. Repercussions will continue for some years as the southern states, Louisiana included, strive to avoid compliance. This tense question of racial justice presents to the Church in Louisiana a grave challenge and a graver opportunity, an opportunity offered but once in a people's history.

Catholic colleges and universities some years back took the lead in desegregation. State institutions of higher education followed suit under prodding from the federal courts. Negro leaders acknowledge the Church as the champion of their rights. With good reason they look to Catholic schools at the elementary and secondary level to pioneer again and set

a working example to the public (state-operated) school system of the whole South. And this responsibility falls primarily upon Catholic Louisiana.

Archbishop Rummel of New Orleans, in his pastorals and
public statements, presses the issue with a rare combination
of prudence and courage. Fifteen years ago he pioneered the
region-wide Catholic Committee of the South to strive for
racial equality and other works of social justice. Despite die-
hard resistance by a considerable number of laymen, our
Catholic schools will probably open to Negroes shortly, offering a working model to the public school system which is
embroiled in a complex politico-legal struggle to retain a
segregated pattern.

But integration among school children does not solve the
more intense and insidious problem of social discrimination
against the Negro. Political, economic and educational progress is not matched by a truly Christian attitude of neigh-
borliness, friendship and love. Rare indeed are the white
homes where a Negro may enter by the front door; rarer
still the family tables at which a Negro may break bread with
white friends. We have far to go on the road to Jericho.

A second social problem results from the current rapid
industrialization of the South. The Church in America
stands out as the exception to the scandal of the nineteenth
century: we did not lose the working man. The thriving
parishes of our great industrial cities of the North were built
up by immigrant laborers—Irish, German, Italian, Central
European. Pastor and bishop came from worker families.
Labor leaders kept close to the Church. The encyclicals provided the *rationale* of the nation's labor movement.

Only now has industry come into the South. Labor organizers today encounter here the same obstacles met by their
predecessors in Detroit and Pittsburgh two decades ago. Anti-
union and "right-to-work" legislation blocks a vigorous labor
movement. The rural population masses into the city slums,
voiceless and unprotected by collective bargaining. Factory
farms, huge sugar and rice plantations, employ tractor drivers

and day "hands" at lowest wages and house their tenant families in rural slums.

In the past four years, the organized labor movement has suffered set backs in its efforts to alleviate this rural and urban proletariat. Their hope lies in the Church with its solid social doctrine and strong moral voice.

This struggle will perdure for some years in the future.

The third problem we choose to comment upon relates closely to the two already mentioned. It is the problem of developing among our lay leaders a Christian social conscience—a moral judgment which extends beyond the individual into the whole of society. Too many practicing Catholics have become so severely scarred by secularism that they not only fail to apply the justice and love of Christ in their work-a-day world, worse yet, they fail to acknowledge that Christ and His Church possess rights within the realm of economic, business and professional life: the "downtown" world of Suhard's City of Man. Religion remains an affair of Sunday and sanctuary. Profits and payrolls, hiring and firing, family income and security are off-limits, beyond the saving touch of Christ and His redeeming justice.

Our Catholic school and college authorities now see this problem; the Newman Club chaplains at our sprawling secular universities like Louisiana State and Southwestern (where most of our lay leaders obtain their degrees) have taken excellent positive steps; some leaders within the vigorous 20,000 man State Council of the Knights of Columbus work at the adult level to awaken social consciences. But as yet no total awareness comes into view. Christ remains an exile from the whole of Louisiana which He died to redeem.

And this Louisiana oasis of the Faith, this citadel within a non-Catholic desert, still retains a Maginot mentality. To preserve a fortress Faith against Protestant or rationalist or masonic inroads has preoccupied the Church for so many years that preservation becomes the principal end. We have still to see the missionary spirit arise. Vocations to the missions of the South and to the world lag deplorably. While we may rejoice that we have preserved the Faith more thoroughly than has France, we are saddened that we altogether lack our old mother country's awing missionary impulse of the past generation. And we have yet to develop an apostolic laity conscious of the call of Christ and the role cast for the laymen of our time envisioned by the Pope Pius.

CHAPTER FOURTEEN

The Catholic Church in Texas

———— ❖ ————

BY ROBERT E. LUCEY, D.D.

Althᴏᴜɢʜ ᴏᴜʀ ᴄʜᴜʀᴄʜ in Texas has a history of almost three centuries, there have been two distinct periods, the second of which has very little continuity with the first. The first period was characterized by the conquest of Texas by the Spaniards with the implanting of the faith among the native Indians and the colonization of the area by Spanish immigrants. This epoch is marked by the heroic zeal of Franciscan missionaries whose work is attested by a number of mission churches built under their direction, several of which are standing today. The Franciscans also attended to the Spanish colonies. As an example, at San Antonio both activities of the missionaries were evident; they were in charge of the parish church of San Fernando in 1750 as well as the

———

Robert E. Lucey, D.D., was consecrated the second Archbishop of San Antonio, Texas, March 27, 1941. He was appointed a member of the President's Commission for Migratory Labor in June 1950 and has served as Executive Chairman of the Bishops' Committee for the Spanish Speaking since its organization in January of 1945.

several mission churches for the Indians in the neighborhood. Most notable of these is that of San Jose, about five miles south of the city. This rugged yet artistic structure is very much admired for its architectural details.

However, towards the end of the 18th century, the Franciscans were withdrawn from Texas to be replaced by secular priests; but as the Bishop of Monterrey, Mexico, (who had jurisdiction over Texas) had not a sufficient number of priests for this remote part of his diocese, the work of conversion of the Indians practically ceased. Likewise parish life among the colonists came to almost a standstill. This situation was aggravated by the separation of Mexico from Spain; the war of Texas Independence in 1836 put a definite end to any properly organized activity of the Church. Most of the Indians reverted to their former savage ways and the Spanish colonists were unfortunately not favored with priests having the zeal of their Franciscan predecessors. The American immigration which began shortly after 1820 and increased rapidly after 1836 was almost entirely Protestant.

The Spanish-speaking Catholics and the few American immigrants of our faith were without proper spiritual care for several years until the Holy See, having been advised of the sad state of the Church in the new Republic of Texas, made arrangements for the Lazarists to undertake the work of restoration. The priest who undertook the task was John Marie Odin, C.M., a native of France, who in the course of time became the first Bishop of Texas, having his episcopal see at Galveston. Under his direction the second period of the history of the Church in Texas began.

As the need of priests was immediate and imperative, Bishop Odin could not wait until priests could be educated from the vocations that might develop among the few Catholics in Texas. With new immigrants pouring into Texas day by day, both from the American Continent and from Europe, it was not long before the Lazarists were unable to supply him with priests. Bishop Odin then turned his thoughts to his native France and particularly to the Diocese of Lyons in which he was born. That city and diocese were the center of a great missionary movement. It was there that the Society of the Propagation of the Faith had been founded and was sustaining missionaries all over the world. Every year scores of young men and women from that part of France were dedicating themselves to labor for Christ in far-off lands.

On his first visit to Lyons, Bishop Odin's quest met with success. He secured several priests and seminarians as well as a generous allotment from the Society of the Propagation of the Faith. Subsequent trips to Lyons, made necessary by the ever-increasing immigration, brought him additional assistance. For the German-speaking immigrants he was successful in obtaining volunteers from Alsace-Lorraine. For missionary work among the Mexican people of the Rio Grande Valley, he obtained a number of priests of the Congregation of Oblates of Mary Immaculate, founded in France by Eugene de Mazenod, Bishop of Marseilles. In San Antonio he founded a school for boys under the direction of the Brothers of Society of Mary, also from France. In 1853 he obtained sisters from the monastery of the Incarnate Word of Lyons. Although he endeavored to establish a seminary at Galveston in order to promote native vocations, his efforts in this field were not successful and during his entire career as Bishop of Galveston, Bishop Odin had to depend on assistance from Europe to take care of his parishes, his missions and his schools. It was from France that he received his greater number of co-laborers. The apostolic laborers of Bishop Odin not only rescued the Catholic Church in Texas from decay and oblivion but brought about a firm and permanent re-organization. Apart from what was done and ended in the previous Spanish period Bishop Odin is the real founder of the Church in our state. He placed a missionary in every city that then existed from the Mexican border along the Rio Grande to the northern frontier beyond which then still roamed the savage Commanche. Among the great missionary bishops who have honored the French nationality in America, Bishop Odin stands high among the saintly and heroic warriors for Christ, such as Blanc, Cretin, Lamy, Machboeuf, Loras, Dubourg, Portier and Flaget, just to name a few. In 1861 he was elevated to the archiepiscopate in New Orleans and in 1870 he died in his native town of Ambierle, department of the Loire.

Towards the end of Bishop Odin's career in Texas, of the 26 secular priests belonging to the Diocese of Galveston 18 were natives of France. This fine French tradition was continued under his successor, Claude Marie Dubuis, also a native of the Diocese of Lyons, who was one of the very first French priests to respond to the appeal of Bishop Odin. Although Bishop Dubuis made many efforts to secure priests from among the Texas Catholics no natives of Texas were raised to the priesthood during his time. So the flow of priests and sisters from Europe had to continue with France again supplying the greater number of volunteers. In the latter part of his episcopate there was an increase in immigration from Germany and the countries of eastern Europe and one observes that from that time on to the end of the century an increase in the diocesan lists of priests from those countries and a decrease of volunteers from France. In fact, after the beginning of the 20th century very few of the younger secular priests were French although many of the important parishes throughout the state were administered by pastors of French birth. France was honored in those later years by two priests both of whom became bishops of San Antonio; these were, John Claude Neraz and John Anthony Forest, his successor, both natives of the Diocese of Lyons. In the various parishes throughout the state the names of French missionary priests are held in honored memory and one may truthfully say that there is not a parish in Texas that had its origin during the 19th century that does not contain in its records the name of a priest from France. In the majority of these places it was a Frenchman who was the pioneer missionary and builder. The predominance of Frenchmen among the secular priests of Texas is shown in the following figures taken from the Catholic Directories: In 1866 of the 30 secular priests, 28 were from France and in 1874 of the 63 secular priests, 42 were from France. During the 19th century at least 75 secular priests who labored in Texas were from France and 66 of these came from the Diocese of Lyons alone.

Although the religious congregations of sisters were blessed by native vocations these were never in a sufficient number to terminate a dependence upon Europe and particularly France for an increase in membership. The demand for sisters for new schools and hospitals was continuous. The religious orders of men likewise had to replenish and increase their numbers by additions from Europe. As mentioned before, the bishops of Texas made many efforts to foster native vocations but were unable to establish seminaries either because they lacked the funds or could not obtain priests to compose the faculties. It was not until the 80's that the first native of Texas was ordained to the priesthood and for many years after this time a priest born in Texas was still a rarity. A small seminary was begun towards the end of the 19th century in connection with the boys' school at Victoria in the Diocese of San Antonio but this came to an end with the death of the founder and rector. The Oblates of Mary Immaculate established a seminary in San Antonio early in this century and a few native priests received their early education at that place. A seminary also was founded in the Diocese of Galveston which resulted in the education of many priests who were of Texan or American origin. Finally a diocesan seminary was begun in San Antonio in 1916. This seminary under the patronage of St. John is a flourishing institution today and has given priestly education to many young men of the diocese and of other parts of the state.

Although the Spanish-speaking or Mexican element which forms a large part of our Catholic population has always received the paternal care of the bishops of Texas, it has only been in very recent years that any priests have come from this source either for the secular priesthood or for the religious orders. Neither have the congregations of sisters received many vocations from among the Mexican population. The care of these people has been almost entirely in the hands of priests of other nationalities.

Without disparaging the work of the priests of European

origin, it may be stated that while they served the Catholic people very well they were unable because of their foreign antecedents to make much progress in the conversion of Protestants, many of whom were imbued with a very strong nativist prejudice against foreigners. Many priests, though laboring zealously among their own nationalities (such as the Germans, Bohemians and Poles), never learned the English language sufficiently well to bring the Church to the attention of the non-Catholics. The Church not having any outstanding priests of Texan or American origin was at a great disadvantage and suffered under the label of being a foreign Church.

It is interesting to note that Bishop Odin visited Ireland in 1849 in search of priests and one hundred years later, in 1949, the present Archbishop of San Antonio and the Bishop of Corpus Christi visited Ireland to recruit seminarians who would volunteer for service in Texas after ordination. During the entire history of the Church in Texas neither English-speaking nor Spanish-speaking families have given a sufficient number of priests, sisters and brothers to the Church. The Spanish-speaking group now number about one million souls and their spiritual care is a heavy burden on the bishops and clergy of Texas.

It would seem that until recently vocations to the religious life were treated in the same manner as convert making among Protestants. As a rule there was no general program or formula for making converts. If Protestants sought instruction in Catholic doctrine the parish priests were glad to instruct them; if they wanted to join the Church the priests were happy to baptize them. But the initiative leading to conversion usually came from the Protestant; not from the priest or the Catholic laity.

Now it is recognized that if a pastor wishes to make converts he must have a program, a policy, a system; and he must work at it and get his laymen to work at it. Conversions to the Church in substantial numbers don't just happen; they are the result of thought, work and prayer.

In much the same way it is now recognized that vocations

in adequate numbers don't just happen. Bishops and pastors must make it their business to foster and develop vocations. They must have a program and they must work at it. A policy of watching and waiting never brought in many converts; neither will it produce vocations.

Specifically, bishops in the Southwest are now appointing a zealous and intelligent priest to be Diocesan Director of Vocations. It is his job to travel around the diocese giving sermons in churches, visiting Catholic schools, personally interviewing likely candidates for the priesthood and the convent, distributing literature and, what is very important, conferring with parents to encourage or persuade them to give a son or daughter to the Church. The Director also recruits laymen as members of the Vocation Society so that they will offer prayers and sufferings to God, asking Him to send laborers into the vineyard.

This program pays dividends and it is hoped that by the grace of God there will soon be many more priests, sisters and brothers to meet the spiritual needs of the laity in the vast State of Texas.

CHAPTER FIFTEEN

The Catholic Church on the Pacific Coast

◆

BY GEORGE N. KRAMER

F ROM A MISSION FRONTIER with a mere handful of non-Indian population to ten ecclesiastical jurisdictions with three million Catholics in a little over one hundred years, that is the phenomenal story of the Catholic Church on the Pacific Coast.

The Pacific Coast here means the States of California, Oregon and Washington. It comprises a total of about 320,000 square miles, an area fifty per cent larger than that of France today.

Geographically, it may be divided into two regions, according to its historical development. The first is California; the second, Oregon and Washington combined.

Logically, too, the historical setting may be divided into

George N. Kramer is research editor on The Tidings, *the official newspaper of the Archdiocese of Los Angeles. A teacher of history for twenty-six years, Dr. Kramer's last teaching assignment was at Loyola University, Los Angeles, where he was Professor of History and Chairman of the Department of History.*

two distinct periods. The earlier one dated from occasional contacts during the age of discovery and exploration to the war between Mexico and the United States, which was concluded with the Treaty of Guadalupe Hidalgo, February 2, 1848; the latter period began with the war and became prominent with the gold rush and the admission of California as a State of the Union in 1850.

California was rooted in Catholic traditions and remained exclusively Catholic during the entire Spanish-Mexican regime. Although the Anglo-American advance which followed was predominantly Protestant, Catholicism has maintained a steady growth to this moment.

Seven years, almost to the day, before the founding fathers of the republic declared the 13 United States of America dependent from England, the Catholic Church was established in the present state of California. On July 1, 1769, a foot-weary caravan from the Spanish province of Baja (Lower) California trudged to the Bay of San Diego, after a trip of 400 miles through unexplored country. Two weeks later the intrepid and saintly Franciscan Junípero Serra founded the first of a chain of 21 missions. Coincidentally, it was near this site that the first recorded Mass in California was said by Fray Andres de la Ascencion, a Carmelite who accompanied Vizcaino's expedition in 1602.

It had been exactly 227 years since the coastline explorer Juan Rodriguez Cabrillo touched these shores, the same year of 1542 that the disillusioned Coronado returned from his fantastic overland search for the fabled Seven Cities of Cibola and the ill-fated DeSoto was buried in the Mississippi River.

The question may well be asked why such a long interval separated these important events, why there was no Spanish settlement in Alta (Upper) California before 1769. Briefly, there had been no previous urgency for it. From the time of the Conqueror of Mexico Hernan Cortes, the empire known as New Spain had experienced a normal, somewhat leisurely growth, pushing continuously northward into an ever-extending and ever-broadening frontier.

Catholic missionaries had an outstanding and indispensable role in this expansion. Religious orders, Augustinians, Dominicans, Franciscans and Jesuits, in addition to preaching the Gospel to the heathen, were serving the Spanish government by civilizing the aborigines and teaching them so that they might become useful loyal subjects of the Crown.

Renowned Jesuits like Kino and Salvatierra had penetrated into the northern vastness, even into what is now the State of Arizona, to the Gila River, but it was yet too early to enter Alta California. In 1697 they began the establishment of a chain of successful missions on the rugged peninsula of Baja California. They were obliged to leave when the expulsion decree of the government in 1767 banished them from Spain and all her possessions. The missions were taken over by the Franciscans in the following year, and shortly thereafter given to the care of the Dominicans.

The orderly progress was disrupted by stirrings of the mid-eighteenth century, with the Seven Years War and the intensification of national rivalries. The far-reaching claims of Spain on the entire Pacific Coast were for the first time endangered when they were exposed to conquest not only by England or France, but by Russia. Having jumped the gap between Asia and North America in 1741 through discovery of Alaska by Vitus Bering, she had been pushing southward. By 1763, at the conclusion of the Seven Years War, her vessels were cruising as far as the Oregon Country.

For more than two centuries Spanish mariners had periodically sailed north in quest of the mythical Strait of Anian, which Spain hoped to fortify against possible interlopers who supposedly could sail the Northwest Passage from the Atlantic. Now the threat was real, with Russian seal-fishing bases at Sitka and Kamchatka. Only by actual occupation could Spain hope to make good her claims to territorial possession.

It was to be expected that missionaries would again be summoned to spearhead this policy. As before, the religious arm would be supported by the military, with expectation that the civil branch of government would follow shortly.

The assignment was accepted by the Franciscans. Thus the gray-robed padres established a chain of missions over a period of 54 years. The last and farthest north was founded in 1823 at Sonoma, above San Francisco, at a time when the zenith of missionary activity had been reached and disintegration was soon to begin. Within a decade destruction was already at hand.

The urgency of advancing northward as rapidly as possible is shown by the fact that the year following the founding of the mission at San Diego, a second one was located at Monterey Bay, and in 1776, the sixth near San Francisco Bay, all of them scattered along the coast for a distance of more than 600 miles.

An account of the 21 missions and their achievements is a history in itself and it has been told and retold in many an interesting volume. But it was not all romance and glamor, for deprivations and sufferings, disappointments and heartaches abounded. On the bright side, the heroism and devotion of the missionaries yielded a rich spiritual harvest, if 100,000 baptisms have any meaning, or officiating at over 28,000 Catholic marriages, or preparing tens of thousands for their last journey and administering the sacraments throughout their lifetime. From 1769 to 1845 a total of 146 Franciscans labored in this spacious vineyard, and 67 of them died there, two of them suffering martyrdom.

The material gains were equally impressive. Although crude flimsy wooden structures with woven grass or tule for roofing were characteristic of the early days of the missions, they were soon replaced with substantial buildings of adobe walls, tile roofs and flooring, and architectural beauty which has become world-renowned. Thousands of acres were producing abundant crops, a quarter million cattle grazed on the hillsides, while thousands of horses supplied transportation and the needs of the ranches. Hundreds of thousands of sheep supplied the spinning wheels and looms, while swine, goats and other livestock were plentiful.

When the supply ships ceased coming to Alta California after 1810, the missions were not only self-sufficient, but sustained the military and civil personnel. It is said that the missionaries had taught the Indians 50 different practical arts and handicrafts.

While it is proper to admire the worldly accomplishments and to recognize that all was to the advantage of the government, it is well to reflect that this was not the primary end of the Franciscans' labors. These were but the means toward their zeal for saving souls. After all, none of these things belonged to the padres; they were only trustees to administer the property until such day when it would be divided among the Indian neophytes, after they could prove themselves capable of shouldering responsibility.

Technically and officially this was known as secularization. It was understood that as soon as the Indian wards were Christianized and sufficiently educated and instructed in the practical arts to be self-supporting, the lands were to be divided among them and civil governments were to be established by them. The missionaries were then to turn over to parish priests their religious authority and advance into the frontier to establish new missions.

At no mission, however, had the natives developed to the point where secularization in its original meaning was feasible. This was true for two reasons: the Califorina aborigine was of an extremely low culture as compared with Indians in other parts of North America; secondly, the productive life span of the missions was too brief to afford that development whereby the neophytes were able to assume the responsibility of civilized life.

Many missionaries looked expectantly toward that day when they would establish new missions in the interior of the country, and already some of them were maintaining *asistencias,* or sub-missions and stations, which were served from the main centers. But facts are facts. The Indians were still irresponsible children.

Although Spain passed the secularization law in 1813, no effort had been made to put it into effect in California. Even after Mexico, which had inherited the law, declared its independence from Spain in 1821, nothing was done about it until 1833, when the government ordered the missions to be secularized immediately.

Over the repeated protests and warnings of the experienced missionaries, commissioners were appointed by the governors of Alta California to administer the properties. Greed, graft and political chicanery resulted in sales at fractions of their true value, the proceeds being shamefully squandered and the Indians wantonly scattered, some of them reverting to their savage life in the wilderness, others corrupted and sometimes practically enslaved by their new masters. There was usually a display of dividing the lands among the Indians, but very few remained in possession of their share. Confiscation, not secularization, was achieved.

Within a decade the mission premises had fallen into disrepair and many of them rapidly into ruins. After the region had been ceded to the United States by Mexico, the U. S. Land Commission during the 1850's partially compensated for the injustices by voiding the fraudulent sales and returning the mission structures and some land to the Church. Most of them became parish churches, although in time some entirely disappeared.

The twentieth century has witnessed a reconstruction of the mission ruins to resemble the originals. This was done through popular contributions and some State aid. Several are now museums, but all have become favorite historic sites for visitors. It is said, for example, that Santa Barbara Mission has been photographed only second to the national Capitol Building at Washington, D. C.

The ecclesiastical history of the Pacific Coast, and of California specifically, dated from the issuance of a bull by Pope Gregory XVI on April 27, 1840, creating the first diocese. Both Californias were included, with the northern boundary at the 42nd parallel, which was agreed upon by Spain and the U. S. in 1819 as the southern limits of the Oregon Country.

It should here be observed that the Oregon Country was an area held jointly by Britain and the U. S., after Spain had been delimited by the 42nd parallel and a few years thereafter Britain had excluded Russia to 54° 40'. It was not until

1846, after sharp controversy that bordered on war, that Britain and the U. S. came to terms by dividing the territory at the present international boundary of 49°.

The erection of a diocese became necessary as a result of secularization, as it was carried out by the Mexican government and California officials. During the Spanish period few non-natives resided in Alta California. Most of them were soldiers, government personnel and a few holders of Spanish land grants. Nearly all of them resided near a mission where their spiritual needs were served by the Franciscan padres.

During the Mexican period there was a substantial increase of white population both at the pueblos and on some 800 "Spanish" land grants, yet up to the time of American occupation, no steps were taken by the government or by the bishop to erect parishes or to place secular priests in charge of the churches. The missionaries carried on as best they could. Father Narcisco Duran, last president of the Alta California missions and one of the few survivors, died in the spring of 1846, blissfully ignorant of the declaration of war a few weeks earlier.

In 1836, the Mexican government demanded that the Spanish padres be replaced with native Mexican priests to become pastors of parishes, and for that reason it petitioned the Vatican for the erection of a diocese. It made rosy promises to support the bishop to the extent of $6,000 annually and make available to him the proceeds from the Pious Fund until the new diocese would afford sufficient revenues for the maintenance of the necessary ecclesiastical institutions.

On June 22, 1839, the Mexican government nominated Father Francisco Garcia Diego y Moreno, O.F.M., from a list of three candidates proposed by the chapter of the Metropolitan Church of Mexico. He was consecrated Oct. 4, 1840. The new see now became a suffragan of the metropolitan see of Sonora. Until 1779 the Californias had been regarded as within the jurisdiction of the Bishop of Guadalajar, but no episcopal visitation to these provinces was ever recorded.

The new bishop at the age of 55 was no stranger in Alta California, but he had spent two years as a missionary and later was Prefect of all the missions there. He planned on making San Diego his see city, for it was located approximately midway between the southern tip of Baja California and the Oregon Territory, a distance of some 1,500 miles.

Arriving at San Diego Dec. 11, 1841, he soon found it entirely unsuitable for the episcopal residence, so on Jan. 11, 1842, he took up his abode at Santa Barbara, from whence he administered the affairs of his vast diocese until his death.

After his consecration, Bishop Diego remained for several months in Mexico, endeavoring to obtain priests for his diocese, but his appeals were in vain, other than enlisting a few students who came with him. At the time there were in the entire diocese only 17 Franciscans in Alta California and four Dominicans in Baja California, with age and illness rapidly depleting their ranks. The missions in Baja California had been as seriously affected as those in the northern province; more so, perhaps, because they were not nearly as extensive or prosperous.

The problems of organizing a new diocese under these circumstances were enormous, particularly on account of the terrible effects of secularization on the only institutions he could hope to use as a foundation. Appeals to the Mexican government were unavailing, but this was not entirely unexpected in view of the political turmoil in that country.

Having almost no source of income, Bishop Diego had every reason to rely at least upon the Pious Fund, a designation given to a method of financial support devised by the Jesuits for their Baja California missions and carried over into the Franciscan enterprises in Alta California. Alms, collections, and gifts had been gathered in Europe over the years and the substantial amount invested, the revenues being used for mission purposes.

When the Jesuits were expelled, the Spanish Crown undertook administration of the funds and held them until the Mexican Republic achieved independence in 1821 and assumed jurisdiction. Bishop Diego accepted the promises of the Mexican government and calculated that the Fund would net an annual yield of about $34,000, half of which would be used in Alta California.

In February, 1842, came a rude awakening in the form of a demand to transfer immediately $40,000 of the Fund to the national treasury, which was perennially in financial straits. Refusal to do so resulted in a decree for the government to assume administration of the entire amount. This, like secularization, was only a thinly-veiled form of confiscation. At the very best, Bishop Diego had to abandon his building program and to struggle on with uncertain meager local resources, which were practically non-existent outside of the Santa Barbara area.

It is true that officially Mexico was as Catholic as was Spain and that in November, 1840, the government had ordered mission buildings and orchards to be placed at the services of the new bishop for the maintenance of public worship. Unfortunately, little could be done for lack of priests and money. Then, within a few years, corrupt officialdom resulted in fraudulent sales or leases of nearly all the properties.

The only measure of success during Bishop Diego's episcopacy was the opening of the Seminary of Our Lady of Guadalupe, May 4, 1844, near Santa Ines Mission. This was the result of Governor Micheltorena's action in setting aside a large tract of land for that purpose. He was well-disposed toward the missions and during his brief term of office he advocated the establishment of schools in California.

During the few years of administration, the Bishop had the satisfaction of raising to the dignity of the priesthood six of the seminary students he had brought with him from Mexico. The first of these was Father Miguel Gomez, ordained June 29, 1842.

The Seminary of Our Lady of Guadalupe remained open for 17 years and was conducted as a school for two decades longer. At the end of 1845 there were 33 students, but unhappily only a few of them were really candidates for the priesthood. Pleasing as it was to the heart of Bishop Diego who ardently desired a seminary, at best it could only be regarded in the historical perspective as a fond hope which must wait nearly a century for fulfillment with the opening of St. John's Major Seminary at Camarillo in 1939.

Desperately Bishop Diego appealed for the last time to the Mexican government in the fall of 1845 for the means to restore religious worship in Alta California. Then, when avaricious politicians proceeded to dispose of even the churches on mission property, all prospects of remedying the situation at an early date faded.

Five days after armed hostilities began between Mexico and the U. S., which resulted in a declaration of war by the latter on May 13, Bishop Diego quietly retired for his last rest and at midnight, April 30, 1846, drew his last breath. His body lies beneath the sanctuary of the church at Santa Barbara Mission.

When the U. S. took over California less than two years later, there were probably not more than 6,000 non-Indian people in what is now the entire State. Secularization had practically undone all the labors of Serra and his co-workers. Religion was at the lowest ebb it had been for half a century. With the entry of the U. S. the work would have to be done all over again, but this time upon a much more permanent basis.

Digressing for the moment, it may be revealing to survey the situation in the Oregon Country. The background and development were quite dissimilar from that of the Californias and much more recent, yet from the standpoint of Church diocesan organization, it was almost exactly contemporaneous. Although the Columbia River was discovered and trading with the Indians along the coast took place toward the end of the eighteenth century, little was known about the interior. Canadian and American trappers were converging in that general direction, but it remained for the first quarter of the nineteenth century to bring them together, as well as to engage them in conflict.

Foreshadowing the Anglo-American overland advance and ultimate occupation, a number of expeditions followed that of Lewis and Clark in 1805. Although there were Catholics in nearly all the parties, including John Jacob Astor's American Fur Company which founded Astoria in 1812, there is no record of Catholic missionaries until many years later. The same may be said of the fur companies coming down from Canada.

It was not until 1824 that any semblance of government appeared in the entire region. This was in the Willamette Valley, sometimes known as the "cradle of Oregon," near the Columbia River, present boundary between the States of Oregon and Washington. At Ft. Vancouver the Hudson Bay Co. established their headquarters for some ten or twelve trading posts in the region, with Dr. John McLoughlin in charge.

Dr. McLoughlin, one of the most outstanding historical figures of early Northwest history, was practically a law unto himself, yet he became benefactor to Canadian and American alike and proved himself a true friend of missionaries, both Catholic and Protestant. He himself became a Catholic in 1843.

In the early 1830's two movements took place which were the beginnings of religious organizations in the Oregon Country, which now extended eastward as far as the Continental Divide of the Rocky Mountains. The Flathead Indians in the eastern portion sent delegations to St. Louis, requesting "Blackrobes" to come and minister to them. They had heard from other tribes and French trappers about the wonderful work of the Jesuits and they wanted to hear the word of God from them.

The results of these delegations were twofold. In 1840 the indefatigable Jesuit Pierre-Jean DeSmet entered upon nearly a quarter century of missionary activity in the Oregon Country. In 1833, the year the Mexican Republic decreed secularization of the California missions, the second Provincial Council of Baltimore petitioned that the Indian missions of the United States be given to the care of the Jesuits, and in the following year the Pope granted the request.

The second result was the excited publicity given the Indian delegation by Protestant missionary societies. The interest this stimulated in the Oregon Country induced Presbyterian ministers Dr. Marcus Whitman and Henry H. Spalding and Methodists Jason and Daniel Lee and others to establish mission centers among the Indians, from 1834 to 1838, although they did not endure for any length of time.

The second movement originated with Canadian Catholics residing in the Willamette Valley who, on July 3, 1834, petitioned the Archbishop of Quebec for priests. At first there were objections from the British government and from the Hudson Bay Co.; however, approval was shortly forthcoming, whereupon the Archbishop on April 17, 1838, appointed Abbe Francis Norbert Blanchet his vicar-general for Oregon, to be assisted by Father Modeste Demers.

Together these two were to be the spiritual guides to the inhabitants and to found missions among the Indian tribes. Setting out from Montreal in a bark canoe of the Hudson Bay Co. May 3, 1838, Abbe Blanchet met Father Demers at the Red River, and from there they completed the 4,000-mile journey to Ft. Vancouver, arriving Nov. 24.

This is but one example of many to illustrate the arduous distances and slow modes of travel in North America little more than a century ago.

On the way, these pioneer priests said the first Mass in Oregon Oct. 14, 1838, at Ft. Bend on the Columbia River; and at Ft. Vancouver their first Mass was on Nov. 25. Here were some 26 Catholic families who, like many others scattered throughout the region, were in great danger of losing their faith, as they had neither priests nor sacraments. It was estimated that Canadian Catholics in the various posts and settlements, with wives and children, numbered about 900.

In January, Mass was celebrated in the Willamette Valley, and from that time the work of the Catholic Church in Oregon Territory showed continued progress down to the present. By Mar. 1, 1840, the two priests had baptized 288 and performed 76 marriages. This was the spring Father DeSmet was making his first trip to the Flathead country in the Bitter Root mountains. Two years later, this famous missionary brought other Jesuit Fathers to assist him and also the first

Sisters of Notre Dame from Namur, France, to open schools there.

So promising was the progress of the Church in Oregon that the Holy See, at the request of the Fifth Provincial Council of Baltimore, Dec. 1, 1843, erected the territory into a Vicariate Apostolic. The Abbe Blanchet was appointed Vicar-Apostolic, May 7, 1844, but the news did not reach him until Nov. 4.

He was consecrated in Montreal by Bishop Bourget, July 25, 1845, and exactly one year later was elevated to the archbishopric of Oregon City then established. At the same time, suffragan dioceses were erected as follows: Nesqually, Vancouver's Island, Princess Charlotte, Ft. Hall, Colville, New Caledonia and Walla Walla. However, to most of these no appointments were ever made, and none of the names as dioceses remains today. They show, nevertheless, the extent of the territory and the hopes that were entertained for Church expansion.

It is important to mention one of the appointees who was none other than the brother of the Archbishop, Augustine Magloire Blanchet, who was consecrated bishop, Sept. 27, 1845, and assigned to the see of Walla Walla. When that was suppressed in 1850, he was transferred to the see of Nesqually, which included all that is the State of Washington today. The name was changed by Papal decree in 1928 and is now the Archdiocese of Seattle. It should be added that the Archdiocese of Oregon City was also renamed and is today the Archdiocese of Portland.

To note all the numerous changes in ecclesiastical jurisdiction would only lead to confusion. Briefly, the brothers Blanchet dominated the scene with their magnificent achievements until 1880, the year when they both retired, having put the Church on a lasting foundation in the Oregon Country.

Before dismissing the subject, it may be well to recall that when Bishop Francis Norbert Blanchet went to Rome in 1846, he returned after a six-months' voyage with six secular missionaries, four Jesuit Fathers, three lay Brothers, and seven Sisters of Notre Dame of Namur. Already 6,000 Indians had been converted and baptized, a dozen Catholic communities were clustered about fur-trading posts, with 1,500 Canadians reclaimed for the Church. He reported 14 chapels and as many stations, as well as two educational institutions, all this within six short years.

In 1848 the First Provincial Council of Oregon was held in the wilderness. The significance of this becomes clear when it is remembered that such an assembly was held within only 40 years after the division of the diocese of Baltimore and the first erection of new sees in the United States.

This was the same year the Oblates came to found a mission in Astoria, which brings to mind the efforts made by Bishop Augustin Blanchet, shortly after his consecration, to induce the Oblates of Mary Immaculate to accompany him to the West. With Fr. John B. Brouillet, whom he made his vicar-general, and others he traversed the plains and rugged mountains for five months in covered wagons to his diocese of Walla Walla.

Back in California, Fr. Jose Maria Gonzalez Rubio, O.F.M., carried on as administrator until a successor to the late Bishop Diego would be appointed.

His difficulties during the war between Mexico and the U. S. and the transition between 1846 and 1850, were somewhat moderated by the friendly attitudes of American officialdom. Even before the sales of missions were declared illegal by the U. S. government, military officers were disposed to regard them as such, and their good will toward priests and divine worship was in happy contrast with the treatment accorded by the presumably Catholic Republic of Mexico.

It was one of the ironical quirks of history that for 350 years Spaniards frantically and for the most part fruitlessly made the pursuit for gold one of the driving forces of their advance. Now, less than two weeks before Mexico, Spain's heir, ceded California to the U. S., discovery of a few nuggets at Sutter's Fort, Jan. 24, 1848, was the beginning of one of the most sensational gold rushes on record and changed the entire course of history on the Pacific Coast.

The floodgates of migration opened wide and the human masses surged West, thousands of miles overland, by way of Panama, and around the Horn of South America. The vast majority headed for northern California and the "diggings." There was even a pronounced emigration from Oregon Country, where the rising churches and Catholic undertakings were greatly embarrassed for several years by loss of population.

All this would affect the Catholic Church and its institutions. The status of California was not altogether clear to the Vatican. The confusion that existed from the Bear Flag Revolt to the advent of the forty-niners, coupled with the 1848 revolutionary movements in Europe during which Karl Marx issued the Communist Manifesto, helps to explain the delay in making an appointment to the vacant see.

Not until May 31, 1850, did Pope Pius IX name Fr. Joseph Sadoc Alemany, O.P., at that time attending a convention of his order in Rome. He was consecrated there one month later, and left immediately for the designated see city of Monterey. This old capital of Spanish California became prominent as the result of the constitutional convention held there the year before and the general expectation that it would become the capital of the State.

When Bishop Alemany reached San Francisco Dec. 6, 1850, he was impressed by the activities everywhere. There could scarcely be any doubt but that this was destined to become the most important metropolis on the entire West Coast. Southern California was still largely pastoral and agricultural, predominantly Mexican in population, and Spanish in speech. It had shown little change from the Spanish mission period, with its sleepy pueblos and antiquated customs. San Francisco was a hub of activity, a seaport teeming with a cosmopolitan population.

As expected, Mexico refused to recognize the new Bishop's authority over Lower California, the excuse being that he was an American citizen, whereas in fact the episcopal see had nothing to do with citizenship. However, the Bishop was advised in 1852 that Rome had removed Lower California from his jurisdiction.

With Bishop Alemany on his return from Rome was Mother M. Goemare, a Dominican Sister, predecessor of members of her community who established the first religious house for women in California, a school for girls opened in Monterey in 1851. In the following year, Sisters of Notre Dame of Namur reached San Francisco en route to Oregon, but at the insistent entreaty of Bishop Alemany, they remained and started a school at San Jose. Sisters of Charity also came from Emmitsburg, Md., in 1852.

It was not until 1856 that the first Sisters came to Southern California when the Daughters of Charity established a girls' school, orphanage and later a hospital.

In 1851 the Jesuits were authorized to open a school at Santa Clara Mission, which has since expanded into the University of Santa Clara.

Although in 1852 there were in the whole diocese of Monterey only 31 churches and 38 priests, the 39-year-old Bishop was elevated to archiepiscopal dignity when he was appointed to the newly created archdiocesan see of San Francisco, with Monterey a suffragan diocese.

Despite mushrooming population, there were only three parishes in the entire city of San Francisco, one at Stockton, and another at San Jose. That was the extent of it in the whole Archdiocese which extended from the latitude of the town of San Jose to the northern boundary of the State.

The vast distances and the increasing mining towns made a division of this area imperative. On Oct. 10, 1860, the first of a series of steps was taken in what today is the diocese of Sacramento. The region north of the 39th parallel, including the territory of Nevada north of that line, to the 42nd was created the vicariate of Marysville. Eight years later this was elevated to diocesan rank and transferred to Grass Valley. It was not until May 28, 1886, that this was abolished and the present diocese was established with Sacramento, the State capital, the see city.

This has been cited as an example of the numerous changes that took place on the Pacific Coast and involved the interior as far east as Montana, Idaho, Nevada and Utah. It makes interesting reading, but it likewise requires lengthy explanation. A history of one suffragan see of a province is often the history of another. The same persons and places and events recur. Then, too, the shifting of political boundaries in the frontier as well as admission of new States affected ecclesiastical jurisdictions.

Changes in the Monterey diocese can be described more easily. At the time Bishop Alemany was appointed to the Archbishopric of San Francisco, Rev. Thaddeus Amat, C.M., reluctantly accepted appointment to the see of Monterey. Consecrated in Rome March 12, 1854, he did not arrive in California until November of the following year. He was trying to secure priests for his diocese, but like other pioneer bishops he met with but small success.

He did bring back with him the pallium for Archbishop Alemany. He also brought the relics, discovered the year before, of Saint Vibiana, which now repose over the High Altar of the Cathedral in Los Angeles named in her honor.

Bishop Amat early saw in Los Angeles what Bishop Alemany saw in San Francisco, the likelihood of it becoming the largest city in the area. After a few years at Santa Barbara, he was permitted in 1859 to make Los Angeles his see city and simultaneously the name was changed to the Diocese of Monterey-Los Angeles. It was here he built the Cathedral which was consecrated in 1876.

In San Francisco, the first Cathedral was dedicated in 1854; the present St. Mary's Cathedral was completed in 1891. Much as Archbishop Alemany desired a seminary, no permanent establishment of its kind materialized until ten years after his death. St. Patrick's famous seminary at Menlo Park was dedicated August 28, 1898.

The diocese of Monterey-Los Angeles was divided for the first time Dec. 3, 1922, when the northern portion was erected as Monterey-Fresno. Bishop Aloysius J. Willinger, C.Ss.R., is the third appointee to the see. On July 11, 1936, it was divided a second time, the southern part being known as the diocese of San Diego. The first and present ordinary of the diocese is Bishop Charles F. Buddy.

These changes took place during the episcopacy of Bishop, later Archbishop, John J. Cantwell, and in 1936 Los Angeles was raised to an archdiocese.

When Bishop Amat passed away in 1878, he was successfully followed by Bishop Francis Mora (1878-1896); Bishop George Montgomery (1896-1903); and Bishop Thomas J. Conaty (1903-1915).

In the Pacific Northwest all the present dioceses and archdioceses were established or had a change of name in the 20th century. Archbishop Edward D. Howard of Portland was appointed to the see of Oregon City Apr. 30, 1926, and the name of the see was changed to that of "Portland in Oregon" Sept. 26, 1928.

Archbishop Thomas A. Connolly succeeded to the Archbishop of Seattle exactly 100 years after it was first created as the Diocese of Nesqually in 1850. The name was changed in 1907, but it was not given archdiocesan status until June 23, 1951.

The Diocese of Baker was erected in 1903. It is now occupied by Bishop Francis P. Leipzig. Bishop Bernard J. Topel is the ordinary of the Diocese of Spokane, which was established ten years later. The most recent is Yakima, Washington, which was activated with the appointment of Bishop Joseph P. Dougherty in 1951.

The recency of their development, the vast stretches of their territory and their comparative sparse populations are indications that the Church in the former Oregon Country can be expected to show great progress in the next several decades.

At the time Bishop Cantwell assumed administration of Los Angeles in 1917, the population growth in the Southland was just beginning to mount rapidly. Before that, it was mostly a matter of real estate promotions, hopes and predictions. When the U. S. entered World War I, Los Angeles had less than half a million residents; today, the city alone

has five times that number and the metropolitan area is estimated at more than the entire population of the State in
1920. Where bean fields and citrus orchards gave the landscape the appearance of an agricultural economy as recently
as 1940, it is now possible to toss an orange from roof-top to
roof-top for a distance of fifty miles.

It was not surprising, then, that the growth of the Church
there impelled Rome to raise Los Angeles to an archiepiscopal see.

In the northern part of the State Archbishop John J.
Mitty was installed as Archbishop of San Francisco in 1935;
and in the Sacramento diocese Bishop Robert J. Armstrong
became the fourth bishop in 1929.

Death of Archbishop Cantwell in 1947 brought to the
Pacific Coast Coadjutor Archbishop of New York James
Francis McIntyre, who was formally enthroned in St. Vibiana
Cathedral by Francis Cardinal Spellman on March 19, 1948.

A greater honor for the Archbishop and a distinction for
the Catholics of the Archdiocese was imminent. The nomination to the Sacred College of Cardinals of the Archbishop of
Los Angeles was announced Nov. 29, 1952. Cardinal McIntyre's elevation to the Sacred College took place in the con-
sistory at Vatican City, Jan. 12, 1953.

The Pacific Coast now has four archdioceses: Los Angeles,
Portland, San Francisco, and Seattle, with a total of about
2,150,000 Catholics. Six dioceses: Monterey-Fresno, Sacramento, and San Diego in California; Baker, in Oregon; and
Spokane and Yakima, in Washington, total almost a million
more.

The greatest problems the Church on the Pacific Coast
encountered were growing pains, vast regions and vicissitudes
of frontier life, complicated by the fur trade, international
rivalries and the discovery of gold. There was the perennial
shortage of priests and Sisters, but the field was a fertile one,
from the wilderness of the aborigines to the industrial centers
today.

The amazing statistics of institutions and religious personnel at present as compared to what they were a century ago

challenges credibility. For the past half century at least, there has not only been a steady growth but one of increasingly rapid progress up and down the Coast, and the Church has been keeping pace with it all. Catholics in the Far West can indeed hold their heads high.

PART III

THE CATHOLIC CHURCH

Her Life and Her Influence
in the United States

CHAPTER SIXTEEN

The Catholic Church and Labor

———— ◆ ————

BY EDWARD MARCINIAK

IN ALMOST EVERY industrialized nation of the world, on both sides of the iron curtain, the official workers' holiday is the first day of May. In the United States May Day is celebrated only by communists and a small remainder of nostalgic socialists. American workers instead celebrate Labor Day, the first Monday in September.

The choice of a September holiday symbolizes the way in which U. S. workers and their leaders have strayed from European working class traditions to accommodate themselves to the U. S. political and economic system. The holiday was not selected for ideological or revolutionary objectives but for highly pragmatic benefits. In choosing Monday, for example, they made certain that a regular working day would be included in a three-day holiday weekend. By picking

———————————————————————————

Edward Marciniak is the editor of Work, *a paper for all who work for a living, published by the Catholic Labor Alliance, Chicago. He is presently Vice-President of the American Newspaper Guild. He is a frequent contributor to leading Catholic publications on labor and social problems.*

September they guaranteed themselves an extra day of rest midway between two established holidays, Independence Day (July 4th) and Thanksgiving Day (the last Thursday in November).

1. The Role of the Church Vis-a-Vis the Labor Movement

A similar accommodation to the facts of U. S. economic life and political life has shaped the part the church now plays in the life of workingmen and the part they in turn play in her life. For example, when Pope Pius XII established the Feast of St. Joseph the Worker on May 1, several U. S. archbishops immediately petitioned Rome for approval to celebrate the new feast on the U. S. Labor Day. And the permission was speedily granted.

In the United States the Mystical Body of Christ seeks to share God's life with a working people who have never developed a strong class consciousness—except in a few instances. The influence of *class* upon workers has been offset by the *mass* impact of American institutions upon the status, occupational mobility, ambitions and religious outlook of workingmen and their families.

While it is dangerous to generalize about workers in a nation as large and varied as the United States, it can be said that any analysis of the American economic system will be inadequate and distorted if it is predicated on the presence of a class struggle. Few factory workers show any enthusiasm to carry on a class war. The impact of movies, radio, press and magazines, advertising, and television upon a worker's attitudes has been immeasurably greater than that of his position as a worker. The country's natural wealth and high productivity, the absence generally of proletarian conditions, public education, the continual influx into cities of new immigrants and migrant workers to take over the menial jobs, all have tended to dull the class consciousness of factory workers. Millions of factory workers who own their own homes regard themselves as "middle class." In addition the most rapidly growing group in the working population (it almost outnumbers manual workers) is made up of white collar employees in offices, commerce, retail establishments, government service and the professions. By and large the aspirations and standards of this white collar population are indistinguishable from those of the U. S. middle class.

(None of the foregoing obliterates the fact that there are millions of low-paid workers, that working and living conditions among most migratory workers are sub-human, and that certain racial groups are deprived of equal economic opportunity.)

As a result, the Church in the United States has never had to face, as it has in many European cities, a dechristianized, hostile working class. The striving for social justice has not been characteristically a class struggle. Church and worker alike have benefited from the absence of rigid class structure in the United States.

It is no secret that the Church and organized labor in the United States are on good terms. Ever since 1887, when Cardinal James Edward Gibbons of Baltimore journeyed to Rome, in the name of the U. S. hierarchy to defend the Knights of Labor, then the most important national labor union in the nation, this relationship of mutual trust has never been successfully challenged. Upon request of the Canadian bishops, the Congregation of the Holy Office had declared the Knights of Labor, then at the peak of their power, a forbidden society. In his successful effort to have that prohibition lifted in the United States, Cardinal Gibbons argued that "social amelioration" was "the inevitable program of the future." Workingmen, he said, "love the Church, and they wish to save their souls; but they must also earn a living, and labor is now so organized that without belonging to the organization, it is almost impossible to earn one's living . . . To lose the heart of the people would be a misfortune for which the friendship of the few and powerful would be no compensation."

As the years went by, that closeness between the Church and unions was cemented by further expressions of good will.

One such instance was the publication in the postwar year 1919 of the Bishops' Program of Social Reconstruction. The bishops proposed a series of reforms which included: minimum wage laws; comprehensive social security against illness, unemployment and old age; laws against child labor; public employment services, government protection of the right to organize; cooperatives; government regulation of monopolies; graduated income, excess profit and inheritance taxes; sharing by workers in profits, ownership and management; public housing for poor families. These reforms summed up well labor's own aspirations—politically and economically. Most of these proposals were later realized in the New Deal legislation of the late 1930's. It was not surprising to find that the president of the National Association of Manufacturers thought these proposals "so radical" that he protested to Cardinal Gibbons against "partisan, pro-labor union, socialistic propaganda under the official insignia of the Roman Catholic Church in America."

It would be expected that many Catholics have been and are now leading union officials. Terrence V. Powderly, leader of the Knights of Labor, was a Catholic until the last years of his life. The late and widely beloved Philip Murray, a Catholic, was president of the Congress of Industrial Organizations (CIO). Also a Catholic is George Meany, incumbent president of the merged AFL-CIO. Yet no special effort has ever been made to elect Catholics to union office. It is also significant that the last three secretaries of labor in the president's cabinet have all been Catholics, Maurice J. Tobin, Martin P. Durkin, and James P. Mitchell.

Today many union conventions open with an invocation by the bishop of the host city. He or some priest active in social action frequently addresses the convention. (Also invited are prominent rabbis and Protestant ministers.) Convention addresses by Archbishop Richard J. Cushing of Boston and Bishop Bernard J. Sheil of Chicago were printed by the CIO, and several million copies distributed. In his 1947 convention talk to the CIO convention, Archbishop Cushing noted that of all the members of the American hierarchy there was not a single one whose parents had a college education. "Every-one of our bishops and archbishops is the son of a working-man and a workingman's wife."

In the last decade laws have been proposed in most of the country's 48 states to weaken trade unions. The most articulate and vigorous champions of the right of free trade unions were priests, bishops, and Catholic lay leaders. In protecting unionism under attack, there was no doubt in their minds that they were continuing the tradition of Cardinal Gibbons. As recently as April 1955, one of the editors of *Fortune,* influential magazine for businessmen, acknowledged that "The Church is today a potent ally of labor . . . By reason of its support (of organized labor) the Church has won respect and important influence in the labor movement."

Supporting testimony during that same month from a union source, the *United Mine Workers Journal:* "Among labor's staunchest allies in this long drawn-out war against big-moneyed ignorance are an imposing number of prominent Catholic clergymen who have denounced 'right-to-work' legislation as 'unsound,' 'schizophrenic' and 'immoral according to Catholic social teaching.' "

In the United States workingmen seldom found any serious reason to share the conviction, popularly held in other countries, that the Church was in league with the wealthy against the poor. "The Church in America," stated a distinguished Protestant theologian, Dr. H. Richard Niebuhr, "has been, with all its wild diversity, very close to the people, much closer than in Europe." And the Jewish sociologist of religion, Will Herberg, observes: "The Catholic Church has remained, by and large, pro-labor and has shown a deep concern for retaining the allegiance of its working people. It very early adopted the approach later formulated by Pius XI in *Quadragesimo Anno*—'The first and immediate apostles to the workingman must themselves be workingmen'—and it could follow this injunction where American Protestantism could not, because so many of its clergy and lay leaders were themselves of working class origin and background. As a result, the Church has managed to develop, especially in recent decades, extensive activities in connection with the labor movement, implemented by a considerable number of 'labor priests' and such agencies as the Association of Catholic Trade Unionists, the Young Christian Workers, and the Jesuit labor schools."

2. *The Changing Labor Movement*

The Church in the United States confronts a labor movement which functions without any religious commitment (as that of the Christian trade unions on the European and African continents) or without any special political allegiance (as that of the socialist unions of Belgium, the now defunct Peronist syndicates of Argentina, or the communist labor movement in Italy). The neutral character of U. S. unions was not an historical accident, but was designed deliberately to fit North American conditions.

When the American Federation of Labor was founded in 1881, it was by no means certain that the new federation would follow a course plotted by non-Marxists. The opening sentence of its constitution dedicated the AFL to the class struggle:

> "A struggle is going on in all the nations of the civilized world, between the oppressors and the oppressed of all countries, a struggle between the capitalist and the laborer, which grows in intensity from year to year, and will work disastrous results to the toiling millions, if they are not combined for mutual protection and benefit."

This preamble remained part of the AFL constitution until 1955 when its merger with the Congress of Industrial Organizations brought forth a new declaration.

The new preamble crystallizes the metamorphosis in U. S. unionism in the intervening years since 1881. Nowhere in the new AFL-CIO constitution is there any ringing call to join the class struggle. On the contrary, the preamble strikes a new tone:

"At the collective bargaining table, in the community, in the exercise of rights and responsibilities of citizenship, we shall responsibly serve the interests of all the American people.

"We pledge ourselves to the more effective organization of working men and women; to the securing to them of full recognition and enjoyment of the rights to which they are justly entitled; to the achievement of ever higher standards of living and working conditions; to the attainment of security for all the people; to the enjoyment of the leisure which their skills make possible; and to the strengthening and extension of our way of life and the fundamental freedoms which are the basis of our democratic society.

"We shall combat resolutely the forces which seek to undermine the democratic institutions of our nation and to enslave the human soul. We shall strive always to win full respect for the dignity of the human individual whom our unions serve."

As a matter of fact, the class-conscious language of the old AFL constitution had been an anachronism since 1900. The swing from a concept of politically-subordinate, marxist-orientated unionism to a pragmatic, bread-and-butter unionism was almost entirely accomplished under the leadership of Samuel Gompers, a founder of the AFL. He was its chief architect between 1881 and 1924, and its president for most of those years. A European immigrant who brought with him current notions of socialist unionism, Gompers learned how little U. S. labor parties and utopian unions had been able to accomplish for workingmen. Resolutely, he steered the American Federation of Labor toward policies which would be effective under American conditions and actually improve the position of working people.

Fighting the doctrinaire theorists of the class struggle, who were more interested in erecting an American working class party than in building a labor movement, Gompers strove to preserve labor's freedom of action—from both the government and the political marxists.

His standard of good unionism was simple: would it bring *more* for the workers? He fought like a tiger against allowing any political clique to dominate the AFL, while at the same time urging unionists to become active in political campaigns. He had a great deal to do with electing Woodrow Wilson president of the United States in 1912; that victory gave the United States its first New Deal. When Gompers died in 1924, it would almost be true to say that "there wasn't an ounce of class struggle in a carload of labor leaders." His legacy to the labor movement was a labor movement committed to business unionism.

The year that Gompers died a young, American-born socialist, Walter Reuther, was just starting to work. His socialism had been handed down from his German-born grandfather. Thirty years later, in 1954, after the most turbulent years of U. S. labor history, Reuther, president of both the Congress of Industrial Organizations and of the United Auto Workers, a union with more than 1,250,000 members, declared:

> "A labor party would commit the American political system to the same narrow class structure upon which the political parties of Europe are built. I believe this very strongly. I believe there is great hope in America. I believe that we have a society that is not rigid in character along class lines. And that is the great hope of America, that is the great hope of freedom everywhere, to keep our society and our social structure in a state of flux so that it doesn't become fixed, so it doesn't snap."

Reuther's shift away from a socialist unionism is an experience through which many U. S. union leaders have gone.

Another index of the labor movement's devotion to business unionism is the strictly pragmatic attitude that union leaders have taken towards nationalization. With few exceptions, union leaders have strenuously opposed public ownership of the basic industries because of their confidence in collective bargaining as *the basic way* to improve the wages, hours and working conditions of workers. Yet these same leaders, in their pragmatic fashion, have not opposed municipal ownership of electrical power, state ownership of the distribution of alcoholic liquor and federal corporations to harness the waterpower of U. S. rivers.

Proud of their business-like concern for immediate improvement in working conditions, union officials claim, with some justification, that the continued pressure upon management for higher wages and increased benefits tended to weed out inefficient and incompetent employers. They also claim that their acceptance of mechanization and technological advancement (but with some exceptions, as in the building and entertainment fields) was, in part, responsible for higher U. S. productivity. Certainly, this pragmatic bent of mind made the labor movement a sturdy stumbling block for the marxist socialists at the turn of the twentieth century and for the communists during the great depression of the 1930's. Today, most U. S. unionists continue to distrust the theorist, whether he be socialist, communist, or capitalist. They have tasted the bountiful fruits of business unionism and will accept no substitutes.

Yet the metamorphosis from class-conscious, marxist unionism of European inspiration to a native, hard-headed allegiance to collective bargaining as the way to produce tangible, sizeable benefits for workingmen is by no means final. The U. S. labor movement has yet to see the day of its maturity. In the last twenty years it has undergone tremendous growth —from four to seventeen million members. Most of these new union members, it is aptly said, are organized but not unionized. Union jurisdiction has yet to be extended to the great majority (65 per cent) of U. S. workingmen who are not members. Furthermore, the nation's 150 national unions, whose membership ranges from 1,000 to 1,500,000 members, differ radically in their militancy, their involvement in political affairs, their policy towards the colored races, and their concern for the welfare of people in other countries. However, postponement of the labor movement's age of maturity is chiefly attributable to two additional factors: the struggle to remove the not infrequent stains of tyranny in *internal* union affairs and the effort of unions to attain some equitable status in their *external* relations.

First of all, the ascendancy of business unionism saw a toleration and, in some cases, a support of violations of human dignity within the unions themselves. Gangster domination of waterfront unions in New York City was an established fact; so was the indictment of union officials for extorting funds from Midwestern contractors; so was the admission of a Chicago union official that his union's insurance brokers had donated $42,000 to help sponsor a girls' baseball team which he personally owned.

Some union presidents acted and talked like corporation executives. "I run the union just like a business. We deal in one commodity—labor," once explained Dave Beck, president of the International Brotherhood of Teamsters, the largest union in the United States. Others, by word and deed, behaved as if the union were their personal property. A few union leaders, following the example of the *nouveau riche,* joined the best country clubs and spent their winters on Florida beaches. Some hired literary hacks to write their biographies arrogantly stuffed with Homeric adjectives.

In some craft unions, especially in the building trades, exclusion of Negroes is still the rule rather than the exception. Such unions have displayed an abominable lethargy about racial discrimination. In collusion with contractors and material suppliers, some local building trades unions still insist on the use of certain building materials and antiquated methods. The leaders of a large factory local in one city, for example, eliminate rank and file opposition by persuading the employer to fire the rebels. And the employer, enjoying a sub-standard contract with the union, is willing to connive.

Such cases of union tyranny are not typical. Yet there are enough of them to make top union leaders like George Meany and Walter Reuther anxious for reform and to create a distrust in the business unionism which has given shelter to such abuses.

Secondly, business unionism has not been able to secure labor's rightful place in American public affairs. For over nine years, unions have unsuccessfully been opposing the Taft-Hartley law, a 1947 national law which imposes severe restrictions upon unions and collective bargaining. Early union demand for absolute repeal has now been replaced by a willingness to accept substantial amendments. Since 1945,

18 states (out of 48) have passed "right to work" laws further restricting union activity—over the militant but highly ineffective protest of unions. State workmen's compensation benefits—in case of occupational disease or accident—are almost without exception pegged to living standards at a starvation level. (Most state legislatures are still dominated by a coalition of middle class farmers and small businessmen.) In some states, a man totally disabled at 22, because of an accident at work, gets small weekly payments until 30, and not a cent thereafter. The combined assets of all U. S. labor unions are still less than those of one corporation giant like American Telephone and Telegraph Co., Metropolitan Life Insurance Company, or General Motors. Twenty times as many businessmen as unionists sit in Congress. Only 84 labor leaders (out of approximately 50,000 full-time union officials in the U. S.) were regarded important enough to be included in a recent edition of *Who's Who in America*.

Achieving for unionism a rightful status in American affairs is complicated further by the fact that the political and economic strength of organized labor is repeatedly exaggerated to exploit fear and confusion for private gain. Most U. S. newspapers, for example, regularly attempt to magnify the real power of unions—implying that such an acquisition of power by workingmen and their leaders is somehow repugnant to American democracy. Objections are constantly being raised to labor's exerting an important and decisive influence in national affairs—even if that power will be democratically determined and used for the common good. Some union leaders, disappointed that the labor movement has only been partially successful in achieving greater political power, are losing faith in the efficacy of business unionism.

These are the reasons, then, why the historical right of business unionism to set the standards for the American Labor movement is being challenged by the "union philosophies" of *democratic unionism and political unionism*. *Democratic unionism* concentrates on reordering a union's internal affairs and its relations with management. It strives vigorously to eradicate the notion that labor is a commodity (by such measures as the guaranteed annual wage), to achieve industrial democracy (by giving workingmen ownership and voice in industry), and by recognizing the justice of each worker's claim to human dignity (by eliminating all discrimination and segregation on account of race or color and by protecting rights of union members against any despotism by some union boss). It regards political action by unions as necessary to guarantee the presence of a government friendly to such objectives; political action stems not from some doctrinaire objective but from economic necessity. Democratic unionism is sparked by some of that mystique which set aflame the native radicalism of the Knights of Labor in the 1870's and the Industrial Workers of the World in the 1910's: *an injury to one is an injury to all.* That is why its supporters, like the late Philip Murray, fought attempts of communists and reactionaries to isolate the U. S. from the world and instead supported the Marshall plan for Europe, technical assistance to underdeveloped countries, freedom for colonial people, and a sturdy United Nations.

Most advocates of *political unionism* would subscribe to these stated objectives of democratic unionism, but would part company by attaching prime importance to labor's role in politics. In many ways today's political unionists are legatees of those who fought against Samuel Gompers fifty years ago. They would tend to stress the social benefits of government action and underemphasize the efficacy of collective bargaining. They would regard the union primarily as a stepping stone to labor's control of political life rather than as an instrument of economic democracy. They would concentrate, through a labor party, on restoring labor to its rightful place in the political sun. By contrast democratic unionism would attempt to establish that place by putting order into the house of labor, and by establishing economic democracy with the aid but not the direction of government.

These three orientations do not represent sharply distinct groupings within the labor movement. They are, rather, tendencies with distinguishable lines frequently blurred. The philosophy of most union leaders would be a blend of these. A recent study of the reading habits of American labor leaders was concluded with these words: "The literary recollections of union leaders are indeed a mixed dish. All sorts of writings—utopian-visions, Irish longings for liberty, documents of the Founding Fathers, and the idealism and collective salvation of both the socialist movement and the Catholic Church—all have been transmuted into organized union protest against social wrongs."

At the risk of some artificial classification, examples might be helpful. George Meany, the president of the recently merged AFL-CIO, began his union career as a "business unionist" but today typifies democratic unionism. Walter Reuther started out dedicated to political unionism but has steadily been moving in the direction of democratic unionism. The purest examples of business unionism are to be found among the union leaders in the building trades, teamsters and coal miners. David McDonald, president of the United Steelworkers of America, a union with more than 1,000,000 members, has until recently made his home with democratic unionism but is now developing many of the domestic habits of business unionism. Most presidents of national unions would represent the philosophy of business unionism while the leaders of national federations would generally reflect the point of view of democratic unionism. The position of political unionism is today the weakest of the competing philosophies.

Unity in the ranks of the 15 million union members who belong to the AFL and CIO accentuates this competition. As this new solidarity enlarges the U. S. labor movement's influence upon national and world affairs, it will be exceedingly important—not only to Americans but also the world at large—as to which of the triad of rival "philosophies" will be more persuasive and ultimately prevail.

3. The Impact of Catholics Upon the Labor Movement

Finally, the Church today is also the heir of a paradoxical development in U. S. history. On the one hand a long stand-

ing friendship exists between the Church and the leaders of
the American labor movement, while on the other hand the
great bulk of Catholic union members know little or nothing of the Church's social doctrine.

In view of the fluid character of the American labor movement—the struggle for hegemony by the conflicting philosophies of democratic, business and political unionism has
not yet been resolved—the absence of a solid base of informed
Catholic union members is portentous. It means that while
Catholic union membership is proportionately high, Christian social teaching will have a disproportionately low influence. It means that democratic unionism, which seems most
truly to represent the thinking of Christians moved by the
Church's social gospel, will have fewer defendants. And the
labor movement will be left, for all practical purposes, with
a choice only between business or political unionism.

Some years ago, in a monthly magazine devoted to pastoral
problems, the question was raised as to whether Catholics
were familiar with Christian social doctrine and whether they
recognized any sacred duty to put it into practice in field,
office, factory, or trade. The magazine published an eloquent
answer from Monsignor Joseph F. Donnelly, full-time director of the Archdiocesan Labor Institute in the highly-indus-
trialized state of Connecticut, who described his experience
with a worker in an evening class which had just been told
about the social encyclicals. The worker said:

"I have been in the labor movement 23 years and that is
the first time I have ever heard anything about the encyclicals. Isn't it the teaching of the church?"

"Yes, of course," the Monsignor replied.

"Well, I go to Mass every Sunday and I have never once
heard anyone mention in Church anything about these encyclicals. If the Church wants things done as they are taught
in the encyclicals, why don't they tell the people?"

In reply the Monsignor said confidently: "It may be true
that the encyclicals have not been mentioned in your parish
as often as they might have been, but you cannot make a

judgment based on your parish and say that they have not
been taught to the people in other parishes."

"I have never heard," the workingman said, "that they
were mentioned in any church." He turned to the fellow on
his right: "Did you ever hear them in your church?"

"No," was the very decided response.

He put the same question to a second, third, fourth and
fifth man. The answer was always "No." Then from the back
of the room a young fellow spoke up:

"I have heard about the encyclicals many times, Father."

Everybody turned around to look at that "strange" person—a man who had heard many times of the social encyclicals.

Summing up his experience, Monsignor Donnelly said:

"It was a rather unique introduction to the charge that I
have heard repeatedly, though in somewhat less striking fashion, many times since. It seems that we are the Church of the
poor and the workers, but workers who for the most part
know nothing of the great documents of Leo XIII and Pius
XI, and workers who have little idea that the Church has any
definite teachings on the problems of organized labor and the
role of organized workers in the reconstruction of society.
Perhaps this ignorance may yet prove to be the greatest
tragedy of the Church in our age."

Efforts to counteract this ignorance have been made
through labor schools, social action departments in various
dioceses, the Catholic press, organizations like the Association
of Catholic Trade Unionists and the Catholic Labor Alliance,
and so on. But the effort has been a very small leaven in a
large loaf. Will Herberg, a staff member of the International
Ladies Garment Workers Union, speaking of the failure of
all religious groups to provide American labor with "a conscience . . . a philosophy, or long-range perspective," says:

"What I want to stress here is how little religion has been
operative in the lives of leaders and rank and file workers
alike in their capacity as members of the labor movement.
Among Catholics, and they constitute a very high proportion
of organized labor, there has been almost total divorce

between their religion and their labor activity. Recent efforts of the Association of Catholic Trade Unionists to make their religion relevant to their responsibilities in the labor movement have met with bitter opposition on the part of the most prominent Catholic labor leaders, who insist that the place of religion is in the church. As for Protestants and Jews in labor's ranks, their outlook on social questions is almost entirely secular, and the relevance of their religion, if they have any, to their labor concerns never so much as enters their minds."

Concentrated in the large industrial cities, Catholics make up the largest single group in the unions. A considerably higher proportion of Catholics are union members than any other religious group. They joined labor organizations for basically the same reasons as did everybody else: higher wages, security of job, a desire for self-expression, preservation of their dignity, and better working conditions. In the unions they joined hands with their fellow non-Catholics *as union members* to achieve these objectives. Like their fellow union members in the big cities, Catholic working people were solidly behind the New Deal reforms under President Franklin D. Roosevelt, and have generally been more socially-conscious than their middle class and rural Protestant brethren. However, Catholic workers have not been as socially-minded as their Jewish brothers.

A 1954 study by a Benedictine monk of the attitude of industrial workers in a Midwestern city revealed that while most of them supported the idea of a living family wage, the necessity of labor unions, the social obligations of private ownership, and so on, the *source* of these attitudes was not the Church—even though all of the men had attended a Catholic high school. Their opinions on vital social and economic and international questions were the result of exclusively secular influences, like the union, political party and public opinion.

These same influences, by and large, determine the position Catholics will take on most public issues. Like their Protestant and Jewish neighbors, Catholics who leave the city to take up suburban residences tend to switch from the Democratic to the Republican party. Like their non-Catholic neighbors, they aim to go up the economic and social ladder. In common, they share a driving ambition to "get along"— which means a higher income, a home of their own in the "better" section of the city or in the suburbs, and a college education for their children.

Under such conditions, it is fatuous to expect Catholic workingmen and women to play a decisive part orientating the American labor movement along the lines of Christian social teaching. Without an informed Christian social conscience, Catholics, even though their number in unions is proportionately quite high, will be followers rather than leaders in the competition among business, democratic and political unionism for the right to chart the future course of the American labor movement.

The future, then, of the Church's closeness to the labor movement is by no means secure. It is quite possible that the Church's great tradition of deep sympathy for working people and their unions, which Cardinal Gibbons began 70 years ago and which has continued to the present day, could be lost to the United States and to the world. Chiefly responsible for such a tragedy would be a failure by the Church to develop laymen whose militancy and philosophy find their source in the gospel of Christ. Through such laymen, and not primarily through bishops and priests as in the past, will this 70-year old tradition be nourished and extended.

CHAPTER SEVENTEEN

The Catholic Church and Racial Segregation

———— ✦ ————

BY JOHN LA FARGE, S.J.

SOME TIME AGO a distressing bit of news aroused a wave of sympathy all over the United States. Junius Kellogg, a youthful basketball star, and a student at Manhattan College, New York City, conducted by the Brothers of the Christian Schools, had been seriously injured in an automobile collision, along with three of his young companions. At the date of writing, Junius is still lingering in a highly critical condition. The incident might have attracted less notice, were it not for two added facts. Kellogg is a Negro, as well as a Catholic. Moreover, he had already won national notice by a moral victory. Alone, and wholly on his own initiative, he

---

John La Farge, S.J., is Associate Editor of America, *the National Catholic Weekly, and former Editor-in-Chief. Father LaFarge has distinguished himself through his interest in all matters relating to the relations of various racial groups in the United States. His latest book,* The Catholic Viewpoint on Race Relations, *was published this year.*

had exposed the actions of a ring of persons who were trying to bribe basketball teams in the various inter-collegiate contests. It was Kellogg's forthright language which revealed a situation which many suspected, but about which little or no direct testimony could be obtained.

But again this interesting fact might have passed with less notice, had it not been for a quite special circumstance in Kellogg's case. The young man who thus stood out before the public eye was a Negro, in a predominantly white institution. This demonstration of his moral courage and integrity was an implicit condemnation of the moral and cultural stigma which the practice of racial segregation has tried to place upon the Negro people in our modern world. It was likewise a fine vindication of the policy now largely adopted by Catholic educational institutions in the United States, of disregarding this stigma, of repudiating the policy of segregation and completely integrating students of all races, colors, and nationalities into their academic bodies.

Incidents of this kind—and in one form or another they are of daily occurrence—keep the interest of the public aroused as to what real estimate is to be placed upon the policy of racial segregation, and they bring it into further disfavor. The word "policy" is used advisedly, for segregation may be considered merely as an act, of itself indifferent in its nature, as in the direction of a line of people waiting for tickets or visas we ask those whose names begin with A to M to apply at one window, those whose names begin from N to Z at the other. Civilized usage segregates and separates people in countless fashions, as we also do in ordinary ecclesiastical usage. Segregation as a social policy, however, is a very different affair. It extends into innumerable phases of ordinary human life, such as employment, residence, education and professional training. Moreover, in the United States, segregation as a social policy is in part institutionalized and sanctioned by law. This law runs through an infinite variety of modalities, ranging from the positive *imposition* of segregatory practices, in certain states of the Union, under severe penalties for any violation, through a complex gamut of legal prescriptions and social customs. Its deepest root is a belief which derives from the former slavery epoch, and has persisted into our own times: that the Negro is naturally a servant of the white man and should be treated as such. But this belief is steadily giving way to the plain realities of the Negro's astonishing progress, especially in the field of education and employment. On the other hand, certain States have adopted the precisely opposite policy; the official prohibition of segregation, with legal penalties imposed for any attempt to put it into effect.

Any attempts to disentangle the complicated skein of law and custom would incur countless details. Hence I merely note a few points that may serve as a guide, and may prevent discussion from becoming pointless and sterile.

1. Evils of Segregation

The objections against segregation as a practice are too familiar to need much elaboration. Some of the more outstanding reasons may be briefly summarized as follows:

1. In the largely industrialized modern world, segregation creates positive hardship for the group upon which it is imposed: an economic as well as spiritual damage.

2. From its nature, it is an offense against the human person, a violation of his natural dignity and rights, *even when he gives to it, as an individual, his full consent.* Stated thus simply, this bald pronouncement makes less impression upon the mind than does the actual experience of the workings of the segregation system, related as it is to the most ordinary events of human existence and intercourse. No person or group of persons can experience it for any length of time without being exposed to a profound psychological scar: resulting from the constant experience of being politely, but always definitely informed that one is simply not a normal human being who can be trusted to eat at the same restaurants, visit the same theatres, sleep in the same public accommodations, as the rest of the world. It is often these smaller matters, the pin pricks, which cause resentment

greater than graver ones that involve tangible economic loss. The Negro New Yorker who drives at will east to west across the continent without thought of encountering any distinction, suffers an unpleasant shock when, but a few hours southward out of New York City, he is suddenly confronted with large signs: COLORED MOTELS, COLORED REST ROOMS, COLORED COFFEE SHOP, etc. Service in these segregated facilities may be almost as good as in the others—or it may not—but the imputation is deeply resented, and uncertainty is always present.

A sense of frustration and injustice is particularly keen when distinctions are applied to the ordinary functions of religious life, to the position within the religious community itself. This would include such practices as the assignment of Negroes to special seating in the churches, exclusion from membership in local units of national Catholic organizations, or from the novitiates of various religious communities for men or—more frequently—for women. It would include also the advocacy of such practices by Catholics in prominent positions, especially by members of the clergy themselves.

With the advance and growing complexity of Catholic life, and the corresponding advance in the Negro's education and general status in the civic community, any such treatment within the Church itself is profoundly resented, and is felt much more keenly than it was in former years. At the same time a profound impression has been made upon the Negro community everywhere in the United States by the vigorous and forthright action taken on this subject by such prelates as Archbishop Rummel of New Orleans, Archbishop Lucey of San Antonio (Texas), Archbishop Ritter of St. Louis (Missouri), and Bishop Vincent S. Waters, of Raleigh (North Carolina), whose dioceses lie in southern or semi-southern regions where segregation, in one form or another, has been the rule in ecclesiastical as well as in civil life.

It is a great mistake to think that the adoption of racial segregation as a social policy is an unmitigated advantage to those who enforce it and only a handicap to those who are its direct victims. Long experience as well as careful sociologi-

cal research reveals the harmful effects of segregation upon
the entire morale of the community. From a practical point
of view it engenders economic difficulties. A thoroughly
organized system of segregation demands duplication to an
appalling degree of facilities of every description. It means
the non-employment in both industry and agriculture of
able and willing workers, something particularly distressing
in a period where manpower is sorely needed. Indeed the
problem of providing a completely dual educational system
on an equal but separate basis has, practically speaking,
been met with only in a very limited number of communities
in those thirteen States where segregation still exists by State
law. In the vast majority of instances the authorities have
simply given up the idea of providing complete service for
both groups. Segregation as a social policy produces, moreover, blighted areas in the cities, ghettos and slums which
are themselves a menace from the standpoint of economic
welfare and of health to the general community. As was recently pointed out, in many such a blighted area the amount
required for various municipal and social services is ten times
the amount of that which can be collected in taxes. In other
words, as a social policy in the civic area segregation is simply
an expensive luxury.

This economic wastefulness is particularly evident in the
residential section, where the attempt to avoid any contact
with those of other races produces depreciation of property.
The fear, indeed the panic aroused over such contiguity is
used by unscrupulous real-estate dealers as a means for producing blighted areas and ultimately destroying fundamental
civil and economic values. Precisely as this point has become
clear, American citizens evidence an increasing readiness to
break away from the segregatory or separatist pattern and to
adjust themselves to the presence of other races in their
midst.

Yet the writer cannot help feeling a certain diffidence in
treating of this topic for readers. No matter how carefully
one's language is qualified, a wrong impression is so easily
conveyed. The mention of annoying and unjust features of

racial segregation in such localities, or in such social milieux, where it is practiced, may fail to give due credit to the extent that it has been officially banned, and in fact largely eliminated, from large areas of Catholic life in the U. S. A. Insistence upon the evils of segregation where it is practiced, is apt to throw into obscurity the fine example of so many of the country's larger dioceses, such as that of New York, Brooklyn, or other dioceses of the great state of New York, where the official policy of the Church is flatly opposed to the entire idea, and where every effort is made to extend this same spirit into every area of Catholic life and worship and ready hearing is given to any complaints on this score. A brief camera tour of many of our large centers is a flat refutation of much current Communist propaganda.

Conversation on this matter with visitors to our country, or while traveling abroad, has led the writer to the conclusion that certain features in the segregation issue may well be emphasized, if a fair picture is to be presented of the case.

These may be summed up under two principal headings: *ambiguities (equivoques)* and *remedies*. The former confuse the issue; the latter vastly clarify it. Let us consider first the ambiguities, particularly as they affect the religious life of the Church.

2. Ambiguities (Equivoques)

I. "SPECIAL" WORKS

A troublesome ambiguity arises from the fact that many of the very practices which today are viewed and resented by the Negroes as implying racial discrimination originally implied precisely the opposite. They were instituted as a simple method of enabling as was thought, people of very different cultural and social backgrounds to live or to worship together peaceably. But practices initiated in good faith can be transformed into instruments of bad faith, into manifestation of racial prejudice, into easy ways of escaping certain elementary duties of Christian fellowship and love.

The seats marked "for colored" in the "white" church assured the Negro that within those confines, at least, he would be freely admitted and enjoy full rights as a fellow-worshipper. The "special" church and special school for the Negro, the special provision for recreation and social life, such as the colored parish hall, was looked upon as an advance from a state of total dependence upon the white majority. The other implication, that of segregation, became apparent only when these same "special"—or separate—facilities, began to be utilized by persons among the clergy and laity as an excuse to exclude the Negro from general participation in Catholic community life. The exclusion was not always felt at the time, but it became painfully evident once a Negro individual or family found itself in circumstances where the "separate" pattern, instead of being a convenience, imposed real hardship. A Negro mother, for instance, found it anything but safe or agreeable to send her children to the "Negro" school across the area of a large city, when the "white" Catholic school was but a few city blocks away.

"Special" works for the Negro, therefore, which were inaugurated as works of selfless condescension and sublime charity for the poor and forgotten black, changed their aspect with the advance of time, and the Negroes came to wonder more and more just why *they,* apart from all other human beings, were unfit for ordinary, routine association with others of their nation or of their faith.

We find then three stages, as it were, in the matter of "special" works for the Negro. In the first stage, that of "benevolence," or *material* segregation, the special undertaking is a pure gift to the member of the minority group. Such, for instance, was the series of institutions for the vocational training of Negroes and for their higher education, set up by private benevolence or by the public authorities as early as 1854 (Lincoln University, Pennsylvania). Such was and is the really sublime mission work of the Catholic Church in the U. S. A., the work of hundreds of devoted priests and nuns, of the various religious communities and many of the dioceses: churches, schools, orphanages, and other institutions. Such, too, were the special organizations for the Negro, such as the Knights of St. Peter Claver, a finely managed national beneficial organization, etc. These same Knights, incidentally, have recently opened their membership to the whites; a deeply significant step.

The second stage, as already noted, is that of *formed* segregation, when the existence of these institutions *is* used by thoughtless or malevolent people as an excuse for exclusion from the main current of religious or civil life and thought, precisely when the Negro has learned to benefit by their ministrations and seeks admission to a wider field.

Those who have heroically labored precisely in the segregated field, the priests, religious women, or laymen who have toiled on behalf of the Negro under social conditions of great adversity, and have identified their lives with those of the poorest of God's poor, are naturally sensitive to criticisms. Hence in many instances the struggle against segregation has been taken as an unfavorable reflection upon the positive ministry of the Church on behalf of the Negro. Insistence upon full equality of opportunity and equal status in the Mystical Body of Christ is sometimes labeled as radicalism or scoffed at as a type of "armchair warfare." In some instances it has been resented as such by the Negroes themselves who are comfortably settled in minor teaching or welfare positions.

Religious communities which are particularly consecrated to work for the Negro and therefore have explicitly avoided ministrations to the white Catholic majority, find themselves in a somewhat difficult position, when the Negro finds himself quite free to avail himself of the same opportunities in the parish or in the school as are provided for the whites. Yet this is simply a question of readjustment. The *raison d'etre* for their work still continues at present, only on a wider, more all-embracing basis, and may continue for many years to come.

Looked at from an historical viewpoint the matter is further complicated by the fact that militant opposition, first to slavery and later, after the emancipation, to the effects of slavery, viz., the inferior position of Negroes in civic life, was in the nineteenth century largely in the hands of groups

in the United States which were for the greater part fiercely
antagonistic to the Catholic Church. The Irish immigrants
to this country a century ago found themselves completely
ostracized by the abolitionist elements in the North, particularly in New England, who in point of fact had introduced
slavery to the United States through their merchant marine,
but later, for largely political reasons, became its opponents.
These same elements forced, as it were, the Catholic Irish
into an alliance with the friends of slavery in the South
producing an equivocation for the Church itself. Hence it
was that some of the Church's most leading prelates in the
ante-bellum days, such as Bishop England of Charleston,
S. C., and Archbishop Hughes of New York City, considered
themselves obliged to take up at least a neutral position in
the struggle against slavery. And even when slavery was past
as an institution, considerable suspicion remained against
those who would take up the cudgels too vigorously on behalf
of the Negro. The Church's mission work for the Negro,
therefore, was begun under these difficult auspices. The Catholic Negro found himself looked upon with suspicion by his
new-found white Catholic brethren and ostracized by his
Negro former religious brethren in Protestantism, and as a
Catholic he was likewise removed from the friendship of
those Protestant white philanthropists who otherwise would
have wished to befriend him.

II. COMMUNIST AMBIGUITY (EQUIVOQUE)

To a certain extent the situation has been confused by the
other element of ambiguity, namely, the militant, supposedly
anti-segregation policies of the Communists and fellow travel-
ers. The effect of these has been to create anxiety in the
minds of many people lest any concerted, systematic attack
upon segregation may be following the Communist line.
In point of fact, this line is by no means as clear as one would
imagine. Individual cases of discrimination have been widely
publicized and used in many instances as an opportunity for
collecting large sums of money. But the Communists have
been singularly wary of committing themselves too freely to

any completely all-out anti-segregation policy for the simple reason that they have never fully succeeded in renouncing one of the two prime elements in their official party line in the United States, which is that of the segregated Negro Soviet state in the so-called Black Belt of the South. Stalin proclaimed this idea apparently in analogy with the alleged treatment of minority groups in the Union of Socialist Republics, and it has been a continual bone of contention among Negro Leftists in the United States. Never too openly proclaimed and yet never renounced, it recently has been revived when many thought that with Stalin's death it would have been abandoned forever.

3. Integration

Hence the problem presents itself of attaining what one might call the third stage in the evolution of special work for the Negro, namely, that of adjusting it to the new conditions, removing from it the poison of exclusivism, separatism and segregation and bringing it to a normal level in the evolution of the entire Catholic community.

Progressive integration of the Negro into the general community has been increasing, one may say, with geometrical progression in recent years and every month adds its quota of achievements. Integration into every form of industrial occupation and upgrading in industrial organizations, integration in education, even in the regions where there has been considerable opposition in the past, indeed in every form of life. Intelligent Negroes in the United States complain that American films exported to foreign countries do not show the degree to which the Negro is actually participating in the complex life of the country as an ordinary citizen; such as a municipal employee, a labor leader, college student, member of a women's civic organization, etc., etc. They are still, as a rule, represented in a pathetic or else in a menial capacity, if they are depicted at all.

Some of this integration is obviously the result of historical development and the experiences of World War II. The in-

evitable consequence, as Gunnar Myrdal pointed out, of the
Negro's advance in education, of his use of the facilities
which were originally provided for him in a segregated form.
But it cannot all be attributed to merely natural and general
progress. Much of it is the result of planned and actively
organized interracial work. Undoubtedly the extraordinary
change which has taken place with regard to the situation of
the Negro in the Catholic Church in the last ten or fifteen
years has been aided by the continued persevering activity of
the Catholic interracial movement, which celebrated on June
6, 1954, the twentieth anniversary of its formal inauguration
in New York City on Pentecost Sunday, 1934. This movement combats and continues to combat segregation directly,
seeking to penetrate to its causes, to solve the practical problems that arise from integration, and particularly to seek
those motives and inducements which will positively help
towards the adjustment of both individuals and groups in
their community.

In point of fact—to permit to myself a certain pragmaticism
—complete integration does "work" to an extraordinary extent: precisely in those humbler phases of life which would
have been noticeable a decade or so ago but pass unnoticed
at the present time. On the very day that I happened to write
these lines I was present at a wedding in St. Patrick's Cathedral in New York City. Of the two acolytes who served the
celebrant at the nuptial Mass one was a white boy, the other
was a full blooded Negro. The striking thing was not that
there was a Negro server, which now would be entirely a
matter of course in the Archdiocese of New York, but rather
the fact that nobody noticed it; neither the bride nor the
groom nor indeed any of the casual visitors to the cathedral.
Yet a few years ago it would have been the cause of much
comment and excitement.

Such phrases as that the Negroes are "happier by themselves," they "want to be left alone," etc., are susceptible of
vastly different meanings. If they mean that every group
enjoys a certain amount of congenial companionship with
those of similar origins and tastes, the expression can pass.

But if it is taken, as frequently it is used, in the sense that being "happier," as it is said, "by themselves," they should be forced legally or ecclesiastically to remain by themselves, the phrase is obviously false. The number of Negroes who are completely happy by themselves when they know that separation is imposed upon them is derisively small. Those Negroes who outwardly accept for reasons of personal advantage, the implication of a permanent servant status, are usually inwardly resentful, and will say so when they can speak frankly.

The opposite policy is the complete integration of the Negro and of all minority groups, such as the various Spanish-speaking groups, the Indians and the Orientals, into the general body politic.

The most powerful single blow ever known to the policy of segregation was delivered by the Supreme Court of the United States when on May 17, 1954 its nine judges announced their unanimous decision, that segregation in State-supported schools is contrary to the Fourteenth Amendment of the Constitution of the United States. This Fourteenth Amendment guarantees to all citizens the equal protection of the laws. The Court's interpretation upset the previous interpretation reached in 1896 which asserted the so-called separate but equal doctrine, and was preceded by half a century of special cases in which the impracticality and unsoundness of the separate but equal doctrine became increasingly apparent. The May 17 decision was uttered in response to the demands of five plaintiffs, in each case Negro children seeking admission to the public schools.

The Court's decision was brief and based not on subtle legal considerations but on the simple sociological fact, namely, that the equality of educational opportunity guaranteed by the nation to all its children could not be fulfilled under a policy of segregation. The Court thus questioned and answered itself saying: "Does segregation of children in public schools solely on the basis of race, even though the physical facilities and other 'tangible' factors may be equal, deprive the children of the minority group of equal educational opportunities? We believe that it does." In confirmation of its position, the Court quoted findings in a State Court which held that "Segregation of white and colored children in public schools has a detrimental effect upon the colored children. The impact was greater when it has the sanction of the law; for the policy of separating the races is usually interpreted as denoting the inferiority of the Negro group. A sense of inferiority affects the motivation of a child to learn."

The Court postponed to a later session in October of the same year the presentation of arguments as to the ways and means by which the people of the various States where segregation prevails could work out an integrated school system. Despite sensational items played up by the public press both in the United States and abroad, the reaction in the segregation States was relatively calm and mild. Since the decision concerned a matter of principle, its effect would naturally be much more far-reaching than the limited area of the public schools and will undoubtedly be felt in the policy of Catholic educational institutions as well.

4. Cooperation: The Local Community

So long and complex has been the fight against segregation that whenever the barrier is broken down and this particular illusion is dispelled, there is temptation to think that the battle is wholly won. Nothing, however, could be more delusive. On the contrary, the removal of this particular obstacle is merely the signal to begin the very much more fundamental work of adjustment between the different groups in the community. Even where segregation is officially proscribed, social exclusion and unfriendliness can be practiced in more subtle form. No matter how many safeguards are created, some ostracism can always be practiced if good feeling is absent. Furthermore, there is need of a positive spirit of cooperation, based upon a firm and intelligent conviction on the part of everybody that they have a common interest in the community's welfare and so are willing to work together.

Two areas in particular are especially critical in the field of interracial relations in the United States at the present day. One of these is in the field of employment; the other is that of residence or housing. In the field of employment there is still a great deal of discrimination to be combatted. In the fall of 1953 a committee of the National Planning Association issued a report on the Negro in Southern industry. It showed that Negroes rarely reached a supervisory status in the Southern States, never over white workers. There was almost complete exclusion from white collar employment. The Negro has been associated with the American economy for a very long time, but until recently his contribution was made mostly in agriculture, not in industry. Great changes, however, are now coming in the economic, social, and political order. The lives of 26,000,000 people will be affected. Hence there is a distinct challenge to American management to practice social justice with regard to the Negro. Even from the purely materialistic standpoint there is the argument of sustained purchasing power. Nearly 16,000,000 Negroes make a market that business cannot ignore. Early employment at decent wages will remove poverty and the fear and despair which poverty engenders.

Discrimination against the Negro does prevail in large sectors of American industry, a fact which is fuel for the fires of anti-American propaganda in many parts of the world, yet there is steady progress towards its removal. In a speech given on October 23, 1953, in Brussels, Belgium, Cardinal Spellman, Archbishop of New York, articulately stated:

Most Americans will agree that the greatest single failure of American democracy has been its failure with regard to the Negro. It does not make inspiring reading to see how many obstacles were placed in his way to secure legal freedom and equality. . . . The status of the Negro has occasioned much interest and critical discussion in Europe, and I am proud to report on the progress that has been made in solving this important problem.

The estimated loss to the consumer market caused by discrimination against the Negro has been estimated at least in a billion dollars a year, namely, ten per cent of the productive potential of the nation. Over against the debit of that loss there is the credit of the advantages found by the employment of Negroes without distinction, as has been shown abundantly by the experience of a large number of outstanding industrial firms in the United States. One of these industrialists, Joseph J. Morrow, personnel director of Pitney-Bowes Postal Meters, Inc., of Stamford, Conn., remarks: "The difficulties one expects to encounter in initiating such a program of full employment materialized to the extent of about 5 per cent of what was anticipated."

Most difficult of all is the question of the residential areas. The question grows more acute as the pressure of population and the corresponding demand for housing increases. This is indeed a front line for Catholic Action along the lines of interracial justice. New communities or neighborhoods spring up by the hundreds and thousands in the vicinity of our great cities and the minority populations, like everybody else, are anxious to move out of crowded ghetto quarters into regions where they can enjoy the benefit of greater space and find a proper environment for the raising of a family. At the same time, inhabitants of older and more settled neighborhoods are alarmed at the prospect of the new strangers moving in. Indeed the better the community or neighborhood is organized the more resentful its inhabitants are apt to be against any change in its racial or national complexion. Hence there is a distinct temptation for both clergy and laity where the neighborhood is fairly homogeneous in the Catholic sense to join resistance to any such innovation.

Yet here, too, the problem is far from being insoluble. Enough experience is at hand to show amply how neighborhood standards of decency and public morality can be maintained despite rapid changes in population, simply through the generous cooperation of all people concerned. This requires, of course, effort and planning sometimes of a more or less professional character. It requires especially the enthusiastic leadership of the clergy and of Catholic organizations. But happily to say such leadership is by no means infrequent. I have personally visited and can personally cite any number of newer neighborhoods where the decided and hospitable stand of the local clergy, as well as of local Catholics and their organizations, have welcomed the newcomers and made them feel entirely at home in their new surroundings. This is a humble sort of work, and it gets very little attention in the headlines. But from the standpoint of Christian sociology it is a matter of profound importance for the increasingly crowded world. Not only the question of material homes but still more the question of human relations between home-owners and home occupants is becoming of more and more crucial importance, so much so that a real science of community relationships is developing.

5. Cooperation: The World Community

Problems of the local community lead to the problems of the world community. The severest judgment upon segregation as a social policy comes from those who see its disastrous bearing on the harmonious relations of the different races of the world, and from the standpoint of the American people themselves the harm it is apt to produce in their relations with foreign countries. More and more embarrassing for Americans are the comments of people from other nations or continents who arrive in the United States and are dismayed when they find themselves confronted by the rigid prescriptions of the States where segregation is the law, or by the less rigid but sometimes more really vicious and hateful subtler ostracisms that are found in the supposedly entirely free parts of the Union. It would be easy to dwell on this unpleasant aspect of the whole matter but it seems better to conclude on a much more practical and constructive note, which is first of all that the *whole question of segregation is the question of a dying cause,* a losing cause, a relic from earlier days. The tragedy, if there is such, is not so much in its existence as in the retardation or the lag of its disappearance. On the other hand, the long battle against it, the complications and the deeper psychological, economic and moral roots of racial segregation and discrimination have earned for the American

people a valuable fund of convictions. These are a *permanent contribution to human relations* within the framework
of our own country and within the framework of the entire
human race. It is my firm belief that the victories that we
have won over this particular evil, even though those victories are not complete and are still imperfect, are sufficiently
meaningful and dynamic to serve as a contribution to the
peace of the entire world. The strongest friendships are
among those whose love has been tried by conflict and suspicion but overcome by right reason and a determination
that such conflicts shall not again occur.

Repeatedly I have heard students from the various non-
white countries, especially those from tropical Africa, tell me
that though they were at first shocked by some of the unpleasant treatment they witnessed in the United States, their
predominant feeling on returning is gratitude for what they
have learned of the better aspects of our racial situation.
They are bringing home with them to their respective countries the practical solution of similar problems at home
which, after all, are rooted in the same fundamental human
weaknesses and passions. For better or worse, the United
States happens to be at the present moment the strongest
nation in the world. We Americans can only pray very humbly and with fear and trembling that by the grace of God we
may not misuse that strength and may live up to its terrific
implications; otherwise God will punish us for neglect as He
has done to so many strong people in the past. But it is com-
forting to think that undoubtedly one of the elements in that
strength has been the presence among us of one-tenth of our
population, namely, of the Negro race. We should not be the
nation we are if we had not had that great contribution, the
contribution of patience, wisdom, strength and hope in
the past; a contribution, I am sure, of joyous and intelligent
cooperation in the future. I pray that this joyous and intelligent cooperation of our own citizens of all races and color
among ourselves may be only a part of our own American cooperation for a world knit together by the bonds of a true
and God-given peace.

CHAPTER EIGHTEEN

The Catholic Church and Religious Freedom

———— ◆ ————

BY JOHN A. O'BRIEN

WHEN THE TRAVELER from the Old World sails into the harbor of New York, he sees the majestic Statue of Liberty holding aloft in her right hand the torch of freedom. It is the sculptural voicing of the Constitutional guarantee of the right of the individual to worship God according to the dictates of his own conscience. Back of this happy culmination, however, lies more than a century of struggle.

It is one of the ironies of history that the early colonial settlers fleeing from the religious intolerance of the Old World so speedily re-established it in the New World. Like so

---

John A. O'Brien, author-in-residence at the University of Notre Dame, has written and edited about twenty-five books on theology, philosophy and science. Some of his best known books are The Faith of Millions, Truths Men Live By, What's the Truth About Catholics?, Bringing Souls to Christ, The Road to Damascus, Roads to Rome, You Too Can Win Souls, *and* Where Dwellest Thou?

much baggage, they carried with them the sectarian prejudices, hatreds and persecution complexes which they had
accumulated in the strife-ridden life of Europe. In 1631 Puritan Massachusetts passed an ordinance limiting citizenship
to conforming church members. Only those in "full communion" could be freemen. This meant that approximately
only one in five adult male residents of the colony had the
rights of full citizenship.

In New England heresy laws cancelled the civil rights of
any person who denied certain religious doctrines. In 1647
an act was passed, as severe as any in England, decreeing the
punishment of any Catholic priest who might be found in
the colony. Writing from England to two friends in Massachusetts, Sir Richard Saltonstall, a Puritan, lamented: "It
doth not a little grieve my spirit to hear what sad things are
reported daily of your tyranny and persecution in New England, as that you fine, whip and imprison men for their conscience."

To Maryland goes the distinction of maintaining a civil
society from 1634 to 1649 without an incident of persecution
because of religious belief or lack of it. This was due to two
pioneering Catholic statesmen—the two Lord Baltimores,
George and Calvert, and his son Cecil. As Catholics, they had
suffered persecution in Virginia, and they were now determined to safeguard religious freedom for everyone in Maryland.

After listening to a bitter attack upon the Jews, the Assembly of New York decided in 1737 that they were not
entitled to vote. Here was an early manifestation of European anti-Semitism that was destined to crop up so often in
American life.

Forty years later John Jay attempted, though in vain, to
have written into the Constitution of New York the exclusion of Catholics from both civil and political rights, "until
such time as they appear in the Supreme Court of this State,
and there most solemnly swear that they verily believe in
their consciences that no pope, priest or foreign authority on

earth have power to absolve the subjects of Rome from their allegiance to same."

Here is laid bare the strange fear that has haunted the minds of many non-Catholics throughout the years. It was this which prompted the American Protective Association a century later to urge the same provision. This apprehension cropped up again in 1928 when Al Smith, a Catholic, was nominated for the presidency.

The continued arrival of an ever increasing number of immigrants of diverse religious beliefs helped mightily in hastening the day when the liberal and enlightened views of Washington, Jefferson and Madison would be woven into the basic law of the land.

"Is uniformity attainable?" asked Jefferson. "Millions of innocent men, women and children, since the introduction of Christianity, have been burnt, tortured, fined, imprisoned; yet we have not advanced one inch toward uniformity." He drafted the statute for religious freedom in Virginia, which became the first law ever passed by a popular assembly providing complete freedom of conscience.

In 1786 was adopted the Federal Constitution which provided in Article VI that "no religious test shall ever be required as a qualification to any office or public trust under the United States." This guarantee was clarified and strengthened by the First Amendment, which declares, "Congress shall make no law respecting an establishment of religion, or prohibiting the free exercise thereof."

Despite these clear guarantees of complete religious freedom, waves of organized bigotry and hatred have periodically swept across our land. Notorious among these were the Nativist movement of the 1830's, and the Know-Nothing campaign of the 1850's, the Loyalty League, the original Ku Klux Klan and allied movements of the post-Civil War period, the American Protective Association of the 1890's, the revived Ku Klux Klan after World War I and the anti-Semitism of the 1930's.

They kindled the fagots of flaming hatreds in a thousand communities, incited mob violence that led to the murder of hundreds of innocent victims, to beatings, brandings and whippings, and to the burning and looting of stores and homes. In the Know-Nothing riot in 1855 in Louisville alone more than a hundred innocent victims were butchered or burned to death, while the civil authorities, all Know-Nothings, stood idly by.

Foremost in seeking to eradicate such hatreds is the National Conference of Christians and Jews. Founded in 1928 on the initiative of Protestant, Catholic and Jewish leaders, chiefly laymen, the Conference seeks to promote justice, amity and understanding among citizens of all faiths. It endeavors to analyze, moderate and ultimately eliminate interfaith prejudices, which disfigure and distort religious, business, social and political relations, with a view to the establishment of friendly human relationships.

Membership in the Conference does not entail any blurring of denominational lines, any least common denominator of religious creeds, or any compromise with the principles of one's faith. While loyal to their respective faiths, the members of the Conference find there are large areas of common interest, where as Americans and as people of good will they can work together for the betterment of the community, of America and of the world.

To ward off any appearance of implying religious indifferentism as the postulate of its operations, the National Conference has officially declared: "N.C.C.J. acknowledges the freedom of the Catholic or the Jew or the Protestant to hold that his faith is the one true faith. It does not affirm such a holding by any one of the three, for it could obviously do so only at the expense of the other two; but neither does it disaffirm. It is not indifferentist, therefore, it is simply, as it must be, non-preferential."

The Conference endeavors to promote affirmative cooperative action among Protestants, Catholics and Jews, in areas of common civic concern. Its efforts in this regard, however, are limited to those things which the members of the three faiths acknowledge to lie within the area proper to such common action. Hence it has no direct business in the area of doctrinal differences, and so scrupulously avoids involvement in the field of theology.

With the branches established in most of our large cities, the Conference sponsors Brotherhood Week each year and brings together representatives of the three major faiths for frequent discussions of problems of common interest. Headed by Dr. Everett R. Clinchy, the Conference has been instrumental in nipping in the bud many explosions of religious rancor and has deepened and consolidated the peace and good will among members of different faiths in hundreds of communities.

Brotherhood Week was first conceived by the late Father Hugh W. McMenamin, the universally beloved pastor of the Cathedral in Denver. Its observance was started by the Conference in 1934 and it promises to become as much a part of the American calendar as Independence Day or Thanksgiving Day. A week in February is designated Brotherhood Week and the President of the United States issues a special message calling upon all the citizens to put into practice the ideals of tolerance, friendship and brotherhood.

As a result of the Conference's appeal, thousands of sermons are preached from the pulpits of all the major faiths during Brotherhood Week on the duty of respecting the beliefs of others and their rights to freedom of conscience and of worship. Even more important are their efforts to get at the sources of prejudice and bigotry, and through education and friendly conference, to eradicate them. Typical of their procedure is their work in many cities, where bi-weekly they bring together six Protestant ministers, six Catholic priests and two Jewish rabbis, who conduct an education program extending throughout the year. The extermination of religious rancors, inherited from centuries of strife in the Old World is no easy task, but education and cooperation by representatives of all the faiths, carried on patiently over the years, is the one method most likely to succeed.

At the present time American public opinion is overwhelmingly opposed to discrimination against a citizen because of creed or color. The decision of the Supreme Court against the practice, common in southern states, of having separate public schools for white and colored pupils, reflects the temper of public opinion against any form of discrimination.

Actual practice often lags behind the norm set forth in legal enactments and enshrined in the ideals of American democracy. Since religious prejudice springs largely from ignorance or misconceptions of other faiths, anti-Catholicism has flourished chiefly in those states and communities where there are few Catholics. As the percentage of Catholics in most of the southern states is still comparatively small, they have had to contend with prejudice for many years. Happily, however, it seems to be decreasing in intensity each year and to be increasingly frowned upon by the better elements in those communities.

For the most part Catholics are urban dwellers. Hence there has been more suspicion of them in country districts and rural hamlets and towns. This seems to be due to the fact that adversaries of the Catholic Church find in those areas a fertile field for the planting of anti-Catholics myths, charges and slanders. Since few of the residents in those areas have had any sustained contact with Catholics, there are few who are in a position to expose the unfounded character of such charges.

What are some of the stock charges? Those which have ranged through virtually the whole nation and have flourished particularly in the South and in rural districts are the following:

1. Catholics owe political allegiance to the pope in Rome and hence cannot give undivided allegiance to the constitution, laws and court decisions of their own country. This is perhaps the most widespread of all the charges and the one most widely believed in whole or in part by non-Catholics.

2. Catholics are looking forward to the day when, on orders from the pope, they will arise and "take over" the country for him to rule. Hence, arms are thought to be stored in the basement of many Catholic churches.

3. The Knights of Columbus take an oath to lead in that

insurrection. This bogus oath has been circulated by the millions. Exposed in the United States Congress, and that exposure duly recorded in the Congressional Record, the caluminators with diabolic deceit now cite the page in the Record which the oath appears as evidence of its alleged authenticity and withhold all mention of its demonstrated falsehood!

4. If Catholics gained ascendancy, they would deprive non-Catholics of their constitutional rights and give their Church a favored position.

5. The Catholic laity are not permitted to read the Bible. It must be read for them only by the clergy.

6. Nuns are kept as prisoners behind convent walls, within which gross immorality prevails.

7. Catholics pay money to priests in the confessional to secure pardon for their sins.

8. Priests charge fees to "pray" the souls of departed relatives and friends out of Purgatory.

9. Catholics adore the Blessed Virgin and worship idols of various sorts.

Though all these charges are utterly unfounded and totally false, though they have been disproven times without number, they have more lives than the proverbial cat with nine, and are resurrected for recirculation year after year. These are the ghosts which still haunt the minds of great numbers, probably millions, of credulous non-Catholics—the tragic victims of the wiles of slanderers who make a business out of peddling calumny. These are the real traitors, the Judas Iscariots who betray the ideals of American life and democracy for thirty pieces of silver.

What is the picture today? In the wake of every war there seems to occur a carry-over into civilian life of the passions and hatreds kindled by the conflict. After the Civil War and World War I, came the Ku Klux Klan with its hoods, veils and fiery crosses. So too in the wake of World War II and the Korean War, there was a recrudescence of religious bitterness and bigotry. The gigantic growth of the Church and the increasing prominence of Catholics in virtually all phases of our national life seemed to inspire once again the age-old suspicions, jealousies and fears.

The forces of religious antagonism, however, are fighting a losing battle. On all sides is heard the condemnation of the fomentors of sectarian strife by leading citizens of every faith. Educated people who have taken the pains to investigate the charges often hurled at the Church know how unfounded they are: they are sick and tired of their constant repetition and they resent the insult to their intelligence implied in the attempts of unscrupulous slanderers to foist willy-nilly their wares upon them. They have learned from experience that the labels which such peddlers of hate pin upon their victims usually turn out to be libels.

The Church in America today enjoys a freedom, vitality, prosperity and growth unsurpassed in any country. The separation of Church and State, with the friendly cooperation of each in areas of mutual interest, has placed the burden of supporting the Church squarely upon the shoulders of its members. With singular loyalty and generosity our laity have responded to the appeals of their consecrated leaders and have built churches, convents, hospitals, and charitable institutions to meet the needs of a constantly growing population —now approaching the forty million mark.

Though bearing the burden of double taxation, they have built a system of schools—grade schools, high schools, colleges, universities and seminaries—which holds the visitor to our shores in breathless astonishment and admiration. That vast system of schools running as an intricate network across the whole American landscape, erected without a penny of state aid by the people who love it, is the greatest moral fact in America today.

Under the wise provision of separation of Church and State, our nation has prospered and all religions have enjoyed the inestimable boon of freedom. Though other nations may prefer a union of State and Church, such an establishment for our country with its variety of faiths would not be only undesirable and impractical, but utterly impossible. In America we want no established Church, no privileged

Church, but simply equal opportunity for all before the law.

Nearly two centuries of experience have proven that religion is most vital and fruitful when its adherents believe in it and love it enough to support it out of their own free will offerings. A free Church in a free land is part of the American dream and we can share no other.

Back in 1909 Cardinal Gibbons, the ranking prelate of the Catholic Church in the United States, admirably reflected the sentiments and the convictions of his co-religionists when he declared: "The separation of Church and State in this country seems to Catholics the natural, the inevitable, the best conceivable plan, the one that would work best among us, both for the good of religion and of the state. . . . American Catholics rejoice in our separation of Church and State; and I can conceive of no combination of circumstances likely to arise which should make a union desirable either to Church and State any closer than they are at present. . . . I thank God we have religious liberty."

There is unanimity among the members of all the faiths upon the desirability and even necessity of separation of State and Church in our country and the bogey that any group, if it gained numerical preponderance, would wish to rescind that arrangement should be buried forever.

The most distinctive contribution which America has made to the world is the ideal of liberty: liberty of speech, of press, of assembly, of worship. Of these none is more precious than freedom of conscience—the sacred right to worship God according to the dictates of one's own conscience. America has not only proclaimed that ideal but is striving by might and main to weave it into the warp and woof of American life. She is struggling earnestly to eliminate the occasional outcroppings of sectarian prejudice and she does not hesitate to brand them as un-American to the core.

What are the principles guiding members of different faiths in cooperating in civil life? At a meeting of the National Conference of Christians and Jews in Washington, the Board of Directors issued a statement, setting forth the principles and ideals which should guide the relations of the members of the various religious faiths in our country. Signed by representatives of the Protestant, Catholic and Jewish faiths, it seeks to accomplish in the field of inter-faith relations what the federal Fair Employment Practices Act seeks to achieve in the domain of industrial relations. The statement is as follows:

This country was founded on the moral principle that all men, under God, are equal.

In a year marking the 300th anniversary of friendly co-existence of Jews, Roman Catholics and Protestants in the United States, we are reminded again that on the basis of this principle we have built a nation of people from many lands who worship, according to the dictates of our conscience, in many religious groups.

Together, we Protestants, Catholics and Jews have hewed the forests, cultivated the soil, built cities, forged a great nation.

In unity for the common good we have revealed the American genius. Respecting one another's differences in religion and origin, we have established a country devoted to the concept of brotherhood.

We have sought to make intolerance alien to our way of life. We have resisted ideas or movements that would set group against group, class against class, faith against faith.

Out of this resistance, 26 years ago, was born the National Conference of Christians and Jews to combat any manifestation of native and foreign brands of intolerance, and to advance education in group relation. Americans of all religious groups learned the lesson of standing together to fight bigotry with the moral and spiritual resources of men who believe in God.

This is the lesson we now bring with us in today's struggle against the forces of Communism which threaten anew the foundations of freedom and brotherhood.

We have watched the agonizing events in the countries behind the Iron Curtain as, at different times, Protestants, Catholics and Jews were persecuted. We have marked the long chain of suffering, horror, abasement and the moral and physical destruction that links all religious groups in a common cause for fear and anguish.

We understand well the motivations of the men of the Kremlin. They are the goals inevitably sought by men to whom the concepts of common brotherhood under the Fatherhood of God is as nothing; to whom the concept of respect for the dignity of each man is as nothing; to whom the concept of responsibility for freedom of each man is as nothing.

In repudiating this totalitarian approach to God and man, we ask all Americans to rededicate themselves to the fundamental spiritual and moral purposes of which the mainspring is our common brotherhood under the Fatherhood of God.

In combatting this newest and most menacing of tyrannies, we set forth these principles of action for Americans:

1. Cooperate as men of good will, each man with his neighbor, toward understanding and toward a republic free of intolerance.
2. Promote the new ideal of human relations—that citizens of many religious groups can work together on matters of common concern without compromise of their religious beliefs and doctrines.
3. Unite in resistance to anti-Protestant, anti-Catholic or anti-Jewish movements, so that no group need "go it alone."
4. Recognize bigotry and discrimination because of religion, race or nationality for what it is: the hallmark of the ignorant, the internal enemy of the United States.
5. Unite with all God-fearing men against the enemies of religion.

These principles harmonize admirably with those set forth on numerous occasions by Pope Pius XII for the collaboration of Catholics with "all men of good will" to promote peace, security, social justice, civil rights and human freedom everywhere. None of these great objectives can be achieved by Protestants, Catholics or Jews working independently. But working together they can accomplish much.

It is heartening to the people of all faiths, races and nations to hear a great world statesman—some think the greatest moral figure in the world today—issuing clarion calls to his vast spiritual family of more than four hundred million to take their place by the side of all men of good will in the struggle for all worthy ends. Such joint action is, of course, a dictate of reason. But it is well to have such a mandate formulated in clear explicit terms by the supreme spiritual authority of the Catholic Church. No longer can there be any doubt, vacillation or hesitation on the part of the most conservative members of the fold.

Taking cognizance of the tendency of some members to hold themselves aloof from a false fear of compromising their religious faith, *America,* a national Catholic weekly, declares: "When it comes to cooperation with non-Catholics, far too many Catholics are 'more Catholic than the Pope.' They shy away from all collaboration with those not of the Faith, even in such purely temporal affairs as the promotion of civil rights and agitation for slum clearance. They suffer, it seems, from a vague fear that to do so would contribute to the spread of religious indifferentism. The Holy Father, on the other hand, has issued so many appeals for cooperation of Catholics with their non-Catholic fellow-citizens during the decade of his reign that he can justly be called the Pope of Cooperation. He has termed such cooperation 'necessary and urgent.' "

The last Religious Census taken up by the government showed there are 255 different religious faiths in the United States—probably more than in any other country. Just about every sect in the world has some of its adherents here. It is obvious therefore that systematic efforts must be made to prevent those differences from carrying over into the civil life of the nation and to enable all to live in understanding, good will, friendship and brotherhood.

This is the ideal to which all the religious organizations in the United States are committed and they have made great strides towards its achievements. In struggling for its achievement in every community in America, Protestants, Catholics and Jews are working hand in hand, and there is every reason to believe that such united effort will be crowned with ever increasing success.

CHAPTER NINETEEN

The Liturgical Movement in the United States[1]

———— ❖ ————

BY SISTER JANE MARIE MURRAY, O.P.
AND PAUL MARX, O.S.B.

HOLY WEEK, 1956! Across the United States Holy Thursday evening finds Catholics—millions of them—in their churches for the celebration of the Mass of the Lord's Supper. Good Friday afternoon they crowd the churches again,

---

1. The data for this chapter are taken largely from the forthcoming *The Life and Work of Virgil Michel, O.S.B.*, written by Paul Marx, O.S.B., and soon to be published by the Liturgical Press. This volume contains full documentation for points here only mentioned.

Sister Jane Marie Murray, O.P., Marywood, Grand Rapids, is an associate editor of Worship *and the author of religion textbooks for primary and secondary schools. She is currently completing work on a four year* The Christian Life *series for Catholic High Schools, to be published by Fides. Paul Marx, O.S.B., a monk at St. John's Abbey, Collegeville, Minnesota, teaches sociology at St. John's University, Collegeville. His doctoral dissertation is entitled* The Life and Work of Virgil Michel, O.S.B.

not for the traditional "Tre Ore" but to participate in the liturgical services and to receive Holy Communion. Greatest crowds of all, perhaps, fill the cathedrals and parish churches in the evening of Holy Saturday to celebrate the Vigil of Easter. For pastors and for the people, Holy Week of 1956 will always remain memorable. Thanks to the greatest liturgical innovation in four centuries, more of the faithful were able to share in the celebration of the liturgy of Holy Week than ever before.

Granting that the degree of this participation may leave much to be accomplished, it remains true that this year's celebration of Holy Week bore witness to a readiness on the part of the faithful for liturgical participation which would have been almost totally absent thirty years ago. What has happened through these past thirty years to make possible such a wonderful popular response as greeted the Decree for the Renewed Liturgy of Holy Week? The answer to this question is to be found in the history of the liturgical movement in the United States. Only a few major events in this history can be touched upon, of course, in this brief account.

The roots of the American liturgical apostolate are to be found in Europe. There they reach back to the year 1841, in which appeared the first installment of Dom Prosper Guéranger's *L'Année liturgique*.[2] Translated into many languages, this monumental work on the liturgical year opened up to countless numbers the riches of the Church's celebration of the feasts and seasons. Pope St. Pius X, in his *Motu proprio* (1903), pleaded for intelligent and active participation "in the most holy mysteries and in the public and solemn prayer of the Church," which he called "the foremost and indispensable fount" of "the true Christian spirit." Six years later Dom Lambert Beauduin initiated in Belgium the first significant response to the urging of St. Pius X, with his publication of a popular missal, *Vie Liturgique*. This missal

---

2. Cf. Dunstan Tucker, O.S.B., "The Council of Trent, Guéranger and Pius X," *Orate Fratres*, X (1936), 538-544.

marked the beginning of the liturgical movement in Belgium, the first country to experience a popular liturgical revival.

With the strong leadership of Abbot Ildefons Herwegen, the Abbey of Maria Laach began its liturgical activity in 1914, when the first liturgical retreat for laymen was held there. In 1920 appeared Father Romano Guardini's *Vom Geist der Liturgie,* the first volume of Maria Laach's famous *Ecclesia Orans* series, edited by Herwegen. While this German abbey addressed itself chiefly to intellectuals and scholars, Austria's Father Pius Parsch, an Augustinian, began his enormously effective popularization of the liturgy in the early 1920's. Dom Gaspar Lefebvre carried on a similar work, though on a lesser scale, from the Abbey of St. André in Belgium. From centers such as these the liturgical leaven soon infiltrated other countries of Europe.

Meanwhile, what of the United States? If the liturgical movement in this country went back to Europe for its inspiration, this was not for lack of any earlier liturgical interest and endeavors in America. On the contrary. For as early as 1778 Father John Carroll—the future first ordinary in the United States—made a strong plea for the use of the vernacular in the liturgy. Later on, as the first Bishop of Baltimore, at a meeting (1810) with his three suffragans, he deplored certain abuses in the use of the vernacular but permitted the maximum employment of English in administering the sacraments, except for the sacramental form itself.[3]

A desire "to instruct the members of the Catholic Church on the nature of the most solemn act of their religion," and non-Catholics, as well, appears in the thinking of the Sulpician Most Reverend Ambrose Maréchal, third Archbishop of Baltimore, and of John England, first Bishop of Charleston, each of whom conceived independently the need of a vernacular missal for the laity. Such a missal, edited by England and largely a reprint of a British missal, was published

---

3. Cf. John Tracy Ellis, "Archbishop Carroll and the Liturgy in the Vernacular," *Worship,* XXVI (1952), 545-552.

here in 1822, with later editions in 1843, 1861, 1865 and 1867.[4]

That this missal was not in general, or even wide, use is evident from complaints of the bishops assembled in 1884 at the Third Council of Baltimore to the effect "that most prayers used by the faithful are anything but literary, and even at times hardly orthodox," and from their insistence on a "careful revision of all the prayers, hymns, psalms, and canticles that are of frequent use in the Church." Nor was this council concerned only with the avoidance of unsuitable prayers, as is evident in this frank and revealing declaration:

> That many Catholics know next to nothing of the Church's standard and form of prayer is indeed most deplorable. Hence, now that in their craving for the things of this world, men find it so hard to realize things divine, it is for clergymen a grave obligation to explain clearly and accurately . . . the rites and prayers of the Church. The holy Council of Trent requests parish priests, and all who have the care of souls, often to explain what is read at Mass and especially to dwell on the Mysteries of the most holy Sacrifice, so that the faithful, who have also a share in the Sacrifice of the New Law offered through the priest's ministry, may derive therefrom greater grace and spiritual benefits. Likewise, in order that the faithful may receive the sacraments with greater respect and devotion, the same Council demands that parish priests explain to the people with skill and piety, in the vernacular, the effects and ceremonies of the sacraments. . . . It is evident how profitable it will be for the faithful to have at their disposal prayerbooks containing an accurate translation of prayers and rites carefully chosen from those of the missal, the breviary, and the ritual. . . . Thus the beauties of the sacred liturgy will be offered to the mind of the readers, as it were a garden of delight.[5]

---

4. Cf. *The Roman Missal Translated into the English Language for the Use of the Laity* (Philadelphia: Eugene Commiskey, 1843), iii; Peter Guilday, *The Life and Times of John England* (N.Y., America Press, 1922), I, 328-333; John K. Ryan, "Bishop England and the Missal," *Ecclesiastical Review*, XCV (1936), 28-36.

5. *Acta et Decreta Concilii Plenarii Baltimorensis* (Baltimore: John Murphy Co., 1886), n. 221-222, pp. 120-122. An excellent *Manual of Prayers* was compiled at the request of the Council; observed the editor of *Worship*: "One

Pleas for the restoration of the chant were made in all the three Plenary Councils of Baltimore, the reason for this being stated succinctly at the Third Plenary Council:

> . . . in order that the number of those able to sing the psalms well may constantly grow larger, until gradually at least the majority of the faithful may, according to the custom of the ancient Church, still observed in some places, learn to chant Vespers and other services in union with the ministers and the choir.[6]

It is to be noted that in this country the chant movement antedated the liturgical movement. Significant events in the development of the chant movement here were: 1874, the foundation of *Caecilia;* 1913, the formation of the Society of St. Gregory at St. Mary's Seminary in Baltimore; 1915, the appearance of the *Catholic Choirmaster;* 1916, establishment of the Pius X School of Liturgical Music in New York by Justine B. Ward and Mother Georgia Stevens, R.S.C.J.; 1920, the Gregorian Congress held in New York.

The important work of the Pius X School in teaching liturgical music is well known. This development of the chant is not to be confused, of course, or identified, with the liturgical movement, which is a far larger thing, of which the chant is but a part, albeit an integral part.

The beginnings of the liturgical movement itself in this country, like the beginnings of most movements, are below the surface. Into the makings of any movement flow many streams. Without doubt it is impossible to identify all those persons who sensed to a greater or lesser extent the tremendous meaning of the liturgy in the life of the Church. The

---

of the tragedies of the Church's history in this country is that the resulting prayerbook was not as generally accepted and promoted as was the Catechism of the same Council, and that its legislation about popularizing the chant was not obeyed. Compliance with the injunctions of the Council would have anticipated the great reforms of Pius X; would have meant a liturgical movement in America a quarter of a century before such a movement made itself felt in any other country" (Godfrey Diekmann, O.S.B., "Lay Participation in the Liturgy of the Church," in *A Symposium on the Life and Work of Pope Pius X* [Washington: Confraternity of Christian Doctrine, 1946], p. 147).

6. *Acta et Decreta,* n. 119, p. 61.

first efforts towards a liturgical revival were made more or
less simultaneously in the early 1920's by Father Martin
Hellriegel of O'Fallon, Missouri, Father William Busch of
the St. Paul Seminary and by the monks of St. John's Abbey,
Collegeville. After firsthand study of the movement in Europe through 1924-25,[7] Father Virgil Michel, O.S.B., with
the support of Abbot Alcuin Deutsch, founded in 1926, the
pioneer organ of the liturgical apostolate in the English-
speaking world: *Orate Fratres,* now known as *Worship.* The
Liturgical Press, established at St. John's Abbey in the same
year, has been the source of a steady flow of popular publications feeding the liturgical apostolate ever since. With the
establishment of *Orate Fratres* and the Liturgical Press the
Liturgical movement is underway.

Into what climate of thought did the liturgical apostolate
seek to enter? Perhaps one of the most obvious indications
of the lack of liturgical awareness appears in the limited use
of the missal even as late as 1926. Today there are millions of
daily and Sunday missals in use. In 1925 the vernacular
missal was practically unknown. When the officials of the
E. M. Lohmann Company of St. Paul approached Archbishop Austin Dowling concerning the feasibility of their
taking over sales for the newly translated *St. Andrew Daily
Missal,* the archbishop

> discouraged us from taking it over, mentioning that although
> it was a very fine thing and should be encouraged, the time
> was not ripe for it yet. He stated that a missal was fine for a
> priest or a nun, but it was expecting just too much of the laity
> to have them use a missal.[8]

7. Cf. Paul Marx, O.S.B., "Virgil Michel in Europe," *American Benedictine Review,* VI (1955), pp. 261-284. While in Europe Michel began organizing a staff of associate editors: Rt. Rev. F. Holweck; Mother Mary Ellerker;
Fathers William Busch, Patrick Cummins, O.S.B., Gerald Ellard, S.J., Martin
Hellriegel, James O'Mahoney, O.F.M. Cap. of Ireland, Richard Power, Jere-
miah Harrington, Leo Miller and Mrs. J. B. Ward.

8. Cf. Diekmann, "Primary Apostolate," in Leo Ward (ed.), *The American
Apostolate* (Westminster: Newman Press, 1952), p. 35. According to official
statistics from companies concerned in the Michel Papers, Kenedy sold a
yearly average of 4,000 missals for 1924-1928; Macmillan for all of the twenties sold a total of 7,000. Paul Bussard estimates that "there were well under

Lohmann's sold 4,826 copies of its daily missal in the following year; 12,800 in 1927, and then, as the liturgical movement continued to progress, the number spiralled so that within the next quarter century the total sales of this missal alone reached well over a million. Today nineteen editions of English daily missals are available. By 1952 thirteen million copies of Father Stedman's *My Sunday Missal*—first published in 1938—had been printed.

Even more limited than the use of the vernacular missal in 1925 was the amount of literature relating in any way to the liturgy. As we examine the ecclesiastical journals for the years preceding 1926, we find practically no articles on the liturgy as we understand it today. Where articles appear, or where the term "liturgy" is used, there is question of "rubrics," or, at best, of the externals of the liturgy. The Liturgical Press was established partly because at that time no publishing firms would risk the publication of books which treated and promoted the emerging liturgical apostolate. It is not surprising that textbooks of religion then in use presented very inadequate studies of the Mass and the sacraments.[9]

As for the doctrine of the Mystical Body, which is the core of liturgical life, this was inadequately treated even in seminaries, it appears. In the introduction to his *Mystical Christ,* written in 1936 and hailed as a "pioneer book," the Reverend John Gruden remarks, "The object of this book is to fill in the complete picture of the Church presented by catechisms and ordinary classroom manuals of theology." [10] Con-

50,000 missals in the U.S. in 1928" (cf. "Why Not the Mass in Your Own Language?," *Orate Fratres*, XXV [1951], 465). For an interesting comparison between the 1920's and 1930's in missal sales, cf. Bussard and Jennings, "How Many Use the Missal for the Laity?," *Ecclesiastical Review*, CII (1940), 61-63. For the latest on English daily missals, cf. John P. O'Connell, "English Daily Missals," *Homiletic and Pastoral Review*, LIII (1953), 809-819.

9. Cf. Bussard, *The Vernacular Missal in Religious Education* (Washington: Catholic University of America, 1937).

10. (St. Louis: Herder, 1936), p. 15. The first complete treatise in English of the Mystical Body appeared in 1931 with Paulist John Burke's translation of Abbé Angé's *The Mystical Body of Christ.*

cerning the doctrine of the Mystical Body, which some hesi-
tated to accept, Pope Pius XII was to say seven years later:

> Some through empty fear look upon so profound a doctrine as
> something dangerous and so they fight shy of it as of the beau-
> tiful but forbidden fruit of Paradise. It is not so. Mysteries re-
> vealed by God cannot be harmful to men. Nor should they re-
> main as treasures hidden in a field useless.[11]

Meanwhile, world conditions in the 1920's grew increasingly critical. Keen awareness of and concern over these
conditions characterized the American liturgical apostolate
from its inception. "We are at the end of an era, . . . in an
age of transition that is questioning all of its old beliefs and
habits," said the editor of *Orate Fratres* in 1927. Of this
period Father Busch wrote in 1939:

> I recall a conversation [with Virgil Michel] prior to the eco-
> nomic depression in 1929 in which we scanned the clouds
> which we discerned upon the horizon at a time when many still
> believed that the sky was clear. And we agreed that the liturgi-
> cal movement had arisen under the providence of God to
> bring in dark days the secret of the world's salvation.[12]

Now "the secret of the world's salvation" lies in the liturgy of the Mystical Body—that is, in the Mass, the sacraments, the sacramentals, the divine office and the liturgical
year. By the proper celebration of, and the active and intelligent participation in, the liturgy, the saving work of Christ
is carried forward through the centuries. The official corporate worship of the Church is, then, of intimate concern to
all—clergy and laity alike, baptized into Christ.

For the promotion of intelligent and active participation
in the liturgy, the liturgical apostolate proceeded to utilize
new means of reaching the faithful. A liturgical summer
school at St. John's in 1929, the first of its kind, had its
official closing in the first National Liturgical Day held at
St. John's Abbey, July 25, 1929.

This Liturgical Day, and two more held in the following

---

11. *Mystici Corporis*, (N.Y.: America Press), p. 7.
12. "An Apostle of Liturgical Life," *Orate Fratres, XIII* (1939), 106.

years, were meant as a prelude to a National Liturgical Week, the first of which, however, was organized only in 1940, in Chicago, by Dom Michael Ducey and Monsignor Joseph Morrison. Objectives of the National Liturgical Week, as originally conceived, were twofold: the popularization of the liturgical movement and the deepening of liturgical knowledge and piety. Endeavors to combine these two aims in the program of the Week presented a problem which finally found a solution in the retention by the Week of a program directed chiefly toward the popularization of the liturgy. For the purpose of fostering scholarly research in the liturgy and at the same time a deeper liturgical piety, the University of Notre Dame instituted its Liturgical Summer School in 1947 under the direction of Father Michael Mathis, C.S.C.

Significant new publications have helped the advance of the liturgical apostolate: the *Leaflet Missal*, 1930; *Liturgical Arts*, 1931; *Altar* and *Home*, 1934; and, finally, *Mediator*, 1949. Under the dynamic leadership of Dom Godfrey Diekmann, O.S.B., *Worship* sustains its role as an effective organ of the liturgical movement in America.

Papal documents appeared which gave strong support to the liturgical renewal and provided impetus for further development of the movement. Chief among these were, of course, the encyclicals, *Mystici Corporis* (1943) and *Mediator Dei* (1947). These were followed by papal sanction of the use of some vernacular in the American ritual, by permission to offer Mass in the evening, by the relaxation of the Eucharistic fast, by the simplification of the rubrics, and finally, in 1955, by the monumental restoration of the Holy Week liturgy.

One should not forget that from its organized beginnings the liturgical apostolate in America moved out from the sanctuary into the lives and activities of the faithful. This was due largely to the vision and leadership of Virgil Michel. Concerning him a well known writer on liturgical subjects has observed:

We had no Virgil Michel in Germany. The close inter-con-
nection of the liturgical revival with social reform . . . was
never expressed in that forceful way in which you see it in the
writings of the late Dom Virgil and *Orate Fratres.* . . . Maria
Laach, Guardini, Pinsk and Klosterneuburg only occasionally
pointed out the necessary social consequences of a true liturgical revival among our Catholic people. . . . America is in an
enviable position. . . . While in Germany the leaders of the
liturgical and social revival, both strong and powerful movements, never really met, and sometimes antagonized and criticized each other—here you have a close cooperation of the two,
a unity of both, right from the start.[13]

The wonderful burgeoning out of the liturgical leaven
into all areas of life and action began, logically, with the
work of education. Interest in the liturgical education of
youth, a concern of Fathers Hellriegel, Busch, Ellard and
Michel from the beginning of the movement, reached its first
practical expression in the publication, in 1929, under the
aegis of the Liturgical Press, of five volumes of *With Mother
Church.* These volumes were written by Dominican Sisters
of Marywood, Grand Rapids, Michigan, guided by Sister M.
Estelle, O.P., under the direction of Dom Virgil Michel and
Father Busch, during the first liturgical summer session at
St. John's Abbey in 1929. *With Mother Church* constituted
the first American effort to orientate religious instruction in
its proper relation to the liturgical revival.

Out of this undertaking, *With Mother Church,* came the
inspiration for a series of basic textbooks in religion for
grades and high school. Outlines for the whole series, comprising twelve volumes, were worked out by Virgil Michel
with Dominican Sisters of Marywood through the fall and
winter of 1929. The eight volumes of the *Christ-Life Series*
for the grades, with two teachers' manuals, appeared in 1934-
35. *The Life of Our Lord* and *Living in Christ,* by Sister
Jane Marie, O.P., designed for grades nine and ten, came
out in mimeograph form in 1938 and 1942, respectively, and
in published form shortly afterward.

---

13. H. A. Reinhold, "Liturgy True Remedy," *Social Forum,* Dec., 1938.

Special mention should be made here of Father Gerald Ellard's *Christian Life and Worship* (1933), the first college textbook in religion reflecting the liturgical revival. This pioneer volume for college students has gone through a number of editions. Father Virgil Michel's *Our Life in Christ* was issued in 1935 and his *The Christian in the World* in 1937.

Liturgical education advanced not only through publication of textbooks, but also, and especially, through active intelligent participation of the faithful in the liturgical life of the parish. Particularly worthy of note in this respect is the work accomplished by Monsignor Hellriegel in O'Fallon, Missouri, and, more recently, in Holy Cross parish, St. Louis.

Not only into education but into all areas of social action the liturgical spirit infiltrated. It is no mere historical accident that St. Pius X pleaded for active lay participation in the liturgical life of the Church and that Pius XI urged the laity to participate actively in the apostolate of the hierarchy. The liturgy and Catholic Action are essentially related. The liturgy, indeed, has a twofold outlet: Godward, in worship, and manward, in Catholic Action. This fact is strikingly evidenced in the historical evolution of the liturgical renaissance in America.

Nearly all the vital lay movements today seem in some way to be related to the primary source of the Christ-Life. In this connection it is interesting that the pioneer organization of Catholic social action, the Central Verein, was the first lay group to endorse and promote the liturgical apostolate (1927). In 1928 the Liturgical Arts Society was charted, thanks to the labors of Father John La Farge, S.J., Harry Binsse, Maurice Lavanoux and others. The heart of the Friendship House movement, which began in 1930, has been, according to Catherine De Hueck Doherty, the liturgical life. Through the 1930's, the *Catholic Worker* (1933)—besides broadcasting the social teachings of the Church as the first Catholic labor paper in this country—also furthered the liturgical revival among the rank and file. Effective work along similar lines was accomplished by English-speaking Canada's first labor paper, the *Social Forum,* founded in Ottawa in 1935. Promoters of the National Catholic Rural Life Conference have always realized the role of the liturgy in their work. Under the inspiration of Archbishop Edwin V. O'Hara, the national center for the Confraternity of Christian Doctrine, established in 1935, has shared in the work of the liturgical apostolate. Cisca (Chicago Inter-student Catholic Action) was founded in 1927 by Joseph Reiner, S.J. About 1934, thanks to the leadership and work of Martin Carrabine, S.J., and Sister Cecilia Himebaugh, O.S.B., Cisca began the active promotion of the liturgy as the basis of genuine apostolic work. Out of this ferment grew the lively *Today* magazine in 1946.

The liturgically oriented Grail Movement began its work at Libertyville, Illinois, in 1940, under Dr. Lydwine Van Kersbergen. Its training center for the formation of apostolic leaders is now established at Loveland, Ohio. From the inspired leadership of Louis Putz,[14] C.S.C., at the University of Notre Dame, and of Monsignor Reynold Hillenbrand, General Chaplain of specialized Catholic Action, derives the effective work of the Christian Family Movement (1946), Young Christian Workers (1941) and Young Christian Students (1940). Various segments of the Cana Movement have also evinced a decided interest in the liturgy.

Promoters of the auxiliary chant movement are showing an increased understanding of the integral part which the chant plays in the celebration of the liturgy. This is particularly evident in the work of the Gregorian Institute of America and in its official organ, the *Gregorian Review,* begun in 1954.

Similarly, the Liturgical Arts Society has furthered a better understanding and appreciation of the sacred arts in the public worship of the Church. The impact of the liturgy as the highest art-form has perhaps left its greatest mark on

---

14. Cf. Vincent J. Giese, "Chaplain to the Working Apostolate," *Today,* X (November, 1954), 3-5.

modern church architecture. Note these words written in 1941 by the famous architect, Charles D. Maginnis:

> A decade ago the liturgical movement had notably aroused the interest and sympathy of many of the hierarchy and priesthood of this country, so that more and more obviously its implications became a challenge to the thoughtful concern of those creatively identified with ecclesiastical art. The first consequence of this was the coming together of a group of Catholic men and women . . . who were prepared to enter on the demonstration that Catholic art could, by studious direction, be restored to something of its historic vitality. . . . But it has been the stirring of the liturgical idea in the mind of the architect which has brought the most notable consequences. . . . This is particularly evident in the sacred precincts of the sanctuary, where the architect is conscious of a new solemnity in the challenge of the altar. . . . The new deference is unmistakable.[15]

Noteworthy also is the fact that in 1955 the Catholic Art Association, in existence since 1937, voted to ally itself more closely with the liturgical movement.

Even this sketchy historical account of the American liturgical apostolate justifies the statement that the future of the liturgical movement is bright indeed, when considered in the light of past achievements and allied current movements. The Liturgical Press sold 25,000 copies of its revised *A Short Breviary* in 1955, and 1,600,000 Holy Week Missals in March, 1956. It seems safe to say that today several hundred thousand of the laity regularly recite some part of the divine office.

The Liturgical Press no longer stands alone as publisher for the liturgical apostolate, as is evidenced by the impressive list of publishers who contributed to the literature on Holy Week, 1956. The total number of Holy Week Missals distributed in 1956 by about sixteen different publishers has been estimated as between six and eight millions. Notable for their liturgical publications are the Pio Decimo Press (initially the inspiration of Monsignor Hellriegel), Concep-

---

15. "A Survey and a Hope," *Liturgical Arts*, X (1941), 3.

tion Abbey Press, and, newest in the field, Fides Publishers. Attendance at the National Liturgical Week has increased yearly; the Proceedings constitute a veritable mine of sound liturgical thought. Publication of the lectures given by experts at Notre Dame University's Liturgical Summer School inaugurated by Father Michael Mathis, C.S.C., in 1947, will make available valuable liturgical research. A report on Holy Week, 1956, in the United States, to be given at the International Liturgical Congress in Assisi is now being drafted by John and Mary Ryan.

Much has been accomplished; yet much needs doing. It is therefore well for apostles of the liturgy to keep in mind the words of Pius XII in *Mediator Dei*:

> Never be discouraged by the difficulties that arise, never let your . . . zeal grow cold. . . . Try in every way, with the means and helps that your prudence deems best, that the clergy and people become one in mind and heart, and that the Christian people take such an active part in the Liturgy that it becomes a truly sacred action of due worship to the Eternal Lord in which the priest, chiefly responsible for the souls of his parish, and the ordinary faithful are united together.[16]

---

16. *Mediator Dei*, NCWC edition, pp. 67, 68.

life among the Catholics of this country. All but the most sanguine of men feel discouragement in circumstances of this kind and the majority usually give way to the natural tendency to slacken their efforts. What is more serious, the presence of so widespread a prejudice among the great majority of the population prompts the minority to withdraw into itself and to assume the attitude of defenders of a besieged fortress. That this situation had such an effect on many Catholics, there is no doubt. Even so brave and talented a man as John Carroll, the first American Catholic bishop, revealed the timidity engendered among the Catholics of his day by hatred of their Church when he was compelled to go into print in 1784 to refute a subtle attack on Catholic doctrine from the first American apostate priest. As Carroll remarked, "I could not forget, in the beginning, progress, and conclusion of it, that the habits of thinking, the prejudices, perhaps even the passions of many of my readers, would be set against all the arguments I could offer. . . ." [6] How many Catholics since Carroll's day could attest to the same reluctance when they sought to exercise their talents in behalf of Catholic truth? And yet anti-Catholic bias should not be advanced as the prime factor in this situation. More damaging than its direct effect on the intellectual shortcomings of American Catholics, has probably been the fostering by this historic bias of an overeagerness in Catholic circles for apologetics rather than pure scholarship.

A second major consideration which helps to account for the failure of American Catholics to make a notable mark upon the intellectual life of their country is the character and background of the major portion of the people who, until a relatively recent date, made up the Church in the United States. From the 1820's, when the Irish began immigrating to the new world in large numbers, to the 1920's, when Congress locked the doors upon all but a small proportion of the immigrants who sought these shores, the Catholic Church was faced with the staggering task of ab-

6. Peter Guilday, *The Life and Times of John Carroll, Archbishop of Baltimore, 1735-1815* (New York, 1922), I, 126.

sorbing an estimated 9,317,000 immigrants of its faith.[7] We
do not need to be told what the immigrant status implied by
way of poverty, hardship, yes, and even illiteracy. Most of us
learned it from tales told by our grandparents within the
intimacy of the family circle. And since we have had the
advantage of a finished education and know what that requires, we can easily understand how impossible it was for
our ancestors to produce anything approaching a thriving
intellectual life. Moreover, the grave responsibility that
these unceasing waves of immigrants imposed upon the leaders of the Church to see that they had the rudiments of religious instruction and the facilities for Mass and the
sacraments, left little time, funds, or leisure for a more
highly cultivated training. Brogan understands that fact. In
1941 he wrote:

> Not until this generation has the Church been given time
> (with the cessation of mass immigration) to take breath and
> take stock. One result of this preoccupation with the immi-
> grants has been that the Catholic Church in America has
> counted for astonishingly little in the formation of the Ameri-
> can intellectual climate. . . .[8]

It is only the exceptional man—for example, John Gilmary Shea,[9] the historian of the American Church—who can
make headway in the world of scholarship amid crippling
poverty and the harassing anxiety of providing a living for
himself and his dependents. That was the lot of most of the
Catholics in this country in Shea's generation and before,
and that there should have resulted a pitifully meager record of accomplishment in the things of the mind is thus
quite understandable.

---

7. Gerald Shaughnessy, S.M., *Has the Immigrant Kept the Faith?* (New
York, 1925), pp. 113-196, contains the most accurate data available for the
Catholic population trends from 1820 to 1920.

8. Brogan, *op. cit.*, p. 65.

9. For a pathetic account of the poverty he experienced and the lack of
support given to Shea during the writing of his great four-volume *History of
the Catholic Church in the United States* (New York, 1886-1892), cf. the correspondence reprinted in Peter Guilday, "John Gilmary Shea," *Historical
Records and Studies,* XVII (July, 1926), 81-146.

But even if the energies of the American Catholic body down to a generation ago had not been so completely absorbed in the primary duty of assimilating the millions of immigrants, any true intellectual distinction—had it been there—would have met with very slight appreciation in the United States. Historically Americans have been wary of their scholars, and it is doubtful if there is a major nation in the world whose history reveals more suspicion of its academicians than our own. It is now 120 years since de Tocqueville published his famous book on American institutions, and among his many wise observations he stated:

> In the United States the people do not hate the higher classes of society, but are not favorably inclined towards them and carefully exclude them from the exercise of authority. They do not fear distinguished talents, but are rarely fond of them. In general, everyone who rises without their aid seldom obtains their favor.[10]

The prevalence of this egalitarian spirit and the leveling process which it inspired prompted Orestes Brownson to inveigh against the American practice of dethroning all distinction when he delivered the commencement address at Mount Saint Mary's College in 1853. On that occasion he pleaded with the graduates to resist with might and main this tendency which he characterized as "the grand heresy of our age." [11] Nor have matters greatly improved since the time of de Tocqueville and Brownson, for it has been our own generation that has given birth to the terms "brain trusters" and "egg heads" to designate the popular concept of professors who have descended from Mount Olympus to engage actively in the realm of public affairs.

In this respect, I regret to say, I can see no appreciable

---

10. Alexis de Tocqueville, *Democracy in America*, edited by Phillips Bradley (New York, 1945), I, 202.

11. Henry F. Brownson (ed.), *The Works of Orestes A. Brownson* (Detroit, 1885), XIX, 439. The title of the address was "Liberal Studies," and it was delivered on June 29, 1853, before the Philomathian Society. Among the six graduates of that year were the future artist, John La Farge, and the later fifth Bishop of Vincennes, Silas M. Chatard.

difference between the attitudes assumed by American Catholics and those commonly held among their fellow countrymen of other religious faiths. The historian looks in vain—
always excepting the lonely few—for a higher evaluation and
a more understanding attitude toward the pursuits of the
mind among those who are Catholics in this country. In that
—as in so many other ways—the Catholics are, and have been,
thoroughly American, and they have shown no more marked
disposition to foster scholarship and to honor intellectual
achievement than have any other group. In this their European coreligionists have often been far in advance of them.
One recalls, for example, the splendid efforts made by the
Belgian hierarchy, their priests and people, in rallying so
bravely—and so successfully—behind Rector Pierre F.-X. de
Ram and his colleagues in 1834 in restoring the great Catholic University of Louvain. In terms of the comparative
attitudes of many American and European Catholics to matters of this kind, it would be gratifying to record that the
Catholics of the United States were an exception to the witty
extravagance of a certain dean who once remarked that "in
the Old World an ordinary mortal on seeing a professor
tipped his hat while in America he tapped his head." [12] But,
alas, as far as my reading and observation enable me to
speak, I find no grounds for the exception.

One of the principal reasons for the lack of such an exception is, I think, the absence of an intellectual tradition
among American Catholics. Obviously the establishment of
such a tradition was impossible amid the stifling persecution
and discrimination which Catholics experienced in colonial
America. With the dawn of religious liberty after the American Revolution there was a brief span of years when it
seemed that a tradition of this kind was slowly taking root
among the families of the Maryland Catholic gentry. For the
personal wealth of some of these families like the Carrolls,
the Neales, and the Brookes, along with their deep and ar-
dent Catholic faith, had enabled them to send their children

    12. Merle Curti, "Intellectuals and Other People," *American Historical
Review*, LX (January, 1955), 259.